# Touring the Wine Country of Oregon

## All 46 Wineries Updated

### By Ronald and Glenda Holden

HOLDEN

PACIFIC

Portions of this book first appeared in *The Weekly, Pacific Northwest, Puget Soundings,* the *Spokesman-Review and Spokane Chronicle,* and *Northwest Gourmet.*

Also by Ronald and Glenda Holden: *Touring the Wine Country of Washington*

International Standard Book Number: 0-910571-02-3
Library of Congress Catalog Card Number: 84-080731

Distributed by Holden Pacific, Inc.
814 35th Avenue
Seattle, WA 98122
(206) 325-4324

*To Trudie Holden, who nurtured this project and provided the base camp.*
*And to the memory of Thyra McPherson (1916-1972).*

## Acknowledgements

This book would not have been possible without the assistance of Oregon's winemakers, whose cooperation and hospitality we gratefully acknowledge. We also express our appreciation for the time and advice contributed by Jeff Isaacson in Salem, Don Marsh in Eugene, Victoria Salter in Vancouver, Nancy Ponzi in Beaverton, and Sherry Lossing in Jacksonville.

Many thanks to David Graham at the Word Processor Store in Seattle, and to Donna Burgess and David Kyle at the Xerox Service Center in Redmond, who came through when the (micro-) chips were down.

Special thanks to Jody and Bob Sheppard.

Last but not least, we are indebted to our children, Michael, David, and Dominic, for their patience and support.

## Credits

Ronald and Glenda Holden have been writing about wine and food for over fifteen years. They are members of the Society of Wine Educators and frequently lecture on wine and tourism in the Northwest.

Ronald Holden, a native of Portland, Oregon, has followed a career in journalism, public relations, and broadcasting; Glenda Holden, a native of Australia, is a physical therapist who has lived in the Northwest since 1967. Their joint byline appears regularly in a variety of prominent publications around the Northwest, including wine columns for *Washington Magazine*, Seattle's *The Weekly*, the *Spokesman-Review and Spokane Chronicle*, and *Northwest Gourmet*.

Their company, Holden Pacific, Inc., specializes in publications about wine and food, and conducts customized, escorted tours of the wine country in Oregon and Washington.

The cover sketch of a vineyard in the hills south of Dundee, Oregon, was rendered in oil pastels by Glenn Carr. Mr. Carr, an architect and artist, lived and practiced in Oregon for many years, and is now based in Seattle.

Maps by Mark Joselyn, a free-lance cartographer and graduate student in the University of Washington Geography Department.

Copy editing by Miriam Bulmer.

Typography, in Century Old Style and Benguiat Bold Italics, was produced directly from personal computer word-processing diskettes by The Type Gallery, Inc., Seattle. Printed by R. R. Donnelley & Co., in Harrisonburg, Virginia.

# Contents

# How To Use This Book

This book includes all Oregon's *bonded* and *active* wineries as well as several wineries which will be bonded within a year of publication. Wineries making fruit and berry wines have been given the same coverage as wineries making wine from premium grapes; indeed, many wineries make both kinds.

The tourist suggestions for each region of the wine country are meant to be impressionistic rather than exhaustive. Several good guidebooks to the Pacific Northwest have been published in recent years; they can steer you to everything from "The Best Places" to golf courses, campgrounds, free attractions, or four-star resorts. We asked winemakers and others to recommend local places, which we then checked personally.

This is an independently researched and published guidebook. No individual, commercial establishment, or trade association paid any fee to be listed or mentioned in this book. We would appreciate hearing from readers with corrections or suggestions for future editions. Please write to Holden Pacific, Inc., at 814 - 35th Avenue, Seattle, WA 98122.

The winery profiles are based on personal visits and detailed questionnaires filled out by the winemakers themselves. Many wineries now welcome bus tours or similar large groups; they usually charge $1 per person to cover the costs of a group visit, but this charge is frequently refunded upon purchase. With any group larger than a carload, it's a probably good idea to call ahead to make sure you can be accommodated. The information about hours open to visitors and wines available is, of course, subject to change at the discretion of the winery.

Most profiles include a map to help travelers find their way from a main road or nearby town. *The maps are meant to be used in conjunction with an Oregon highway map.*

1

The state has put up highway signs for several wineries; it's part of a new awareness that Oregon wineries have an impact on tourism, but the wineries have to pay for the signs.

We have abbreviated the names of most of the wine festivals in the charts listing each winery's recent awards. The festival's host city, rather than the full name of the festival, is used. For instance, the Enological Society of the Pacific Northwest is "Seattle;" the American Wine Competition in Ithaca, New York, is "New York;" the International Wine and Spirits Competition is "London."

Finally, we have included three Washington wineries in this book because they are on the Oregon border and easily accessible to anyone touring Oregon wineries. Complete profiles of all Washington wineries are found in *Touring the Wine Country of Washington*, which we published last year.

We've tried to keep our recommendations on a scale that matches the wineries themselves: intimate and welcoming. We haven't listed any chain-operated motels, for instance. (You don't need this book to find a Holiday Inn, do you?) There's an emphasis, instead, on "bed-and-breakfast" lodgings and independently run hotels and inns. We have listed independent Bed & Breakfast inns with other touring information for each area (especially in Ashland, where there are over a dozen); we have listed Bed & Breakfast registries separately at the back of the book.

We tried to find restaurants for each region in a variety of styles and price categories: dinner houses, lunch counters, breakfast places, hamburger stands. We eliminated many "fancy" restaurants because their wine lists gave short shrift to local wines; we feel that a restaurant making a big to-do about "fresh" ingredients and "local" materials has an obligation, a responsibility, to offer the product of local vineyards.

Generally speaking, restaurants that are part of hotels are listed in the lodgings category. Our own preference is for little restaurants (places like Nick's in McMinnville, Chata outside Ashland, the Central Cafe in Eugene), with an owner-chef at the helm if at all possible. This isn't meant to be snobbish, but to encourage the entrepreneurial spirit of a family-run restaurant where the welcome and attention to detail are personal.

Delicatessens and wine shops come in all stripes: take-out places, sit-down places, a complete wine selection, a meager wine selection. We've tried to find those which sell picnic makings to take out, or have a decent selection of Northwest wines, or both.

Most wineries have their own picnic areas, but you may not be visiting a winery at mealtime. So we've come up with a few nice parks and out-of-the-way picnic places in the wine country.

**Out-of-state readers should note that all Oregon telephone numbers are in area code 503.**

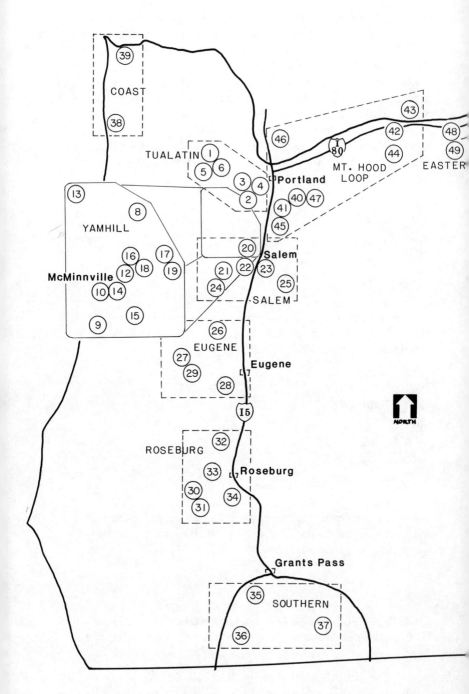

COAST

39

38

TUALATIN

1

5 6

3

4

2

Portland

I 80

MT. HOOD
LOOP

46

42

44

43

48

49

EASTER

40 47

41

45

13

YAMHILL

8

16 17

12 18 19

McMinnville

10 14

15

9

20

21 22 23

24

25

Salem

SALEM

26

EUGENE

27

29

28

Eugene

I5

ROSEBURG

32

33

30

31 34

Roseburg

Grants Pass

SOUTHERN

35

36 37

NORTH

# OREGON WINERIES

## *(and Washington Wineries close to the state line)*

### Tualatin Valley
1. Cote des Colombes
2. Mulhausen Vineyards
3. Oak Knoll
4. Ponzi Vineyards
5. Shafer Vineyard Cellars
6. Tualatin Vineyards

### Yamhill County
7. Peter Adams Wines (*)
8. The Adelsheim Vineyard
9. Amity Vineyards
10. Arterberry
11. Century Home Wines
12. Chateau Benoit
13. Elk Cove Vineyards
14. The Eyrie Vineyards
15. Hidden Springs Winery
16. Knudsen Erath
17. Rex Hill Vineyards
18. Sokol Blosser Winery
19. Veritas Vineyard (*)

### Salem Area
20. Bethel Heights Vineyard (*)
21. Ellendale Vineyards
22. Glen Creek Winery
23. Honeywood Winery
24. Serendipity Cellars Winery
25. Silver Falls Vineyard

### Eugene Area
26. Alpine Vineyards
27. Forgeron Vineyard
28. Hinman Vineyards
29. The Honey House

### Roseburg Area
30. Bjelland Vineyards
31. Girardet Vineyards
32. Henry Estate Winery
33. Hillcrest Vineyard
34. Jonicole Vineyards

### Southern Oregon
35. Rogue River Winery
36. Siskiyou Vineyard
37. Valley View Vineyard

### Oregon Coast
38. Nehalem Bay Wine Company
39. Shallon

### Mount Hood Loop
40. Big Fir Winery
41. Henry Endres Winery
42. Hood River Vineyards
43. Mont Elise Vineyards (+)
44. Mount Hood Winery
45. St. Josef's Weinkeller
46. Salishan Vineyards (+)
47. Wasson Brothers Winery

### Eastern Oregon
48. La Casa de Vin
49. River Ridge (+)

*(\*) Winery not bonded at press time*
*(+) Winery in Washington State*

# *Introduction*

The purpose of this book is to take the mystery and pretense out of wine *and* travel without destroying their inherent romance.

This totally updated edition, designed to remain current for 1984 and 1985, is the most complete guide to the wineries and wine country of Oregon. We have added almost twenty new wineries; updated the tourist listings for lodgings, restaurants, wine shops, delicatessens, and picnic spots; provided new maps; compiled new information about the wineries, what they grow and what they sell; and revised the profiles of the wine-makers, who they are and why they make the wines they do.

Oregon's wine country is unique. In some parts of the world, the vine-yards sit next to one another like cornfields; Oregon's wine country is checkerboarded among the orchards and row crops of the Willamette and Umpqua valleys. In some parts of the world, a quaint wine country Bed & Breakfast inn is likely to have a four-month waiting list of city folk anxious to snuggle up among the vines; in Oregon, a visitor risks getting lost on coun-try roads. In some parts of the world, three-star French chefs prepare hun-dred-dollar meals for wine country visitors; in Oregon's wine country, the meals are honest and unpretentious. In some parts of the world, they think "theirs" is the only wine; in Oregon, the wine industry recognizes both its youth and its enormous potential.

Oregon wines are winning well-deserved, worldwide recognition, and have contributed immensely to the region's evolution from frontier outpost to vanguard of civilization. How? It's partly the devotion of the winemakers to their craft, but it's primarily Oregon's weather. Oregon's climate is ideal for growing premium wine grapes. (You can grow some varieties of grapes in a parking lot, but they won't make decent wine.) The grapes that go into California and Italian jug wines come from hot climates, where they ripen early and produce enormous quantities of sweet juice. Oregon's best grapes, Pinot Noir and Chardonnay, require a long, relatively cool growing season, just like the Pinot Noir and Chardonnay grown in Burgundy. Every growing season is suspenseful; not until October do the growers know whether the vintage will ripen successfully or if cold weather and rain will ruin the crop.

Climate is everything, or almost everything. The growing season pro-duces warm (but not hot) days, and (because Oregon is further north than California) an average of two more daylight hours every day. The nights are cool compared to California, allowing the grapes to retain more of their natural acid, which produces wines with more character and potential for aging.

The need to age wines puts enormous financial pressure on the wine-makers. It means they must buy barrels and tanks, and build a facility big enough to store them; it means they must exercise skill in caring for the wines until they're ready to be released. All this costs money, which explains why Oregon wine is more expensive than California jug wine and some cheap imports. The grapes themselves are also labor-intensive, which gives vineyards a high value per acre. Willamette Valley alfalfa or grass seed farmers probably couldn't even turn their combines around in the space that winegrowers need to plant a successful vineyard; they can't imagine investing a grape-grower's labor investment into such a small piece of land.

In agriculture as in any business, you're either very big or very spe-cialized. You either produce a commodity that's sold to a processor, or you have an item that's marketed directly to the consumer. Scott Henry (of Henry Winery in Umpqua) was selling his prunes to a cannery; he tore them out and planted Riesling, because he can sell the wine directly to con-sumers. This emphasis on old-fashioned direct marketing may sound con-trary to the way California and Italy sell wine, but Oregon emphasizes only small volumes (a little more than 300,000 gallons a year, roughly one-tenth of Washington's output, and a mere drop in the country's 100-million-gallon wine consumption). Gallo and Riunite, to name only two producers, proba-bly spill more in a day than Oregon bottles all year. In fact, the Gallos and Riunites are doing Oregon a favor; their efforts to open new markets are creating new wine drinkers, some of whom will one day become more selective drinkers and choose Oregon wines.

Still, it will be a long, long time before any Oregon wine is produced in large quantities. Two years ago, we wrote that volume alone is anathema to many of the smaller-scale wineries. Nancy Ponzi, co-owner of Ponzi Vine-yards in Beaverton, confirmed this sentiment to us in the spring of 1984, pointing out that her winery, for one, is actually reducing its production. She wrote to us that "with more [wine production], everything increases . . . the costs, the labor, the overall work, the promotion, and, because of the need to meet all these overhead costs, the winery is pressed with a need for cash flow, which means expediting the wines, compromising, [bank] loans, dropping prices, and ulcers. The equation of more wine equaling more profit simply doesn't work. I'm not privy to anyone's accounts, but I suspect there are only a tiny handful of wineries actually making a profit, and further suspect it's not those producing large quantities. The American concept of big is better is not necessarily true, profitable, or civilized."

It is precisely the civilizing quality of winemaking—and wine touring—that we find so appealing. Oregon's tiny wine industry hasn't attracted the interest of Corporate America. We hope the industry will remain small scale, attractive to small investors, small growers, small producers, small innkeepers, small restaurateurs. This will keep it accessible to tourists, environmentally attractive, and contributing to Oregon's very special quality of life.

# Questions & Answers About Oregon Wine

### "Tell me about wine touring."

Until recently, "wine touring" implied a trip to California. No more. There's now a sufficient concentration of wineries in western Oregon to provide a variety of interesting tours, whether you've never visited a winery before or consider yourself a sophisticated world traveler whose last stop was Chateau Lafite.

You can come from nearby or from far away; you can stay in first class hotels or in campgrounds; you can dine in ritzy restaurants or cook hotdogs over a campground barbecue. If you are open to new experiences, to the beauty of Oregon's scenery, to back roads and byways, and to meeting interesting new people along the way, then you have the right idea. Wine touring, in other words, is an attitude of curiosity, of appreciation for the world around you.

Wine touring can be the sole reason for a vacation, or an added attraction to a trip that's already underway, or even a day trip from wherever you've made your base in Oregon.

### "Don't I have to know a lot about wine?"

Not at all. Wine touring will make you more knowledgeable about wine, and that will let you enjoy wine all the more. Besides, wine touring lets you learn about a fascinating (and rapidly growing) Oregon industry. Visiting a winery is every bit as interesting as visiting a brewery or an airplane factory. And the surroundings are much, much more beautiful.

### "Is there a lot of wine country in Oregon?"

Yes, and it's growing all the time. Oregon's acreage is nothing vast, nothing like the vine-covered mountainsides along the German rivers, or like the expanses of vineyards along the famous French hillsides of Burgundy, or even like the lush acreage of central California, but they are premium vineyards, producing many superb wines.

The difference in Oregon is that its patches of grapevines are planted amidst other crops: among fruit orchards, nut groves, and wheat in the Willamette Valley; among oak trees and more fruit orchards in the southern parts of the state. This keeps the views more interesting, we think. You get to see real agricultural countryside while you drive from the freeway to the vineyards: pastures full of cows, fields full of corn, orchards of fruit and nut trees, barns, and farmhouses in the shade of a few tall trees.

## "How many wineries are there in Oregon? How many vineyards?"

We've identified over 46 wineries around the state, most of which are open to the public. There are many independent growers, too; some of them grow nothing but grapes, some grow grapes along with other crops. About 2,000 acres of grapes are currently planted in Oregon, and about half of those vineyards are mature enough to produce a commercial crop. There are thousands and thousands of acres of fruits and berries, too, which go into Oregon wines. We've included all active and even prospective bonded wineries (licensed by the federal government to sell alcoholic beverages to the public), whether they make grape wine, fruit wine, or both.

## "What's a varietal wine?"

It's any wine made from one of the recognized grape *varieties*, such as Pinot Noir, Chardonnay, or Riesling. Fruit wines, jug wines, and proprietary blended wines don't count; the wine must be named for the grape variety that is in the bottle. The classic European wine grapes are generally referred to as varietal, and are generally of higher quality and more expensive than blends.

## "Why so many small wineries? Can they all make it?"

The wineries are small because their owners want to keep personal control over the entire process, something they couldn't do if the winery produced huge volumes. Oregon's fiscal structure, furthermore, taxes wineries making less than 100,000 gallons at a lower rate, specifically to encourage small wineries.

Because they're not huge, the wineries don't really compete with each other, except at wine festivals. Instead, they share a growing market for high-quality wines; they identify their own customers, their own restaurants, their own distribution channels. And even though most winemakers are concentrating on Pinot Noir and Chardonnay (the great grapes of Burgundy), we think there's plenty of room for a diversity of winemaking styles and labels in Oregon.

## "What are Oregon wineries like to visit?"

Most of Oregon's wineries welcome visitors, though they are not geared to a high volume of tourist traffic. If you've ever visited any of the larger California wineries, where the driveways are designed to allow tour buses to turn around, you'll notice the contrast soon enough! Most of the wineries described in this book are "mom and pop" operations: very, very small, although quite ambitious, undertakings. The winery itself is often part of the family home; provisions for large group tours are the exception, not the rule.

The Oregon Winegrowers Association has published a handy booklet that tells you how to get to the wineries, but that doesn't necessarily mean that the winemaker has paid for space in the booklet or put up any signs to direct you once you leave the main road. Once you pull up to the winery itself, though, you will receive a genuinely friendly welcome, especially if you show a sincere interest in the winemaker's activities.

## "What does a tour consist of?"

When the winery is open to the public, the winemaker, family, or staff members will be on duty to conduct tours and tastings. If the winemaker is away (at a festival or on a trip), a knowledgeable employee takes over. Your questions about the wines, the grapes, the winemaking process, and the marketing of the wines are welcome.

You may be asked, if you're in a small group, if you'd like to see the winery itself; accept, by all means. The winemaker will proudly walk you past a lot of equipment: stemmer-crushers, presses, fermenting tanks, oak casks, stainless steel barrels, hoses, and what not. He'll talk about the sources of his grapes and the number of gallons he's got going through malolactic fermentation in French oak. He'll tell you about last year's harvest and next season's grape supply. He may ask you about your own interest in wine and where you might have seen his label. Don't be surprised, by the way, if the winemaker turns out to be a woman. Women are responsible for winemaking and cellar work in many Oregon wineries.

### "Hold on: we've got youngsters under 21 with us. What about them?"

Kids are welcome at wineries. Chances are that they'll enjoy a tour of the facilities. And they'll certainly enjoy the drive through the countryside and the picnic or hamburgers before or afterwards.

You don't have to make a major production out of wine touring. It's a casual affair, not a formal exercise, and many visitors bring children. The kids just don't participate in the actual wine tasting.

### "Okay, let's get on to the wine tasting."

The tasting itself follows a fairly standard procedure. You will be offered the driest white wine first (like the least sweet Riesling or Semillon), then perhaps a fuller-bodied white (such as Chardonnay), perhaps a rose, and then the red wines (such as Pinot Noir).

Many wineries offer pieces of bread or cheese to chew between wines. Some also put out buckets or other receptacles if you don't want to swallow the wine. (Professional tasters never do; they spit . . . discreetly.) If you're going to visit more than one winery in a day, you probably shouldn't swallow too many tastes and drive.

### "Can we buy wine at the winery?"

Indeed you can, although you certainly aren't obligated to buy anything. You'll see a sign that says "Tax Paid Room" somewhere in the vicinity of the tasting room; that's where they keep the wine that's available for retail sale.

In addition to their regular line of wines, most wineries sell a few limited bottlings only at the winery, and they're almost always good buys. Case discounts vary from 10 to 20 percent.

### "How many wineries do people visit in a day?"

We think it's unrealistic to visit more than two or three in an afternoon. It takes time, at least an hour, for even a casual visitor to do a winery justice. We also think it's more fun to visit wineries in conjunction with a picnic or more traditional sightseeing. We're appalled that some people think of wine touring as an opportunity to guzzle free wine before charging down the road to the next winery. We don't encourage wine touring as an excuse for drinking and driving.

### "I don't like wine all that much, and I'd be embarrassed to take up a winemaker's time and taste his wines if I know I won't buy anything."

The winemakers realize that they're operating tasting rooms as much for tourism and self-promotion as for retail sales. They don't have to open to the public at all, if they don't want to, but many believe that wine touring is a good way to acquaint visitors with their wine. Some sell all their output at the winery; many also sell T-shirts, books, and souvenir glassware, too. Who knows, you may even find something you like!

### "What about the price of Oregon wines? Aren't they terribly expensive?"

Not really. You're buying "handmade" wines from premium grapes, not Gallo Burgundy, after all. It costs a lot of money to buy acreage, to buy grapes while waiting for your own vines to reach maturity, to build and equip a winery. The winemaking process itself is very labor intensive: planting, fertilizing, pruning, picking, crushing, checking fermentation, racking, transferring, bottling, warehousing, marketing. Still, it's less expensive to do this in Oregon than in California because land and labor costs are lower here; Napa Valley vineyards cost up to $20,000 an acre, twice Oregon's going rate.

The price tags on most Oregon wines have not changed much in the past two years, and there are some very good bargains to be had. But remember that vintages change, a winery's cash flow needs may fluctuate, and that your tastes may not agree with ours. We found Scott Henry's Umpqua Red Table Wine to be a real bargain at $4.50, Mulhausen's Pinot Noir Rose to be well worth $4.50, the non-vintaged Pinot Noir, Chardonnay, and Riesling at Knudsen Erath to be fine values at $7.99 per magnum, and some of the Ponzi bottlings, available only at the winery, to be excellent buys. The important thing, when looking at the price of a wine, is to relate it to the wine's quality (or the other way around); a wine can be a terrible buy despite its low price.

### "How can you tell from the label what's in the bottle?"

With Oregon wine, you're in luck. Oregon has the strictest, most consumer-oriented wine-labeling regulations in the country. The vintage date, if there is one, guarantees that at least 95 percent of the grapes used to make the wine were harvested during that year. The name of the wine, if it's a varietal grape, guarantees that 90 percent of the grapes are indeed that grape; federal laws promise only 75 percent. One exception is Cabernet Sauvignon, which is traditionally blended with other varieties. Wines can also have "proprietary" names, such as Sokol Blosser's "Bouquet Blanc" or Henry Winery's "Umpqua Red," but no Oregon wine can have a "generic" name; in fact, no European geographic names (like Chablis or Burgundy) may be used at all. Any wine with a varietal name, such as Chardonnay or Pinot Noir, must also carry an "appellation" or statement of its geographic origin. This appellation can be a state (Oregon or Washington) or a federally approved region within a state (such as Willamette Valley), and all the grapes involved must come from the region named. Finally, all labels must indicate the name and location of the winery that produced the wine.

## "What else is Oregon doing to promote its wine?"

The state legislature recently created a Wine Advisory Board to direct research and marketing efforts for the wine industry. The board's funding comes from an assessment on the tonnage of all grapes produced in Oregon, and a portion of all the wine taxes collected, whether it's Oregon wine or not. The advisory board is required to spend one-third of its funds on research, one-third on marketing, and one-third at the discretion of its members. What's remarkable about this is that the state has become aware of wine as an important symbol of Oregon's quest for the highest standards in its products and its environment.

## "What's the best time of year to go wine touring? And which wineries should we visit?"

Go anytime. There is beauty even during a downpour, and most of the wineries are open year-round. There's more to see during harvest and crush, but the winemakers themselves will probably be too busy to show you around. New releases come out in spring, usually beginning with the Rieslings of the previous harvest. Summer weekends can get crowded, and some of the festivals are nothing short of madness. Go when you can, and enjoy yourselves.

Which winery? That's like asking which child you like best. They all have their distinctive selves to offer. Scenery, wine, people. Go.

# *Tualatin Valley*

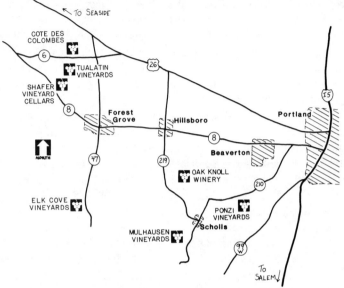

The fertile soil of the Tualatin Valley extends westward from metropolitan Portland like a great green blanket, enriched centuries ago by the mineral deposits of lava flows from the Cascades and by prehistoric sand, clay, and silt. The Tualatin River—its name, given by the valley's native American inhabitants, means "lazy river"—meanders across the valley floor toward the Willamette. Less than 200 years ago, the Twality Indians hunted deer, elk, bear, and geese along the shores of the river; within fifty years, they had succumbed to smallpox epidemics brought by the white men who came to settle the Oregon Territory.

Today Washington County, which encompasses most of the Tualatin Valley, is the fastest-growing jurisdiction in Oregon. The timbered plains are no longer pristine, dotted now with homes and shopping centers. Housing developments cascade from the West Hills of Portland, gobbling up farmland; electronics companies like Tektronix, Floating Point Systems, and Intel are turning Highway 8 (between Beaverton and Forest Grove) into Oregon's "silicon valley." And yet, the western half of Washington County has retained its agricultural character, boosting farm income fourfold in the past fifteen years, giving rise to several new vineyards, and permitting half a dozen wineries to flourish.

15

The proximity of these vineyards to metropolitan Portland allows for satisfying, uncomplicated wine touring. The wineries themselves have banded together in an association of Washington County Winegrowers to encourage weekend touring by Portland residents and visitors.

Still, the most popular festival in the region is no doubt the annual sausage and kraut dinner held on the first Saturday in November at Verboort, about two and a half miles north of Forest Grove. Thousands of people converge on this little Dutch community every year for the sausage feed, which raises money for local good works.

Washington County's proximity to Portland has left its small towns with a charming quality of isolation and innocence. Hillsboro, the county seat, has a museum that includes an intriguing miniature replica of a pioneer farm. It also hosts two festivals: Happy Days in June, and Western Days in July. Forest Grove, home of Pacific University (founded in 1849), sponsors an annual Barbershop Quartet/Gay Nineties Festival. Among the sights in Forest Grove are the campus of Pacific University, attractive old homes, and the Prune Exchange.

A popular activity in Washington County is antique hunting by urbanites looking for country bargains. Tiny places like Banks, Cornelius, Brookwood, and Scholls have antique shops or flea markets, as do the larger towns such as Forest Grove, Hillsboro, and Beaverton. The widely available *Mapbook of Antique Shops* has addresses and hours.

Another Washington County destination, not as widely publicized, is the Trolley Park on Gales Creek at Glenwood, along Highway 6. It's a living museum for turn-of-the-century trolley cars, managed by the Oregon Electric Railway Society in a twenty-six-acre park. Among the trolleys running on a track through the park are a double-decker from Blackpool, England, an open car from Sydney, Australia, and a closed city streetcar. Some souvenirs and picnic supplies are available. Overnight camping and picnic sites can be reached only by riding the trolley to the far end of the little valley. For information on schedules and charter possibilities, phone the park at 357-3574 in Glenwood, or the Electric Railway Historical Society in Portland at 284-6236.

Because so much of the wine country is virtually in the Portland suburbs, it would be tempting to turn this section into a guidebook to Portland, where we lived for many years. Although many travelers to the wine country will make Portland their base, we feel that a catalog of Portland lodgings, restaurants, and delicatessens is beyond the scope of this volume, and we've limited our tourism recommendations in this edition to Washington County establishments.

And what a pleasure it can be to tour Washington County's wineries! The Tualatin Valley offers easy access from the Portland metropolitan area, leisurely driving along country roads, the archetypal country store (Petrich's, near Scholls), some of the most pleasant surroundings to be found anywhere in Oregon, and excellent wine at the end of gravel driveways.

*Notes:*

*The Washington County Winery Association will sponsor two events in 1984 of special interest to the public. And because all the wineries participate, we have not listed them individually in each of the winery profiles which follow.*

*Fourth of July weekend brings the annual "Barrel Tasting Tour," a fascinating opportunity to taste wine "before it's time" directly from the barrel, to meet the winemakers, to learn why some wines are aged in wood, and what qualities to look for in young, "unfinished" wines. Admission to the wineries is free; light snacks and appetizers are available during the tour, and mixed-case discounts are given to buyers during the tour.*

*The three days of Thanksgiving weekend, a traditional time for wineries to show off their wares after the harvest has finished, is the occasion of another "Valley Wine Tour."*

# Cote des Colombes

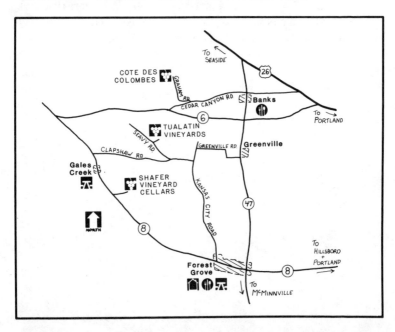

Perhaps the most remarkable thing about Joe and Betty Coulombe's tiny Cote des Colombes ("Hill of the Doves") vineyard, on a quiet, flowered hillside in Washington County, is that they are successfully growing Cabernet Sauvignon—a variety that the Tualatin Valley's climate doesn't normally support. But Joe Coulombe spent ten years in the U.S. Air Force as a weather researcher, and he *knows* about microclimates. *His* little patch of hillside, a few miles from the sleepy community of Banks, receives just the right amount of warm air rising from the valley floor to allow his Cabernet Sauvignon vines to grow to maturity.

The vineyard was inaugurated in 1969, while Coulombe was still working at Tektronix and running a couple of wine shops called "The Progressive Winemaker" on the side. The Coulombes leased a plot of land once used as a hog farm at the end of Graham Road and started planting their cuttings: Cabernet Sauvignon from Concannon Vineyard, Pinot Noir from The Eyrie Vineyards, Chauche Gris (often called Grey Riesling) from Wente Brothers. While the vines were maturing, Coulombe confined his winemaking

---

**COTE DES COLOMBES VINEYARD**
Graham Road
Route 2, Box 13
Mail: P.O. Box 266
Banks, OR 97106
324-0855

| | |
|---|---|
| Open to the public | 12-5 daily |
| Tour groups | yes |
| Charge for tour groups | $1 per person (groups over 10) |
| Picnic facilities at the winery | 3 picnic tables and benches under tree overlooking the valley |
| Festivals/special events | Medieval Wine Festival, July 8-9; Open House, Thanksgiving weekend |
| Wines available (1984) | Chardonnay |
| | White Riesling |
| | Pinot Noir Blush |
| | Pinot Noir |
| | 1980 Cabernet Sauvignon |
| | Chenin Blanc (late harvest) |

---

ambitions to teaching enology courses at the wine shops and selling wine-making equipment to his students. Before long, though, "complete insanity" (as he describes it) took over. He closed the wine shops and bonded Cote des Colombes in 1977: the commitment to full-time, commercial winemaking had been sealed.

Coulombe used Cabernet Sauvignon grapes grown by others in Yamhill County and in Washington so he would know what to do when his own grapes were ready. The key questions involved the wine's exposure to oak. Big barrels, small barrels? For how long? And what kind of oak (Limousin, Allier, traditional "American" oak, or even *Oregon* oak)?

All of the Cote des Colombes experimenting with Cabernet aside, Joe Coulombe recognizes the public demand for white wines, and will be making more Chardonnay, Gewurztraminer and White Riesling. He's also making jelly from Oregon vinifera grapes, selling it at Portland's Saturday Market and other outlets as "Oregon Vintner's Pride Wine Jelly."

Marketing in the traditional, commercial sense is not Joe Coulombe's strong suit. He is a wine*maker*, not a wine seller. But his serious calling does not overshadow a smiling, affable nature and a love of fun. Joe and

## COTE DES COLOMBES

| | |
|---|---|
| Owners | Joe & Betty Coulombe |
| Winemaker | Joseph R. P. Coulombe |
| Year bonded | 1977 |
| Year first planted | 1969 |
| Vineyard acreage | 5 |
| Principal varieties | Pinot Noir |
| | Cabernet Sauvignon |
| | Gewurztraminer |
| | Pinot Blanc |
| | Chance Gris |
| Year of first crush | 1977 |
| Production capacity | 8,000 gallons |
| Production in 1983 | 4,000 gallons |
| Awards, 1983 | |
| 1980 Cabernet Sauvignon: | Silver, Oregon State Fair |
| 1981 Pinot Noir: | Silver, Oregon State Fair |

Betty open the vineyard regularly for festival weekends, and in July there's a Medieval Wine Festival that always gets lots of attention. A new winery building and tasting room were added in 1982, making the little vale at the end of Graham Road even more attractive to visitors.

And if the grass grows a bit high around the vines and outside the entrance to the tasting room, we must remember that wildflowers and field mice flourish in the high cover, and dogs seem more playful when their bellies are tickled by taller grasses. The vines don't care; they are influenced only by waves of air flowing unseen up or down the slope.

# Mulhausen Vineyards

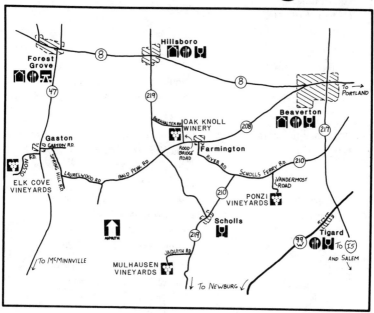

The drive from Newberg over Chehalem Mountain to Mulhausen Vineyards is one of the most magnificent in all of Oregon. Newberg itself is a busy little town of about 10,000 people that seems to be full of one-way streets and gas stations, but a stone's throw past George Fox College (Herbert Hoover's alma mater), along Highway 219 to Scholls and Hillsboro, the road becomes quiet as it travels through yellow grassland and into deep woods. As the road climbs, there are occasional, ever-changing glimpses back down into the magnificent valley; if you are lucky, you may even see a few deer in the brush. Then, at the heady altitude of 1,212 feet, the road crests and there is a spectacular view into the Tualatin Valley. Oregonians whose only sight of the Tualatin Valley has been housing tracts covered with smog (the usual view from Portland's West Hills) will be particularly surprised; the perspective from Chehalem Mountain is totally unexpected.

The dense woods are left behind as the highway descends toward the orchards and farmland of the valley, but a sharp turn onto Jaquith Road takes you back uphill again. The Mulhausen Vineyards winery is almost at

---

**MULHAUSEN VINEYARDS**
(formerly Chehalem Mountain Winery)
Jaquith Road
Route 1, Box 99-C
Newberg, OR 97132
628-2417

| | |
|---|---|
| Open to the public | 12-5 weekends & holidays (except Thanksgiving & Christmas) |
| Tour groups | by appointment for more than 25 |
| Charge for tour groups | $1 per person |
| Picnic facilities at the winery | lawn and gardens adjacent to the winery; several tables; view of Mt. Hood, Mt. Adams, Mt. St. Helens, Mt. Rainier |
| Festivals/special events | Mai Weinprobe, May 19; New England Lobster Feed, July 7; Oct. weekends, crush celebration; Novemberfest, Nov. 23-25. |
| Wines available (1984) | 1982 & 1983 Estate Riesling<br>1982 & 1983 Oregon Riesling<br>1982 & 1983 Pinot Noir Blanc<br>1981 Pinot Noir Rose<br>1982 Pinot Noir<br>1982 Gewurztraminer<br>1982 Chardonnay<br>1982 Vin Blanc |

---

the end of the road. The driveway passes some twenty acres of vineyards planted with Pinot Noir, Riesling, and Chardonnay before arriving at the Mulhausen home, which Zane and his wife, Pat, have built rather like a French country estate. You park in an area patrolled by wandering ducks; to reach the tasting room, you walk around the side of the house, along a lovely shaded veranda that surrounds a quiet, flowered garden. Then the door opens, and you are admitted to a great hall with high, sloping ceilings, surrounded by a gallery. Oriental rugs lie on wide-planked hemlock floors. The whitewashed walls set off remarkable pieces of antique furniture. A refectory table for the wine tasting is to one side, but your eye is drawn to the windows, which overlook a green swath of lawn set with picnic tables, more vineyards, the entire Tualatin Valley and the mountain peaks of Hood,

## MULHAUSEN VINEYARDS

| | |
|---|---|
| Owners | Zane & Pat Mulhausen |
| Winemaker | Zane Mulhausen |
| Year bonded | 1979 |
| Year first planted | 1973 |
| Vineyard acreage | 35 |
| Principal varieties, acres | Pinot Noir, 10 |
| | Chardonnay, 8 |
| | Sylvaner, 7 |
| | Riesling, 7 |
| | Gewurztraminer, 3 |
| Year of first crush | 1979 |
| Production capacity | 20,000 gallons |
| Production in 1983 | 7,000 gallons |
| Production in 1982 | 18,000 gallons |
| Recent Awards | |
| Estate White Riesling: | Bronze, Oregon State Fair (1983) |
| Sylvaner: | Silver, Seattle (1982) |
| | Silver, Oregon State Fair (1982) |

Adams, Saint Helens, and Rainier. The setting is more than splendid; it is unparalleled.

To take a glass of wine in hand in these surroundings—to admire the color and taste of the wine while appreciating the terrain—is soulstirring. To be a winemaker here, we feel, must give Zane Mulhausen some of the satisfactions of a feudal lord.

Of course, there is also some of the serf's sweat in winemaking, and that must be counted as one of its satisfactions, too. Trained as a mechanical engineer at the University of Washington, Mulhausen had worked at Tektronix (where his job involved water purification), and as a contractor. An interest in European wines triggered his interest in winemaking, and the prospect of living in the country and making a reasonable living established his commitment to winemaking. So Mulhausen Vineyards, planted in 1973, was bonded in 1979 (at first it was called Chehalem Mountain Winery) and the winemaking began in earnest.

It would be nice to think of this kindly gentleman in his magnificent home atop Chehalem Mountain as a sort of guru to the younger winemakers in both valleys below. But Mulhausen is not part of the winemaking fraternity; he does not subscribe to the mystique of winemaking at all. "All winemaking is easy and simple with good grapes and reasonable equipment," he says. He proceeds with common sense: one year, he puts his money into the vineyards, the next into the winery. When he had the opportunity to buy extra Riesling grapes in 1982, he made 18,000 gallons of wine; now he's got extra Riesling to sell in 1984, and fortunately, Riesling ages beautifully. Meantime, he's planted five more acres of Sylvaner because he couldn't get a guaranteed outside supply. Ironically, Mulhausen has had great success with Sylvaner as a varietal wine, but a competitor outbid him for the only Sylvaner grapes and used them in a blended wine.

Mulhausen wines offer excellent value. One of the best is the 1980 Mulhausen Pinot Noir Rose, a rose in name only. The grapes were intended for a full-bodied Pinot Noir, and were fermented on the skins to extract extra color and tannin, but the color wasn't quite deep enough to satisfy Zane Mulhausen's standards. Instead of transferring the wine to oak barrels for aging, he put the wine into stainless steel tanks and bottled it with just a little residual sugar. The result is an immensely flavorful wine which (by the case at the winery) costs only $3.60 a bottle.

The winery welcomes visitors on weekends and holidays, and has an added attraction for groups: a chef, Steve De Angelo, who gives cooking classes at the winery and does catering for visiting groups. Mulhausen has also added several festivals to its schedule, including three weekends of "Crush Celebration" in October. And despite the Newberg post office address, Mulhausen has decided to align himself with the Washington County winemakers, a decision that makes enormous sense considering that he's only eleven miles from the Washington Square Shopping Center.

Zane Mulhausen reminds us of a tough but fair high school coach, or of the leader of a scout group. A man who keeps to himself but whom you'd like to know better. How fortunate that he is making *wine*, the one commodity that quickens friendship. His wine deserves a greater audience; his winery is the undiscovered jewel of Oregon.

# *Oak Knoll*

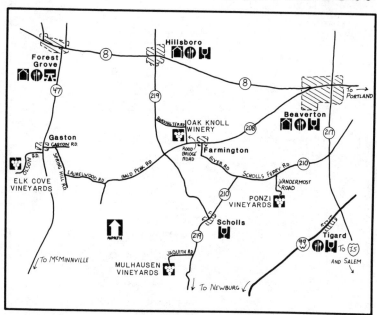

Oak Knoll Winery looks like it ought to be a dairy farm—except that there are no cows on this five-acre spread of yellow grassland along Burkhalter Road, southwest of Beaverton. Instead, the visitor finds a stand of black oak trees, a big house for the owner's family, several outbuildings, and a dairy barn that once held 108 cows. But there are no cows in sight, and no vineyards, either, for that matter. So what is going on here?

The answer lies inside the barn, where oak barrels from Chateau Lafite and stainless steel fermenting tanks occupy the heifers' stalls, and lengths of hose and tubing run along the concrete troughs and drain channels used by dairymen only a dozen years ago. In fact, the barn is no longer large enough to contain all the gear and to store all the wine produced by Oak Knoll; a new warehouse has been added on, containing the bottling operations, offices, and a comfortable tasting room, freeing up enough space in the barn to increase the winery's capacity to 70,000 gallons a year. As recently as 1978, Oak Knoll was making one-third of all Oregon's wine. With more wineries in production, that percentage has gone down, but Oak Knoll's production has gone up. Increasingly, Ron Vuylsteke is becoming

---

### 🍇 OAK KNOLL

Burkhalter Road
Route 6, Box 184
Hillsboro, OR 97123
648-8198

| | |
|---|---|
| Open to the public | 12-5 Wed.-Sun. (11-5 Sat.) |
| Tour groups | yes, by appointment |
| Charge for tour groups | $1 per person |
| Picnic facilities at the winery | 10 picnic tables adjacent to the winery |
| Festivals/special events | Bacchus Goes Bluegrass, May 19-20; Niagara Fest, Aug. |
| Wines available (1984) | 1980 Cabernet Sauvignon |
| | 1982 Chardonnay |
| | 1981 Pinot Noir |
| | 1982 Vintage Select Pinot Noir |
| | 1983 Pinot Blanc |
| | 1983 White Riesling |
| | 1983 Muscat of Alexandria |
| | Bacchus Blanc |
| | Raspberry, Loganberry, Blackberry, Rhubarb, American Niagara |

---

known and admired for his vinifera wines.

A case in point: Andre Tchelistcheff, dean of American winemakers and the senior wine judge at the Oregon State Fair in 1983, stood up at the end of the tasting, held a glass of Pinot Noir on high, and pronounced, "I am prepared to defend this wine with the last breath in my little body." With that kind of backing, the wine went on to win a gold medal and the Governor's Sweepstakes for the best vinifera wine in the state. And as soon as he found out that it was Oak Knoll's 1980 Vintage Select Pinot Noir, Tchelistcheff telephoned the Vuylstekes to offer his congratulations. "One of the greatest Pinot Noirs I have come across in fifty years of tasting," he said.

That heady honor wasn't all. Oak Knoll won the *other* Governor's Sweepstakes as well, for the best fruit wine, for their Oregon Raspberry. It was the second year in a row that Oak Knoll won the sweepstakes for fruit wines.

Why should one of the state's most honored wineries continue to make

| OAK KNOLL | |
|---|---|
| Owners | Ron & Marj Vuylsteke |
| Winemaker | Ron Vuylsteke |
| Year bonded | 1970 |
| Year of first crush | 1970 |
| Production capacity | 70,000 gallons |
| Production in 1983 | 50,000 gallons |
| Expansion plans | to 100,000 gallons by 1990 |
| Awards, 1983 | |
| 1980 Vintage Select Pinot Noir: | Gold & Governor's Sweepstakes, Oregon State Fair Gold, New York |
| 1982 Gewurztraminer: | Silver, Oregon State Fair |
| Oregon Raspberry: | Gold & Governor's Sweepstakes, Oregon State Fair |
| Loganberry | Silver, Oregon State Fair, Bronze, London |

fruit wines? The Vuylstekes cite three solid commercial reasons. First, they allow the winery to use its production capacity more efficiently, because fruit can be purchased when it's ripest (and cheapest) and frozen until it's needed without any loss in quality. Second, the fruit wines cost less to make, and can be sold quickly, thereby improving the winery's cash flow. Finally, fruit wines broaden Oak Knoll's range of wines, allowing the winery to produce a wine for every palate, a wine for every occasion.

Because over half of Oak Knoll's output is fruit and berry wine, the amount of vinifera grapes it purchases and vinifera wine it produces can vary considerably from year to year. Oak Knoll can afford to buy more grapes in "good" years, when quality or quantity is high; 1983 was one such year, with the best crop of Pinot Noir and Chardonnay in memory. Most of Oregon's vinifera winemakers, on the other hand, are tied to the production of their own vineyards—supplemented by outside growers—and are almost obliged to make enough wine every year to justify their substantial investment in vineyards, facilities, and equipment. No such obligation confronts Oak Knoll. Nor is fruit and berry winemaking as intensely seasonal as the annual harvest and crush of grapes: as the crop arrives, it is frozen and stored in 400-gallon drums in nearby Hillsboro if it's not needed right away.

Oak Knoll's Niagara is a wine that's finding a lot of buyers these days. It's a labrusca, or native American grape wine, and very popular as a "stepping

27

stone" wine for new wine drinkers and fruit wine drinkers switching to grape wines; Oak Knoll's production of Niagara has gone from 300 gallons in 1978 to 5,000 gallons in 1983.

Ron Vuylsteke was an electronics engineer who designed switches for Tektronix when he and his wife Marjorie started making wine at home one summer, as a hobby, to use up a bumper crop of blackberries. Encouraged by his early success, Vuylsteke eventually began thinking of winemaking less as a hobby, more as an art, and bonded Oak Koll in 1970. He is a truly curious man, always keenly interested in his wines. He seems to learn avidly from every glass and bottle he savors, and he probably has no equal when it comes to the chemistry of enological smells.

Now, even as the winery turns out a wide range of wines and provides employment to several members of his family, Vuylsteke continues to aim at the premium end of the market. The trend, he recognizes, is for wines that complement food, and he foresees a renaissance of red wines as Oregon's accomplishments with Pinot Noir receive their due recognition, including Michael Broadbent singling out Oak Knoll's as one of the top Pinot Noirs in the United States. He even intends to plant some Pinot himself. And he remains steadfast in his determination to make "the finest wines humanly possible."

# *Ponzi Vineyards*

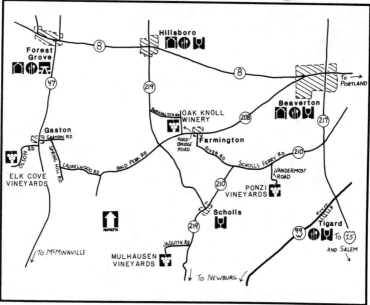

What makes an Oregon winery different? In many cases, it's the care that the winemakers take. With the vineyard, with the winemaking, with the marketing. Dick and Nancy Ponzi, who own the winery closest to metropolitan Portland, take extraordinary steps in all three aspects of the business.

The first indication you get of the care that goes into Ponzi wines comes while you're still in the driveway and observe that there's a rosebush growing at the end of every row of vines in the seventeen-acre vineyard. They're not there for beauty alone, or simply to pay homage to the classical standards of European viticulture; the rosebushes are prone to the same mildew that afflicts the grapevines, and if the vines have been affected, the mildew will show up in the rosebushes first.

To prevent the mildew while adhering to their intention to make the most natural wine possible, the Ponzis dust the vines with a traditional mildew-inhibiting sulfur spray, early in the morning while the air is still moist and the sulfur particles attach themselves more readily to the damp grape leaves. There's a more modern spray, more convenient to use, but the Ponzis feel it's more likely be absorbed by the fruit rather than remain-

---

### 🍇 PONZI VINEYARDS
Vandermost Road
Route 1, Box 842
Beaverton, OR 97007
628-1227

| | |
|---|---|
| Open to the public | 12-5 weekends and by appointment; closed Jan. |
| Tour groups | by appointment only |
| Charge for tour groups | $1 per person |
| Picnic facilities at the winery | large lawn; "we've been known to provide a picnic blanket for a picnic beside the Riesling..." |
| Festivals/special events | Early Summer Wine Festival, May 26-28 |
| Wines available (1984) | 1982 Chardonnay<br>1982 Chardonnay Reserve<br>1983 Riesling<br>1980 & 1981 Pinot Noir<br>1983 Oregon Harvest |

---

ing on the leaves.

This extra work, like the netting the Ponzis use instead of a chemical spray to discourage birds, produces fruit that is harvested in better condition. Berries that are not broken, oozing, or fermenting require much less of the antioxidant chemical sulfur dioxide at crush. And this, in turn, produces a more natural wine, a wine less "gunked up" with preservatives and chemicals.

Furthermore, the Ponzis don't subject their wines to extremes of temperature, especially the cold stabilization that many wineries use to stop fermentation and precipitate the harmless (but "commercially objectionable") tartrate crystals. Too much temperature variation can only damage wine, they say, so they are trying to educate the public to the possible presence of these "wine jewels."

Now, it takes time and effort to do things right, and it can't be done on a large scale without an enormous escalation of costs. That's why the Ponzis have found that their winery is more efficient on a smaller scale, and why they're actually reducing their production.

Dick Ponzi was a mechanical engineer in northern California who designed rides for Disneyland—serious man, but with a good measure of

**PONZI VINEYARDS**

| | |
|---|---|
| Owners | Richard & Nancy Ponzi |
| Winemaker | Richard Ponzi |
| Year bonded | 1974 |
| Year first planted | 1970 |
| Vineyard acreage | 11 |
| Principal varieties, acres | Pinot Gris, 4 |
| | Chardonnay, 2 |
| | White Riesling, 2 |
| | Pinot Noir, 2 |
| Year of first crush | 1974 |
| Production capacity | 18,000 gallons |
| Production in 1983 | 7,000 gallons |
| Expansion plans | 2 more acres of Pinot Gris |
| Awards, 1983 | |
| 1980 Pinot Noir: | Silver, New York |
| | Silver, Seattle |
| | Silver, Oregon State Fair |
| 1982 Riesling: | Silver, Oregon State Fair |
| 1981 Riesling: | Gold, London |

daring in him. When the fun went out of the fun-making business, he moved to Portland and took a job teaching engineering at Portland Community College while he and Nancy started planting an eleven-acre vineyard of Pinot Noir, Chardonnay, White Riesling, and Pinot Gris not far from then-rural Scholls Ferry Road. Pinot Gris is the grape to watch, they say.

From the beginning, Nancy Ponzi has been responsible for marketing, and has assumed a high profile in the community as an advocate for a greater female role in the winemaking business. Not only has she worked alongside Dick in the vineyards (the Ponzis have only one outside employee), and researched firsthand the viticultural practices of their beloved Alsace, she has also taught classes in wine appreciation for women and written wine columns in suburban newspapers. She points out that women buy more wine than men (in supermarkets, and increasingly in restaurants). She has designed the special wine-tasting programs offered by Ponzi Vineyards. And she spearheads the Washington County Winery Association, sponsors of the annual Fourth of July barrel tasting tour of Tualatin Valley wineries, an event that drew 2,000 participants last year.

With wine touring becoming increasingly popular, Ponzi Vineyards' location so close to Portland is an asset. What is now the tasting room was originally the Ponzis' first (tiny) house on the property; the winery itself is a vastly expanded version of the original garage, rebuilt in stone and covered with a copper roof.

Groups of ten or more visitors, for $1 per person, will be treated to an hour-long winery tour hosted by one of the Ponzis themselves; the tour includes a walk through the vineyard and winery, and a sampling of premium wines.

There is also a $5 "tasting program" lasting two to three hours, which offers a more formal presentation, with wine served at tables (again, a ten-person minimum). And for groups up to 100, the Ponzis offer wine tasting parties ($65 minimum, plus the retail price of the wine.) These programs can be tailored to the specific interests of each participating group: Wine and Women, Introduction to Wines of the World, A Practical Approach to Wine.

Nancy Ponzi's obvious understanding of the elements necessary to run a successful business enterprise complement Dick's ability to make good wine. And their mutual success proves that Oregon's Department of Agriculture didn't know what it was talking about when it told the Ponzis in the late 1960s that it was impossible to grow vinifera in the Willamette Valley. The Ag Department obviously hadn't heard about microclimates, sandy subsoils, or the determination of Dick and Nancy Ponzi.

"There are no winemaking traditions to break in Oregon, only those to set, and styles to evolve," Nancy says.

# Shafer Vineyard Cellars

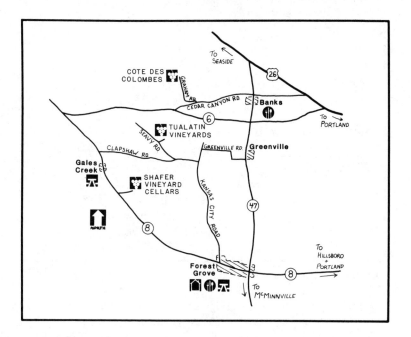

Harvey Shafer is the cheerful owner of one of Oregon's most attractive wineries on a seventy-acre property overlooking Gales Creek, near Forest Grove. Beside the road, five and a half miles from Forest Grove along Highway 8 toward Tillamook, there stands an elegant, carved sign; you turn right up an unpaved road, toward the spic-and-span winery on the hillside and the picture-perfect vineyard planted with twenty acres of carefully tended grapes.

By training and background, Harvey Shafer is a farmer and builder, a man who works out-of-doors. But he is also a fastidiously clean person, whose hobby of home winemaking led him to appreciate good grapes. And there he was in 1972, with this sloping Tualatin Valley acreage ideal for planting vinifera at a time when a growing number of commercial winemakers were willing to pay good money for grapes. So Harvey built himself a vineyard.

For almost ten years, Shafer Vineyards remained "just" a vineyard, supplying Pinot Noir, Chardonnay, Riesling, Gewurztraminer, and Sauvignon Blanc grapes to winemakers with insufficient plantings of their own. As

---

**SHAFER VINEYARD CELLARS**
Star Route, Box 269
Forest Grove, OR 97116
357-6604

| | |
|---|---|
| Open to the public | weekends, 12-5 |
| Tour groups | yes |
| Charge for tour groups | $1 per person |
| Picnic facilities at the winery | 6 redwood tables in small oak grove adjacent to winery |
| Festivals/special events | New Release Event, May 20; Jazz Festival, second weekend in Aug. |
| Wines available (1984) | 1983 White Riesling |
| | 1983 Pinot Noir Blanc |
| | 1980 Pinot Noir |
| | 1980 Chardonnay |
| | 1982 Dry Riesling |
| | 1982 Gewurztraminer |

---

such, Shafer played a crucial role in the economics of winemaking in Oregon. And yet. Even though the sale of grapes brought Harvey Shafer a deserved measure of recognition as a supplier of superb grapes, he increasingly felt as if he were giving away his children at birth.

Eighty percent of a wine's quality, he felt, was in the growing of the grapes. In 1978, Harvey Shafer used some of his own grapes to make a wine of his own: a 1978 Pinot Noir. The quality of that wine is what changed his mind about remaining forever a supplier of grapes; it wasn't long before he started building a winery for the vineyards: Shafer Vineyard Cellars.

In 1978, Shafer's grapes were crushed at Elk Cove; in 1979 and 1980, he used Oak Knoll's facilities. It wasn't until July, 1981, that his own winery and tasting room were finished, with a wide picture window overlooking the valley and a big oak tree just outside the veranda.

One quickly gets the feeling from Harvey Shafer that everything he does will be done properly, at the right time. When we first talked to him, he was looking forward to the 1981 crush: he had planted 740 Pinot Noir vines to the acre and knew that his annual crop per acre would rise from 2.6 tons to 3.5 tons as the vines matured; Gewurztraminer grapes are hard to pick and have a low yield; Sauvignon Blanc is easy to grow. He would like to see a lot more experimentation with red grape growing in Oregon, specifically Cabernet Sauvignon and Foch. But the future of Oregon's wine industry, he

**SHAFER VINEYARD CELLARS**

| | |
|---|---|
| Owner and winemaker | Harvey Shafer |
| Year bonded | 1981 |
| Year first planted | 1972 |
| Vineyard acreage | 20 |
| Principal varieties, acres | Pinot Noir, 6 |
| | Chardonnay, 4 |
| | Riesling, 3 |
| | Sauvignon Blanc, 1.5 |
| Year of first crush | 1981 |
| Production capacity | 15,000 gallons |
| Production in 1983 | 13,000 gallons |
| Awards, 1983 | |
| 1982 White Riesling: | Silver, New York |
| | Silver, Oregon State Fair |
| 1981 Chardonnay: | Silver, San Francisco |

recognizes, is with the potential of the Pinot Noir grape. "There's an erroneous concept that Northwest wines are *supposed* to be different from California's—the myth of cool-weather wines," Shafer believes. "On the other hand, I do believe that wines should be made according to their potential. And the best potential is with the Pinot Noir grape."

Shafer has done well with his wines in competition: a silver for the dry Riesling, and bronze medals for the Pinot Noir and the Chardonnay. Still, Shafer views competitions wryly: "Judgings give us exposure, but most winemakers know it's a crapshoot," he says. "We could make wine for the judges—or wine to sell."

His 1980 Pinot Noir is now available, and aging beautifully in the bottle. The 1981 Chardonnay is a delicate but complex wine with fine flavors from the fruit. Shafer's 1982 Pinot Noir Blanc has picked up a blush of color from the dark grape skins and has a just-detectable sweetness to it; it's a nicely balanced, clean wine. The 1982 Willamette Valley Reserve Riesling was made from botrytis-infected grapes. The smell is honeyed; the taste is grapy, luscious, not overly sweet, with a bright, acidic finish. It's a wine to seduce non-wine drinkers from their stance.

A warm welcome awaits you. Harvey Shafer is assisted by a full-time marketing director, Michael Harris, and on weekends by his daughter Stephanie. You will learn a lot here, taste fine wines, and survey yet another splendid and panoramic view of the lush Oregon wine country.

# Tualatin Vineyards

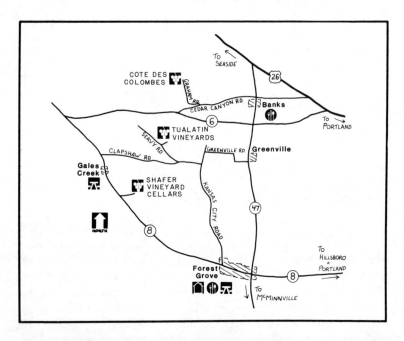

The Tualatin Vineyards, named for the Tualatin Valley, are planted on the south-sloping hillside of an old farm near Forest Grove: it's one of the prettiest sites for a vineyard picnic in the state. The wines of Tualatin Vineyards are among the two or three most widely distributed Oregon labels; the winery produced 40,000 gallons in 1983 and is capable of bottling 60,000 gallons. Bill Fuller, winemaker and part owner, thinks nothing of hopping on a plane (to Denver, Miami, or Boston) with a sample case and a sales pitch for a distributor.

Fuller is a chemist who has been in the wine business since 1958, when he graduated from San Francisco State College. After getting a master's degree in enology from the University of California at Davis, he became chief chemist for Louis Martini's Napa Valley winery. Eventually, he became restless, went into partnership with financial manager Bill Malkmus of San Francisco, and scoured the country for the right piece of property, which he found in Oregon's Washington County.

Fuller founded Tualatin Vineyards in 1973, planting sixty-five acres of rolling farmland in vinifera: twenty-four acres of White Riesling, another

---

🍇 **TUALATIN VINEYARDS**
Seavey Road
Route 1, Box 339
Forest Grove, OR 97116
357-5005

| | |
|---|---|
| Open to the public | 1-5 weekends; weekdays by appointment |
| Tour groups | yes, by appointment |
| Charge for tour groups | $1 per person |
| Picnic facilities at the winery | seating for 40 in a grove overlooking the vineyard and the Willamette Valley |
| Festivals/special events | Estate Release, late summer (by invitation); Annual Art Show, Nov. 24-25 |
| Wines available (1984) | 1983 White Riesling |
| | 1981 Chardonnay |
| | 1980 Pinot Noir |
| | 1983 Pinot Noir Blanc |
| | 1982 Gewurztraminer |
| | 1982 Early Muscat |
| | 1983 Muller Thurgau |

twenty-six acres shared between Gewurztraminer and Chardonnay, eleven acres of Pinot Noir, and some Muscat, Flora, and Muller Thurgau to round out the vines. He immediately began to make wine, using grapes from Washington: a 1974 White Riesling and a 1974 Dry Muscat. By 1981, he was making 60 percent of his wine from his own grapes, and since 1982 his wines have been exclusively "Estate Bottled." Tualatin's vineyard is now the second-largest in Oregon, second only to the Knudsen Erath property, and the Tualatin winery is the largest in Oregon making wine only from grapes grown on its own estate.

Virginia Fuller, a registered nurse, continues to work at Saint Vincent Hospital in Portland. When the Fullers return home, it is to an elegant old farmhouse set amid the vines; the view from the porch is spectacular, especially at sunset. A picnic area for visitors is close by.

The 1981 Chardonnay is a dry, well-balanced wine with an aroma of ripe fruit enhanced by French oak, very smooth in the mouth. The White Table Wine is dry, light-bodied, with a floral nose. It is made from a number of

---

**TUALATIN VINEYARDS**

| | |
|---|---|
| Owners | Bill & Virginia Fuller; Bill Malkmus |
| Winemaker | Bill Fuller |
| Year bonded | 1973 |

| | |
|---|---|
| Year first planted | 1973 |
| Vineyard acreage | 83 |
| Principal varieties, acres | White Riesling, 33 |
| | Chardonnay, 21 |
| | Gewurztraminer, 14 |
| | Pinot Noir, 11 |

| | |
|---|---|
| Year of first crush | 1973 |
| Production capacity | 60,000 gallons |
| Production in 1983 | 40,000 gallons |

| | |
|---|---|
| Awards, 1983 | |
| 1980 White Riesling: | Gold, London |
| 1978 Pinot Noir: | Gold, London |
| 1980 Chardonnay: | Gold, Oregon State Fair |

white wine grapes, so different nuances of aroma and taste will probably reveal themselves as bottle aging continues.

Tualatin Vineyards received two out of the fifteen gold medals awarded to U.S. wines at the 1982 International Wine and Spirits Competition in England for its 1978 Estate Pinot Noir and the 1980 Estate White Riesling.

At first, Fuller was almost alone among Oregon winemakers in his concern over marketing issues, especially the need to develop sales of Oregon wine *outside* of Oregon. "Oregon may be fifth in per capita consumption of wine," Fuller says, "but there aren't that many 'capitas' in Oregon!" So Fuller takes sample case in hand, climbs on a plane, and goes off to sell. First the concept of Oregon wine, then his own brand.

Ordinary wine is better today, thanks to technology, chemist Fuller points out. Thus the object becomes making wines that are *better* than ordinary, that are special enough to justify the higher price tags that Oregon's premium wines require. The paradox is that consumers are still buying wines to drink tomorrow, today, *now*. Fuller is fond of quoting the British writer and wine authority Hugh Johnson: "Most great wines will (again) be consumed before their time." Fuller adds, "We're trying to speed up the aging process, to get the *flavors* there, to make the wine drinkable *yesterday*."

# *Lodging*

## *Beaverton*

### *Greenwood Inn*
10700 S.W. Allen Boulevard
643-7777

This stylish motel complex just off Highway 217 makes a good (and rather luxurious) base for wine tours of both the Yamhill and Tualatin valleys. Many amenities, including wake-up service with coffee, and a pleasant swimming pool. There's a good restaurant, the Pavillon Bar & Grill, decorated in greenhouse style, serving champagne brunches on Sunday.

## *Hillsboro*

### *Dunes Motels*
452 S.E. Tenth
648-8991
622 S.E. Tenth
640-4791

Two similar, moderately priced motels in a town without many fancy accommodations.

## *Forest Grove*

### *Holiday Motel*
3224 Pacific Avenue
357-7411

Conveniently located near Pacific University.

# Restaurants

## Aloha

### Nonna Emilia
17210 S.W. Shaw (one block from the Tualatin Valley Highway)
649-2232
    A good restaurant to consider for a family feast. Options include complete Italian dinners, various huge pasta dishes, and homemade pizza, calzone, and manzo. There are combination plates for the undecided, and an inexpensive children's menu. Family-style seating at tables with checkered cloths. Very popular, often crowded.

## Banks

### Brown Derby
181 N. Main Street (on Highway 47)
324-8121
    An inexpensive and handsome restaurant with traditional American dishes, a children's plate (chicken with mashed potatoes and gravy), a fine Sunday brunch, and a "country" atmosphere. A lace-curtained window separates the pretty dining room from the bar (decorated with old lumberman's tools) and dance floor. All this and a good wine list, too.

## Beaverton

### Pier 101
12525 S.W. Canyon Road
641-3701
    This looks like a big, old country house built with river stones. In fact, it's a very pleasant, modern restaurant with half a dozen rooms, cheery fireplaces, a something-for-everyone schedule of "activities" (including vintage wines poured as house wines once a week), vast and reasonably priced menus, and an informal oyster and sandwich bar.

## Echo
6175 S.W. Lombard
643-5252

Many of the winemakers in the Tualatin Valley continue to recommend this rustic little place, which has a new owner and chef, Jim Van Buren. It's been "discovered" of late, so be sure to call for reservations.

## Brannigan's Restaurant & Bar
116500 S.W. Canyon Road
626-2223

A pleasant setting, and a fine wine list make this place near Beaverton Town Square attractive to wine-country visitors. There's another Brannigan's on Burnside in Portland.

## Le Trianon
9225 S.W. Allen Boulevard
245-2775

A rather fancy place just down the road from the Greenwood Inn. The owner, Fred Harder, has put together an ambitious menu highlighted by classic French specialties in an elegant, five-level building. The wine list is ambitious, too.

## McCormick's
9945 Beaverton-Hillsdale Highway
643-1322

This is a very up-to-date restaurant, specializing in fresh seafood, with a well-trained staff and an admirable wine list that includes many local bottlings. McCormick & Schmick and Jake's Crawfish, both in downtown Portland, and McCormick's in Seattle are under the same ownership.

## Greenway Pub
12272 S.W. Scholl's Ferry Road (at Greenway Shopping Center)
621-4699

Thirty beers on tap at this establishment not far from Ponzi Vineyards. You might consider ordering their beer sampler, a trayful of six or eight beers to taste and compare. Hardly dark or gloomy, as you might expect a pub to be, the Greenway has a restaurant license, so you can bring children, and serves both "regular" and "irregular" hamburgers. Same ownership as McMenamin's, in Hillsboro. These folks take their beer seriously.

## Giovanni's
12390 S.W. Broadway
644-8767

Not a fancy place, mind you, but a popular one; it has the best pizza in town, and not expensive, either.

## Forest Grove

## Anthony's Old Fashioned Eatery
3018 Pacific Highway
358-6989

A conveniently located family restaurant with a menu that includes omelets, burgers, a sandwich bar, and full dinners. There's a fine wine list besides, featuring local wines. It's good food, clearly a notch above Denny's, at an affordable price.

## Jan's Food Mill
1819 19th Street
357-6623

A pleasant place, with a respectable and moderately priced menu served in a ranch atmosphere. A good wine list. Open seven days a week.

## Gales

## Bonanza Cafe
Highway 6 (just west of its intersection with Highway 8)
357-3893

A very unpretentious truck stop, but a great find if the weather is too poor for a picnic. The decor, which consists of hundreds of souvenir ashtrays, is unpromising, and it's probably better to avoid the higher-priced, more ambitious items on the menu (like salmon or chateaubriand). Concentrate instead on the burger basket, the pork tenderloin sandwich, or the breakfast special (biscuits, sausage, and gravy for $1.50), and you'll be delighted.

## Hillsboro

### Anthony's Old Fashioned Eatery
640 S.E. Tenth Avenue
640-2024
   The same food, service, and congeniality, especially for families, as the Anthony's in Forest Grove.

### Helvetia Tavern
Route 1, Helvetia Road
647-5286
   Twenty minutes from Portland along Highway 26 is Hillsboro, county seat for Washington County and unofficial capital of the Tualatin Valley. The old Helvetia Tavern has stood here for generations, serving virtually legendary hamburgers and french fries.

### McMenamin's Pub
2020 N.E. Cornell Road
640-8561
   Here's a jovial spot, not unlike an English country pub, with 16 sorts of beer on tap, hearty sandwiches, and a steak that comes topped with peppers, mushrooms, cheese, and sauteed onions.

## Manning

### Java
Sunset Highway (Highway 26, two miles west of Highway 47)
324-0781
   The bus from Portland to Seaside always used to make a pit stop in Manning. Now there's every reason to make a pilgrimage. The Java is an authentic Indonesian restaurant, stuck out in the middle of logging country, serving exotic curries, *sates*, and a mouthwatering *rijstafel*. Prices are great. Be warned that the Java does not serve burgers.

## Multnomah

### Marco's
7910 S.W. 35th (at Multnomah Boulevard)
245-0199

A very pleasant cafe. Breakfasts are leisurely, with copies of the *New York Times* on racks for patrons, good espresso drinks, and hearty "continental" breakfasts of croissants, Westphalian ham, Swiss cheese, and cappuccino or orange juice. Soups, salads, and quiches are served later in the day. Dinners might include moussaka, breast of chicken in a cream sauce, or fettuccine. Desserts are home-made. Prices are moderate, and the wine list is more than adequate.

## Tigard

### L'Ecurie
12386 S.W. Main Street
620-5101

Portland's suburbs are not notably endowed with fine French restaurants, but l'Ecurie, under new ownership, tends to disprove that contention. The rustic setting is agreeable, and the menu includes some interesting items, like veal with scallops, to go along with the classical French recipes. A sorbet follows the appetizers, and the salad is served after the entree. Rather expensive.

## Tualatin

### Rich's Kitchen
18810 S.W. Boone's Ferry Road
692-1460

This country restaurant creates a French auberge setting in a fine brick building, one of the oldest structures in Tualatin. The upstairs balconies have window boxes, the tables are draped in white, the staff gives you a warm welcome. The meals are moderately priced, and Oregon wines are well-represented.

# Wine Shops & Delicatessens

## Beaverton

### Anderson's

9525 S.W. Beaverton-Hillsdale Highway
643-5415

One of the oldest, most respected delis in the Portland area, and right on the road to the wine country. A good selection of imported cheeses and top-quality cold cuts. Wonderful ready-made sandwiches, and facilities to sit down and enjoy them, too. Excellent selection of fine wines.

### Beaverton Bakery

12375 S.W. Broadway
646-7135

Very high-caliber baked goods, including bagels, French breads, a new Italian country bread, quiche, even wedding cakes. Telephone orders are accepted, probably a good idea for a large group.

### Fetzer's German Sausage & Deli

2485 S.W. Cedar Hills Boulevard
641-6300

There aren't many places like this around anymore: a true German *Metzgerei* (butcher shop) where the sausages and cold cuts are made by the owner himself. Lots of imported mustards and candies, but the main attraction is the real, homemade garlic salami and liverwurst. Delicious breads and rolls are available to take into the wine country.

### The Grapery

4120 S.W. Cedar Hills Boulevard
646-1437

A quiet, well-stocked wine shop that now serves lunches (and even dinners), too. Wine tastings are held regularly.

## Valley West Grocery & Country Deli
18450 N.W. West Union Road
645-1650

Nick and George Athnasakis run this incredible place near the Rock Creek campus of Portland Community College. The thing to order, if you're game, is the Mad Greek Sandwich. They won't tell you what's in it, but it's indescribably delicious: olive oil dribbled over four different meats and Greek cheese on a foot-long sesame roll. (There's a Mad American version, too, for more timid souls, with mustard and mayonnaise replacing the Greek seasonings.) It's just the thing to take on a trip into the wine country.

The shop also serves wonderful Greek fries: cut potatoes that are floured, seasoned with garlic and heaven knows what else, and cooked in a pressure cooker. Many, many wines from around the Northwest, California, and Greece, with an emphasis on Cabernet Sauvignon, and the largest selection of imported beers in Oregon. The Athnasakis brothers have been here for over six years now, getting better all the time.

## Nelson Brothers Cheese & Wines
13496 N.W. Cornell Road
643-1140

A deli well-recommended by the winegrowers (who don't always want to drive all the way into "downtown Beaverton"). Good wine selection, nice cheeses.

## Forest Grove

## Creative Kitchen
2834 D Pacific Avenue
357-6366

This is a combination cookware store (with cooking classes and demonstrations), wine shop, and delicatessen; the owners are very conscious of Oregon products.

# Hillsboro

## Laurel Valley Store
Laurel and Bald Peak Roads
628-1574

A pleasant rural location on a back road near Forest Grove, with a gas pump out front and the sort of quaint appearance that gets used in commercials.

## Petrich's General Store
Scholls Ferry Road at Sherwood Road
628-1626

This is the real thing, an old-fashioned country store. It's a bustling, vital place, where the bulletin board is full of community notices (it's where you advertise if you've lost your cow). The Petrich family has raised ten children over the twenty years that they've been here; the children often work in the store, selling everything from plumbing parts to dog fod (and chicken feed, too). The best deal is on cheeses. *Everybody* shops here, from migrant workers to local squires.

## Southwest Portland suburbs

### Bardee's Deli
8836 S.W. Hall, Progress
646-9992

A fine little deli, where breakfast includes wonderful bran muffins. The emphasis is on Jewish items as well: pickled herring, white fish spread on bagels. Wines are available, too.

### Comella & Son & Daughter Produce Center
6959 S.W. Garden Home Road
245-5033

The Comella family has assembled a remarkable collection of fruits, vegetables, flowers, nuts, and wines at this roadside complex (the old Garden Home station of the Oregon Electric Railway). One entire wing is devoted to Northwest wines.

### Crane & Company
8610 S.W. Terwilliger Boulevard
246-4323

Steve Cary conducts the best wine classes in the Portland area here. Good by-the-case values here, as well as high-quality meats and poultry. Deli meals, too.

### Strohecker's
2855 S.W. Patton
223-7391

This small supermarket caters not only to the neighborhood (with deliveries, charge accounts, and custom cuts of meat), but to wine afficionados from all over town. It's also a fine place to buy cold cuts, breads, and cheeses for wine-country picnics.

## Tigard

### The Wine Master
9612 S.W. Washington Square Road
620-2324

This shop in the busy Washington Square shopping center specializes in Oregon and Northwest wines. Karen Grimm also sells picnic baskets.

### Made in Oregon
Washington Square Mall
620-4670

This is one of several stores featuring Oregon products, wine among them. You'd be surprised how many items are made in Oregon (besides Pendleton blankets and Tillamook cheese).

# Picnic Spots

Picnic facilities are available at all the wineries in the Tualatin Valley; we particularly like the view from Mulhausen Vineyards, where you can see four Cascade peaks from the lawn outside the tasting room.

Bald Peak State Park, which is in Yamhill County, also offers a spectacular view of the Tualatin Valley. Follow Bald Peak Road from Highway 219, southwest of Scholls. Some additional suggestions follow.

## Gales

### Balm Grove Park

Six miles west of Forest Grove, this campground offers swimming and sports facilities (softball, volleyball, horseshoes, swings), and handles company picnics as well as family outings.

## Forest Grove

### Rogers Park

A pleasant spot in downtown Forest Grove. The town has its own institution of higher learning (Pacific University, founded by the Congregational Church in 1849) and community theater (the Grove Players); a walking tour of Forest Grove has much to recommend it. Maps are available from the Chamber of Commerce at 2417 Pacific Avenue.

## Glenwood

### Glenwood Trolley Park

Highway 6 at milepost 38
357-3574

Excellent picnic grounds at this site. From the parking lot, the only way in is to ride one of the park's historic trolleys. The park is actually a museum operated by the Oregon Electric Railway Historical Society, so there's a modest admission charge. Open to the public on weekends and holidays from Memorial Day to October, and to groups at other times.

## Gaston

### Cherry Grove

Patton Valley Road

Six miles out of Gaston, this is a campsite and picnic ground on the banks of the Tualatin.

### Hagg Lake

A reservoir northwest of town (along Highway 47) with picnic facilities at several sites.

# Yamhill County

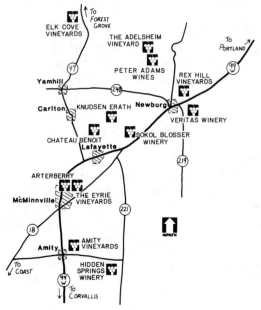

Mornings in Yamhill County seem to be overcast and cool. Not until noon, after the low gray clouds have burned away, does a strong, warm sunshine bathe the lowland fields and gently rolling hills with a pleasant, golden glow. The valley's rich harvest of fruits, nuts, and grain flourishes in this moderate climate, as does a relatively new crop planted among the orchards: grapes.

This is a county of small towns, hillside orchards, and prosperous farms, whose rich soil gives root to crops as diverse as filberts, strawberries, cherries, row crops, pole beans, hops, wheat, and rapeseed. It is also exceptionally good country for grapes: almost 50 percent of Oregon's wine grapes are grown in Yamhill County, not only because the climate is right, but also because the Jurassic clay around Dundee is an unusually salutary soil for the vines. In fact, the "Red Hills of Dundee" may one day become as famous as the Cote d'Or (or "Hills of Gold") in the Burgundy-growing region of France.

Travelers who whip through the Willamette Valley along Interstate 5 can only guess at the richness of the land. Fortunately, the countryside is criss-crossed with scenic back roads and byways that wind around deep-shaded filbert orchards and through fields of tall-growing grass. From every village crossroads rises the abrupt silhouette of a silo, guarding a cache of filberts or walnuts or grain like a silent sentinel, its shape bringing to mind the belfry walls of the church or cathedral that might dominate a wine village in Europe. But the wine country of Europe is often flat and uninteresting; rows upon rows of vineyards unrelieved by trees or row crops. The vineyards of Yamhill County are but one element of a diverse economic and artistic patchwork.

McMinnville, Yamhill's county seat, is a charming town that has escaped the roar of traffic zooming along Highway 18 between Portland and the coastal beaches. A visitor easily gets the feeling that McMinnville has retained a delightful 1950s character: a picture-postcard campus (Linfield College), peaceful shopping streets, a shaded city park, a respected municipal art gallery, restored and spruced-up downtown buildings. The second week in July brings round a city-wide Turkey Rama (this used to be the turkey-growing capital of the country), complete with turkey races, barbecues, carnival rides, sidewalk sales, and all the local color you'd expect. McMinnville also has a flourishing Little Theater group (the Gallery Players) whose technically advanced new theater is supported by local businesses. And, although accommodations are sparse, there are several fine restaurants. In all, the town makes a fine headquarters for visiting the nearby vineyards.

Many of Yamhill County's towns have some connection with the history of the valley, but the sleepy, old-fashioned, altogether charming character of the county is evident everywhere: in the roadside stands selling local produce; in Dayton, where the first fort in Oregon stands on a tree-lined square; in Lafayette, where a museum about the early days of the western settlement is now housed in an old church. The plains along the Willamette River were originally settled by fur trappers, then by wheat farmers. A forty-mile scenic loop, marked by fleur-de-lis signs, traverses the valley's historic districts; the Visitor Center at Champoeg State Park near Newberg has details.

The single blinking traffic light in Yamhill is evidence that there are few urban attractions. If you're looking for "downtown," you'll have to go back to Portland. The attraction is the very absence of urban attractions, both in the small towns themselves and in traveling along the narrow roads between one town and another. Take the time to drive slowly along these roads; roll down the window and smell the dark, rich earth under the walnut groves. Look at the wildflowers growing up amidst the grassy weeds at the roadside, or at the hawks above a field of prancing lambs, or at the brilliant green color of a nearby hillside as sunshine burns through the morning haze and washes over the land. To the visitor who takes the time to savor the countryside, Yamhill County offers rich rewards.

*Note:*

*The wineries of Yamhill County have formed an association to sponsor an annual Wine Country Thanksgiving, when they open to the public from 11 to 5 on Friday, Saturday, and Sunday on Thanksgiving weekend and offer special case discounts. It's the only time of year that the public can visit Adelsheim Vineyard and The Eyrie Vineyards, which release their new wines on this occasion.*

*All of the active wineries profiled in the following pages are expected to participate in this Wine Country Thanksgiving again in 1984.*

# *Peter Adams Wines*

Portland Adams, age two, walks through the comfortable living room of the Adams home in the southwest Portland hills wearing a T-shirt that reads, "Real Wine Throws Tartrates." She seems to symbolize her parents' intellectual involvement with wine.

Peter Adams, a Portland business consultant and Newberg-area vineyard owner, got into the wine business ten years ago when he and his brother owned a retail wine shop in suburban Portland. The store didn't last, but Adams's fascination with wine did. He took short courses at the University of California at Davis, attended seminars in San Francisco, and took a wine-tasting course from David Adelsheim, whom he had known in high school in the late 1950s. When some property close to Adelsheim's vineyard came up for sale in 1976, Adams bought it; he planted Pinot Noir and Chardonnay. The 1981 harvest of Adams's vineyard was crushed and vinified at Adelsheim's winery, and was released late in 1983.

The Chardonnay, which included some botrytised grapes, was aged in Limousin oak, and has an unusually deep color. The aroma is a fine, complex blend of fruit and oak, and the flavors are balanced. In the tradition of great Chardonnays, it understands that less is more. The Pinot Noir is a glorious, medium red color. It smells of cherries and blackberries, is smooth in the mouth, and finishes with some tannin and the promise of further development with bottle aging. Only 200 cases of Pinot Noir and 400 cases of Chardonnay were turned out. Both varieties sell for $9 a bottle.

The label was created by Peter's wife, Carol Adams, a food columnist and artist. She designed a sumi wash of a grapevine, with a single tendril curling off the gray stem. The label is silver, with blue-green accents for the Chardonnay, burgundy trim for the Pinot Noir, a color combination that suits the wines—and their creators—very well. "There's a male mystique to wine," Carol Adams complains. She's the taster, a cooking instructor (with a master of fine arts degree in painting) who appreciates the creative act of cooking as well as its immediate feedback. Peter talks about syndicating a thirty-five-acre Pinot Noir vineyard and philosophizes about enology: "Why not just pick in mid-October and make what the *grapes* indicate?" he asks. "We should harvest for *acid* levels, not for *sugar*," he muses.

Adams, who had been working as a controller for Esco Corporation, was recently elected to the company's board of directors, and has since set up a consulting practice in computerized accounting and inventory control systems. He's not tied to a time clock, and he has the luxury to apply his business skills to the financial planning that precedes the fateful decision, whether to acquire a facility for winemaking on his own, and get bonding for Peter Adams wines.

Peter and Carol ask themselves where the winery might be, at their vineyard or closer to the city? A winery with a restaurant, perhaps. They could live upstairs. With a hundred qualms and doubts, they approach the inevitable. If only the wines weren't any good, quitting would be easy. But it's not. A decision will have to be made. Soon.

For the time being, Peter Adams has a telephone answering machine in his Portland home for wine-related business. The number is 294-0606.

They are almost at the point that the other winemakers of this book have reached at some point in their careers: total commitment. We'd understand if they backed off, but we think the industry would be richer if they forged ahead.

# Adelsheim Vineyard

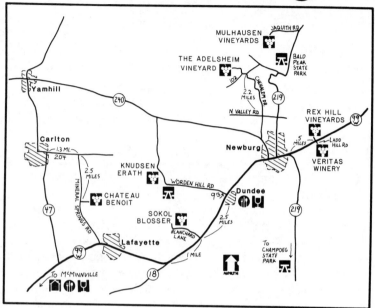

The Adelsheim Vineyard, a gently-sloping, nineteen-acre property in the hills behind Newberg, overlooks a wide expanse of the Yamhill Valley. It is almost totally planted with Pinot Noir, Chardonnay and Riesling, and is tended with great care and dedication by David and Ginny Adelsheim. Their house is set amidst an undulating sea of vines, and the winery itself hugs the side of the house. In this setting of remote, yet splendid privacy, David Adelsheim has, for the past several years, been studiously developing some of the best wines in Oregon; he has also emerged as one of the industry's foremost innovators, a tireless experimenter who applies his research to virtually every aspect of the business: grape growing, winemaking, marketing.

Like most of Oregon's winemakers, David Adelsheim has managed to turn his avocation into a livelihood. Perhaps more than most, he also brings to it a serious sense of mission.

Adelsheim, now 41, came to winemaking rather late in life. He graduated from Portland State University with a degree in German, served in Korea during the mid-1960s, and went into banking, while Ginny, a gifted artist, made pottery and intriguing sculptures. They planned to supplement their

---

**⚏ ADELSHEIM VINEYARD**
Route 1, Box 129 D
Newberg, OR 97132
538-3652

| | |
|---|---|
| Open to the public | by invitation |
| Festivals/special events | 2 per year; write for invitation |
| Wines available | 1983 Yamhill Riesling |
| | 1983 Washington Semillon |
| | 1982 Yamhill Chardonnay |
| | 1981 Washington Merlot |
| | 1981 Yamhill Pinot Noir |

---

income with a vineyard that they began planting in 1972 on their property near Newberg.

"It was a romantic delusion," Adelsheim admits. "We had to spend huge amounts of time working on the vineyard, planting, pruning, training, and trying to stay ahead of the weeds." Even today, he finds the vineyard work the hardest part of winemaking, although the Adelsheims bring some of it on themselves by insisting on expensive and time-consuming methods: theirs is one of the few vineyards to cover all the vines with nets, rather than spray them with chemicals to keep away birds and other pests. The vineyard has full-time managers; Dr. William Doan, a former psychologist, and his wife, Terry, a nursery consultant, have looked after the vineyard since 1975. And Adelsheim himself has just published in the *Oregon Wine-grape Growers Guide* a definitive, fourty-four-page paper on vineyard training and trellising systems. He's also been carrying out an eleven-year project in conjunction with Oregon State University to import and evaluate clonal material from European test stations, the only such research of its kind in the country.

Back in the 1970s, to get a feel for winemaking, David Adelsheim worked for a season with David Lett at The Eyrie Vineyards, and traveled the following year to France. After returning to Oregon, he eventually took a job as wine steward at Horst Mager's l'Omelette restaurant in Portland, but quit after he became exhausted by the late-night commuting. He then took over the management of an urban rehabilitation project in Portland while Ginny ran the vineyard; she also applied her artistic talents to the design of labels for the bottles. Adelsheim Vineyard was bonded as a winery in 1978, producing Semillon, Pinot Noir, Chardonnay and two styles of Merlot in its first releases, accompanied by Ginny's now-classic labels: the "Spirit of the

| ADELSHEIM VINEYARD | |
|---|---|
| Owners | David & Ginny Adelsheim |
| Winemaker | David Adelsheim |
| Year bonded | 1978 |
| Year first planted | 1972 |
| Vineyard acreage | 18 |
| Principal varieties, acres | Pinot Noir, 7 |
| | Chardonnay, 6 |
| | Riesling, 4 |
| Year of first crush | 1978 |
| Production capacity | 18,000 gallons |
| Production in 1983 | 14,000 gallons |
| Awards, 1983 | |
| 1981 Chardonnay: | Gold, Oregon State Fair |
| 1982 Semillon: | Gold, Seattle |

Vineyard" for the very first Semillon, the winter vineyard landscape to celebrate the first Adelsheim harvest.

Adelsheim Vineyard wines are memorable. "Forget everything you ever learned about Pinot Noir [from Burgundy] having to age for years before it's any good," Adelsheim says. "Oregon Pinot can be drunk as soon as two years after harvest because the cool climate produces wine that's smooth even when it's young." Even now, his 1981 Pinot Noir is as much a tactile experience as it is one of smell and taste. Its warm, earthy flavors and silky texture caress the mouth and linger long.

The 1982 White Riesling is made in the German style, first fermented dry, then sweetened with some unfermented Riesling juice; the botrytis which affected some of the grapes is noticeable in the rich color, the honey smell, and the complex flavors.

Perhaps the most distinctive of Adelsheim's wines is the 1982 Chardonnay, which even in its youth has a complexity of flavors that comes from picking the grapes at their ripest and vinifying them in a Burgundian style by giving the crushed grapes lengthy skin contact before pressing, then aging the wine on the lees for some time in three different kinds of French oak barrels. The result is a wine that is rich and soft, with a hint of essence of pear and oil of lime in the long-lasting flavor. The label for the 1982 Chardonnay is a portrait of Barbara Setsu Pickett, a textile artist and professor of weaving who has also been a chef at Portland's Genoa Cafe. She and Ginny Adelsheim laid out the vineyard's original Chardonnay rows in 1974.

Adelsheim experiments endlessly with the effects of different oak barrels. (He also acts as a broker for many Oregon winemakers buying barrels from Europe.) In the winery's crowded barrel room, Adelsheim carefully notes the nuances of smell and taste contributed by the various French oaks—Alliers, Vosges, Nevers for the Pinot; Limousin, Vosges, Nevers for the Chardonnay; both Eastern and Oregon oak for the Merlot.

For a relatively small winery, Adelsheim wines are widely distributed. We think there are several reasons, the first being the elegant and distinctive packaging created by Ginny Adelsheim's beautiful and easily recognized labels. (They are being released as posters, too.) Then there's Adelsheim's deliberate decision to limit the varieties he produces. Only five are in general distribution: Pinot Noir, Chardonnay, and White Riesling (all from Yamhill County grapes), and Semillon and Merlot (from Washington State grapes). The result is that Adelsheim Vineyard wines are available throughout Oregon, plus Washington, California, Texas, Minnesota, Montana, and New York.

None of this would mean much without the quality of the wines themselves. It takes more than quality, though, to get a wine distributed; it takes the recognition of quality, the perception of quality, the promotion of quality. Here again, Adelsheim Vineyard wines hold a remarkable record. Every Adelsheim wine entered in a competition in 1983 won a gold or silver medal. David Adelsheim is quick to point out, though, that he does not make wines to impress judges at competitions. He makes them to be enjoyed by his public, and not just for special occasions, either. They're superb wines, but they're not intimidating. You can drink them "for everyday" without feeling guilty. And that is perhaps the ultimate compliment you can pay a winemaker.

# Amity Vineyards

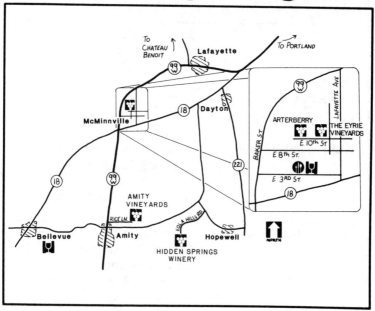

Amity is a village on Highway 99W, five or six miles south of McMinnville, in the heart of Yamhill County farmland. It's the sort of town where the feed store on the outskirts of town stays open all day on Sundays.

At the northern boundary of Amity, Rice Lane turns eastward off the highway, passes the elementary school, and angles sharply uphill. The gravel road passes through some of the seventy-acre property until it crests 400 feet above the valley floor at the Amity Vineyards winery (and adjacent house trailer) where its founder, winemaker, and guiding spirit, thirty-eight-year-old Myron Redford, makes his home.

The setting is spectacular. Amity's view is toward the south, into both the Yamhill and Willamette valleys, which look like storybook landscapes from its vantage point atop the vineyards. Small wonder that Redford chose this location when it was offered for sale. He had been a research assistant for the University of Washington's vice-president for academic affairs, and then worked on the staff of the Battelle Institute in Seattle, doing research on the social aspects of contraception before he met Lloyd Woodburne, who led him on the path that brought him to this mountaintop.

---

### 🐾 AMITY VINEYARDS
Route 1, Box 348-B
Amity, OR 97101
835-2362

| | |
|---|---|
| Open to the public | June-Sept., 12-5 daily |
| | Oct.-May, 12-5 weekends |
| | (closed Dec. 24-Jan. 30) |
| Tour groups | yes |
| Charge for tour groups | $1 per person |
| Picnic facilities at the winery | tables adjacent to the winery |
| | overlooking Willamette Valley |
| Festivals/special events | Summer Solstice Festival, third |
| | weekend in June; Pinot Noir |
| | release, third weekend in Sept.; |
| | Winter Solstice, third weekend |
| | in Dec. |
| Wines available (1984) | Solstice Blanc |
| | Oregon White Riesling |
| | Oregon Gewurztraminer |
| | Oregon Chardonnay |
| | Oregon 1982 Pinot Noir |
| | Oregon 1980 Winemaker's |
| | Reserve Pinot Noir |
| | Nouveau Pinot Noir |

Over lunch one Saturday in 1974, Woodburne lured him into part-time (and unpaid) work at the burgeoning Associated Vintners operation. Redford had become acquainted with fine wines during a hitchhiking trip through Europe in the late 1960s, and was ready to make a change in the direction of his career.

Myron Redford is one of the industry's more analytical and verbal spokesmen. He has staked a claim to uniqueness with one specific wine— the "Nouveau" Pinot Noir—designed to be the first wine of the new harvest; it is a wine he has been making with increasing skill since 1976. In 1983, Redford's Nouveau was served alongside French Beaujolais Nouveau that had been flown to the Northwest for several banquets.

But Redford's winemaking skill doesn't revolve around that one wine; indeed all the wines of Amity Vineyards have an extraordinary record of

---

**AMITY VINEYARDS**

| | |
|---|---|
| Owners | Myron Redford, Ione Redford, Janice Checchia |
| Winemaker | Myron Redford |
| Year bonded | 1976 |

| | |
|---|---|
| Year first planted | 1970 |
| Vineyard acreage | 15 |
| Principal varieties, acres | Pinot Noir, 5.5 |
| | Riesling, 3 |
| | Chardonnay 2 |
| | Gewurztraminer, 1 |

| | |
|---|---|
| Year of first crush | 1976 |
| Production capacity | 20,000 gallons |
| Production in 1983 | 17,000 gallons |

| | |
|---|---|
| Awards, 1983 | |
| 1980 Winemaker's Reserve | |
| Pinot Noir: | Gold, Reno |
| | Gold, Tacoma |
| | Silver, San Francisco |
| 1982 Oregon Dry White | |
| Riesling: | Double Gold, San Francisco |
| | Silver, Oregon State Fair |
| 1982 Gewurztraminer: | Silver, Oregon State Fair |
| | Silver, Tri-Cities |
| | Silver, Seattle |

---

success. The 1978 Oregon Pinot Noir was cited for its outstanding quality by *Vintage* magazine in 1981; two years later, the 1980 Pinot won the same rating. In 1983, Amity did better than any other winery from the Pacific Northwest at wine competitions in California and Reno; Amity's Dry White Riesling was the only non-California wine to receive a "double gold" for quality beyond the usual gold medal. Furthermore, every wine Redford entered in Northwest competitions also won.

Most recently, the English wine writer Michael Broadbent cited Amity's 1979 and 1980 Pinot Noir in *Decanter*, a British wine publication, along with Pinots from Oak Knoll and Knudsen Erath. "It is time for our friends in Burgundy to sit up and take note," Broadbent wrote.

People whose palates are adjusted to European tastes, Redford feels, will prefer Oregon Pinot Noir to a California Pinot, because the cooler climate produces grapes with a higher level of acid. This will help Oregon winemakers sell their products outside of California, mostly to Eastern markets, too. Redford believes wines should be made to go with food, and on the labels of his wines he recommends specific foods that his wines will complement. When there's a festival at the winery to release a new wine, it's always with appropriate food.

In June, the Summer Solstice Festival introduces the Dry White Riesling and the Solstice Blanc, a proprietary blend. Amity's Riesling is dry, in the Alsatian style, to accompany meals, rather than in the sweet, German style for sipping. The Amity Riesling makes an excellent accompaniment to seafood dishes. The Winter Solstice, at the Lawrence Gallery, features the "Nouveau" Pinot Noir and heartier food.

Best of all, perhaps, is the Pinot Noir festival in September, when the latest releases of Pinot are unveiled. These aren't necessarily the vintages other winemakers are releasing; Redford will wait until *his* wine meets his own standards, not the market's. Redford's commitment to quality is why Amity Vineyards continues to be one of the wineries that people watch; he doesn't follow the market, he shows the market where it *should* be.

# Arterberry

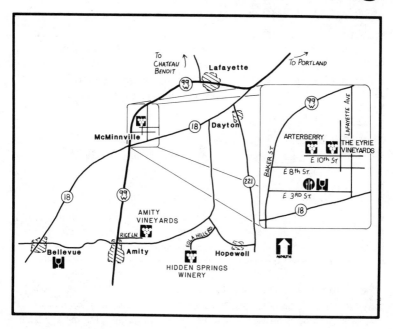

"Even as a kid, I thought wine was neat stuff," says Fred Arterberry, who was scooting around his small winery in McMinnville recently, supervising the construction of a new tasting room and office, showing visitors the tanks and fermenters, helping pour wines in the tasting room.

The first commercial wine Fred Arterberry made was sparkling cider, back in 1979. He made a sparkling Chardonnay that year as well, which he liked well enough to continue making. Although he was trained in classical enology ("fermentation science" is the name of the degree program) at the University of California at Davis, he has no reservations about working with apples as fruit; in fact, he has made his reputation with sparkling ciders, and it is only within the past few months that he has begun making a full line of varietal wines and opening his winery to the public.

He recognizes that other wineries are now making sparkling wines, that imitation is the sincerest form of flattery. He's proven that it can be done, that there *is* a market for Northwest sparkling wines. Indeed, at least ten wineries in Oregon, Washington, and Idaho, are currently making sparkling

---

**▓ ARTERBERRY**
905 E. Tenth
Box 772
McMinnville, OR 97128
472-1587

| | |
|---|---|
| Open to the public | 11-5 weekdays, 11-6 weekends |
| Tour groups | by appointment |
| Charge for tour groups | $1 per person, refunded with purchase |
| Festivals/special events | Spring Open House |
| Wines available (1984) | 1980 Sparkling Wine (limited) |
| | 1982 Sparkling Chardonnay |
| | 1982 Pinot Noir |
| | 1982 Chardonnay |
| | 1982 Rose of Pinot Noir |
| | 1983 White Riesling |
| | Cider |
| | Apple-Berry wines |

---

wine. Arterberry will continue to make the cider, the sparkling Chardonnay, and a limited quantity of a sparkling wine (containing a blend of Chardonnay and Pinot Noir like the best French champagnes), but his emphasis may have changed.

All good young wineries should experiment, the Arterberry brochure states. "We would like to produce White Rieslings in a big way in 1984," he tells us. "I think it will sell well." He bought five tons of Riesling grapes in 1983, and has access to as many as thirty.

This is very much a family operation. Fred's mother, Margaret, is president of the company, his father is the winemaker's advisor. Brother Kelly does sales and marketing. And father-in-law James Maresch owns the vineyard (Red Hills Vineyard in Dundee) that provides the grapes for Arterberry's new line of vinifera wines, including the Rieslings.

One of Fred Arterberry's proudest moments came at the Oregon State Fair in 1981, when his cider won a gold medal. He doesn't enter competitions except for the fair, an understandable plan for a small winery. Among those "in the know," Arterberry's ciders have been sought after from the beginning as splendid examples of the craft. Now vinifera and sparkling wines will be added to the list. One thing you won't find here is a lot of

**ARTERBERRY**

| | |
|---|---|
| Owners | Fred Arterberry family |
| Winemaker | Fred A. Arterberry, Jr. |
| Year bonded | 1979 |
| Year first planted | 1968 (Red Hills Vineyard) |
| Vineyard acreage | 37 |
| Principal varieties, acres | White Riesling, 15 |
| | Pinot Noir, 15 |
| | Chardonnay, 7 |
| Year of first crush | 1979 |
| Production in 1983 | 4,755 gallons |
| Expansion plans | 2,100-gallon tank; tourist signs |
| Awards, 1983 | |
| Cider: | Silver, Oregon State Fair |
| 1982 Rose of Pinot Noir: | Silver, Oregon State Fair |

wines aged for years in oak barrels. "I hope consumers will begin to shy away from a lot of oakiness in wines," Fred Arterberry says. "I think it's overdone in some wines and detracts from varietal character."

There are "varietal" differences in the cider, incidentally. The current bottling has a hefty percentage of Gravenstein apples, harvested in August, which lend more acidity to the finished product.

# *Century Home Wines*

Springbook Road at Highway 219
Route 2, Box 111
Newberg, OR 97132

David and Peggy Maze are the current owners of this low-profile winery, housed in a hundred-year-old barn just south of Newberg. Maze is not actively selling wine at this time, although he continues to crush and produce vinifera wines (Pinot Noir Blanc, Rose, Pinot Noir, Chardonnay, and a white table wine) as well as fruit wines. If you were to drop by the winery (there's no phone), Maze would probably invite you to taste his wines; he hopes to resume a full marketing effort within a year or two.

# *Chateau Benoit*

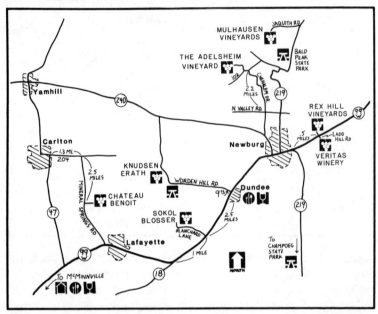

Not long ago, at a restaurant in Seattle, we enjoyed a most remarkable salmon dish. The fish had been broiled, seasoned with a bit of fennel, butter, and lemon, and served with a *red* wine sauce: a sauce that had been finished with a Pinot Noir from Chateau Benoit. The wine served with the meal was that same Pinot Noir. And both the salmon and the wine were wonderful.

We suspected that the meal would be memorable when we began with *two* sparkling wines, also from Chateau Benoit: a fine Blanc de Blanc made entirely from Chardonnay grapes, and an even better Brut, made with 60-percent Pinot Noir grapes, which had lovely soft and tiny bubbles. Clearly, Chateau Benoit has come of age.

Fred Benoit's great-great-grandfather was the first white settler in the Yakima Valley; the fields where he grew alfalfa are now vineyards. From this agricultural background, Fred Benoit went to medical school; he got into winemaking, he says, "because I don't like golf." Having graduated from home winemaking, he planted his first vineyard, near Veneta in Lane County, with Pinot Noir and Chardonnay. When he and his wife, Mary, really got serious about participating in Oregon's emerging wine industry, they found an even better parcel near McMinnville, sixty acres of Wal-

## CHATEAU BENOIT

Mineral Springs Road
Route 1, Box 29B-1
Carlton, OR 97111
864-2991 (winery), 864-3666 (home)

| | |
|---|---|
| Open to the public | 1-5 weekends, weekdays by chance |
| Tour groups | yes, by appointment |
| Charge for tour groups | $1 per person, refundable with purchase |
| Picnic facilities at the winery | 3 redwood tables overlooking the valley |
| Festivals/special events | Bastille Day, July 14-15; Red-White-Blue sale, July 4 |
| Wines available (1984) | Sauvignon Blanc |
| | Benoit Blanc |
| | White Riesling |
| | Pinot Noir Rose |
| | Merlot |
| | Blanc de Blanc (sparkling) |
| | Brut (sparkling Oregon wine) |
| | Select Cluster Chardonnay |
| | Pinot Noir |
| | Pinot Noir Nouveau |

lakenzie soil that had southern exposure and a warm 2,300 heat units during the growing season. The Benoits hired a full-time winemaker, planted more grapes, built the beginnings of an enormous winery, and eventually moved their home and his medical practice to the new site.

The winemaker was a young Swiss, Max Zellweger, who brought the popular European styles of winemaking to Chateau Benoit: light white wines with some residual sweetness. Zellweger's success at Chateau Benoit soon attracted the attention of the huge German firm of F. W. Langguth, and he was hired away to build and run Langguth's enormous new winery at Mattawa, the second-largest winery in Washington.

Hired two years ago to replace Zellweger was Rich Cushman, who had apprenticed in Germany with Weingut Dr. Burklin-Wolf and worked for a season with Dick Erath. Many of the techniques he learned in Europe were applicable to Oregon grapes and to winemaking that produced lighter wines of moderate alcohol levels. "Wine is a basic part of everyday life, to be

**CHATEAU BENOIT**

| | |
|---|---|
| Owners | Fred & Mary Benoit |
| Winemaker | Rich Cushman |
| Year bonded | 1979 |
| Year first planted | 1972 |
| Vineyard acreage | 42 |
| Principal varieties, acres | Riesling, 12.5 |
| | Muller Thurgau, 12 |
| | Pinot Noir, 10.5 |
| | Chardonnay, 7 |
| Year of first crush | 1979 |
| Production capacity | 25,000 gallons |
| Production in 1983 | 24,000 gallons |
| Expansion plans | to 35,000 gallons |
| Awards, 1983 | |
| 1982 Select Cluster | |
| Chardonnay: | Gold, Seattle |
| | Gold, Oregon State Fair |
| 1982 Sauvignon Blanc | Gold, Greatest of the Grape |
| 1982 White Riesling: | Silver, San Francisco |

enjoyed with meals, but not an object of worship," Cushman believes. He has helped expand Chateau Benoit's line from the original concept of two wines (Chardonnay and Pinot Noir) to the current, more commercial range; he was the one who tackled the assignment of making sparkling wines.

Visitors might be forgiven for seeing Chateau Benoit as a winery still in transition: the building appears unfinished, the tasting room nonexistent. The approach to the winery, from Mineral Springs Road, climbs a long, gradual hill past the still-maturing vineyard. The great concrete winery stands almost forlornly atop the rise, the shell of what will eventually be one wing of a U-shaped chateau. Wines are currently poured for tasting at a refectory table beside the barrels and stainless steel tanks.

You do get a feel for the potential of the place standing just outside the winery. Though the rise can't be more than a hundred feet or so from the road below, the modest altitude provides a totally different perspective on the farms of the Yamhill Valley. McMinnville, Lafayette, and the busy highway lie somewhere in the green creases below; your eyes are drawn to the undulating hills and soft golden horizon. It is a landscape of bounty, of optimism, of reassurance.

# Elk Cove Vineyards

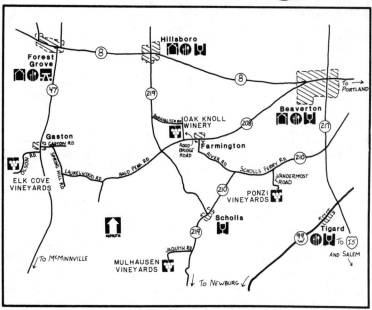

The "cove" of Elk Cove Vineyards is a sheltered fold of trees just off Olson Road, nestled high in the hilltops that separate Yamhill and Washington counties. Gaston, a little town on Highway 47 between McMinnville and Forest Grove, is where Olson Road begins; as it climbs through the evergreens and alder, marvelous panoramas of the Tualatin Valley are succeeded by wonderful vistas of the Willamette Valley. Three miles from the highway, there is a mailbox at the driveway of Elk Cove Vineyards; one last turn down the driveway, and the vineyard itself comes into view: twenty-four acres of Pinot Noir, Riesling, and Chardonnay vines surrounded by more than a hundred acres of sloping forestland. The handsome new winery with its octagonal, skylit tasting room complements the magnificent setting. No wonder that herds of Roosevelt elk migrate here every spring!

Elk Cove is owned and operated by Pat and Joe Campbell, natives of the Hood River area, who have found in this idyllic setting an opportunity to put their hands as well as their minds to work. They share the vineyard chores, the winemaking decisions, the cellar work. Pat, who is descended from Swiss farmers, earned a degree in French and German, and sold hand-

---

### 🍇 ELK COVE VINEYARDS

Olson Road
Route 3, Box 23
Gaston, OR 97119
985-7760

| | |
|---|---|
| Open to the public | 12-5 daily |
| Tour groups | yes |
| Charge for tour groups | $1 per person (groups over 12) |
| Picnic facilities at the winery | 2 tables with view of vineyards |
| Festivals/special events | Riesling Festival, May 26-28 |
| | Pinot Noir picnic, Sept. 1-3 |
| Wines available (1984) | 1982 & 1983 Riesling |
| | 1982 & 1983 Select Harvest Riesling |
| | 1982 & 1983 Gewurztraminer |
| | 1981 Chardonnay |
| | 1981 & 1982 Pinot Noir |

---

crafted jewelry before she became interested in winemaking. Joe, a physician with an undergraduate degree in chemistry and biology from Harvard and an M.D. from Stanford, commuted to the emergency room at Saint Joseph's Hospital in Longview during the winery's early days. Now he shares a family practice at a clinic in Hillsboro. Despite Elk Cove's substantial, 20,000-gallon annual production, this is perhaps Oregon's ultimate *family* winery, with all of the Campbell children joining in the winery duties.

As with any endeavor, the results are what count, and Elk Cove's wines are being acclaimed around the country as representative of the best Oregon vintners can produce. When Robert Drouhin, the leading shipper of Burgundy, visited Oregon in 1981, he picked Elk Cove's Chardonnay and Pinot Noir to be served at a banquet in his honor. When Richard Olney, the noted food writer, visited Oregon, he singled out Elk Cove's Pinot Noir as one of America's best red wines. Of the several Rieslings Elk Cove produced in 1981, the one made from selected clusters of botrytised grapes was Elk Cove's most successful wine last year, winning gold medals in San Francisco, Tri-Cities, and the Oregon State Fair. In 1982, Elk Cove's 1981 Dundee Hills Riesling won the Governor's Sweepstakes Trophy at the Oregon State Fair. The Elk Cove Pinot Noirs won gold medals in Tacoma and the Oregon State Fair last year. Even the labels have won awards.

The Campbells are scrupulous about keeping the grapes from their vari-

**ELK COVE WINERY**

| | |
|---|---|
| Owners | Pat & Joe Campbell |
| Winemakers | Pat & Joe Campbell |
| Year bonded | 1977 |
| Year first planted | 1974 |
| Vineyard acreage | 24 |
| Principal varieties, acres | Pinot Noir, 8 |
| | Riesling, 7 |
| | Chardonnay, 5 |
| | Gewurztraminer, 4 |
| Year of first crush | 1977 |
| Production in 1983 | 20,000 gallons |
| Expansion plans | improvements in picnic area |

Awards, 1983

| | |
|---|---|
| 1981 Select Cluster Riesling: | Gold, San Francisco |
| | Gold, Tri-Cities |
| | Gold, Oregon State Fair |
| 1982 Estate Riesling | Silver, New York |
| 1980 Estate Pinot Noir | Gold, Tacoma |
| | Silver, Seattle |

ous suppliers separate because they believe that the soil where the grapes were grown imbue the wine with unique characteristics. They don't (as many others do) blend wines from various vineyards in an effort to achieve a uniform "house wine" for a given year. It's a philosophy not often adhered to among Oregon winemakers. Actually, the greatest problem the Campbells have with their grapes is controlling the birds that eat or peck at the ripe grapes just before harvest. *Making* the wine is relatively easy, and certainly more satisfying, Pat Campbell reports. Especially with Elk Cove's spacious new winery, which replaced a cramped facility in an old barn on the property.

In addition to their success with Riesling, the Campbells are forging ahead with superb Pinot Noirs. Their favorite wine to date is the 1982 Pinot Noir Reserve, which won't even be released until the fall of 1984. In a recent tour of the winery, Pat Campbell explained how the Pinot had been fermented in small totes, with the "cap" of grape skins being punched down by hand several times a day during fermentation. The wine goes into small barrels of French oak for aging before it's released, and Pat says, "We hope the customers will *also* age our wines."

# *The Eyrie Vineyards*

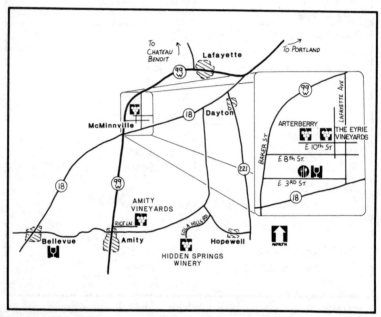

He is an intense, reserved man with smiling eyes and a trim white beard, at the same time the most famous of Oregon's winemakers and the most private. He is, of course, David Lett, founder and owner with his wife, Diana, of The Eyrie Vineyards. The attention that is paid to Lett's affairs is the price he pays for having been here first, and for being the man who showed the world the potential of Oregon wines.

David and Diana Lett came to the Willamette Valley in the mid-1960s, before anyone else knew, believed, or cared that wine grapes could be grown in this region. They established the beginnings of a thirty-acre vineyard in the now-famous Red Hills of Dundee, between Newberg and McMinnville, and converted a former turkey-processing plant in McMinnville into their winery.

David Lett grew up on a farm in Utah before getting his first degree, in philosophy, at the University of Utah, then got a second degree, in viticulture, from the University of California at Davis. After a stint at Souverain Cellars in the Napa Valley and a year of travel in France, he went looking for a cool climate in which to grow Pinot Noir—the noble grape of

---

**THE EYRIE VINEYARDS**
Winery:
935 E. Tenth
McMinnville, OR 97128
472-6315
Vineyard & mail:
P.O. Box 204
Dundee, OR 97115
864-2410

| | |
|---|---|
| Open to the public | by appointment |
| Tour groups | space for groups under 15 only |
| Festivals/special events | Open House and release of new wines on Thanksgiving weekend |
| Wines available (1984) | 1982 Pinot Noir |
| | 1982 Chardonnay |
| | 1982 Muscat Ottonel |
| | 1983 Pinot Gris |

---

Burgundy. To support his vineyard, planted with Pinot Noir, Chardonnay, Riesling, and Pinot Gris, David Lett worked as a publisher's representative for eight years, selling Scott Foresman textbooks during the academic year and tending the vineyard "on the side." Diana Lett worked on the vines while he was on the road. It wasn't a good time to be a "pioneer" in the Oregon wine country; the weather was miserable, and it would be years before there was any company.

In 1970, the Letts bonded their winery, and David's wines started to get some attention, first as a curiosity, then as outstanding wines, period. When his 1975 Pinot Noir was entered in a blind tasting in Paris, against the greatest Burgundies, the results surprised the judges, who rated it second only to one of the very best wines in France; they promptly ran the tasting again, in Beaune, and the results were the same. The Eyrie Vineyards' reputation was established internationally, and David Lett's patience was rewarded.

An article about Oregon wineries in the *Wall Street Journal* pointed out, though, that the business of running a small winery involves a lot of hard work; much of it is farming, after all, and the return on investment is small. "I'm not in the wine business to make money," David Lett told the newspaper reporter. "I'm in it to make wine."

Profit or not, he is still very much his own man. Lett went so far as to

| THE EYRIE VINEYARDS | |
|---|---|
| Owners | David & Diana Lett |
| Winemaker | David Lett |
| Year bonded | 1970 |
| Year first planted | 1966 |
| Vineyard acreage | 30 |
| Principal varieties | Pinot Noir |
| | Chardonnay |
| | Pinot Gris |
| | Muscat Ottonel |
| Year of first crush | 1970 |
| Production capacity | 10,000 gallons |
| Production in 1983 | 7,000 gallons |

remove the Riesling vines he had been growing—a variety whose grapes are in high demand, and which produce a wine that is ready for market in only six months—and grafted Pinot Gris instead. Riesling, Lett believes, ripens too late and takes too much technology to make properly. Even though Pinot Gris is almost unknown to Northwest wine drinkers, Lett thinks it's the road to profitability. It's a grape that reaches its peak of quality when planted in a region with a long, relatively cool growing season. Even so, The Eyrie Vineyards and Ponzi Vineyards have almost all of the commercial acreage in the United States. That's surprising, considering that Pinot Gris is conceivably the ideal wine for Northwest salmon. The bottles we've tried tend to confirm Lett's thesis; it's a clean, strong, pleasing wine with a pale straw color.

Lett's willingness to experiment is further exemplified by his interest in developing new Pinot Noir clones (minor mutations) that would be particularly suited to the Willamette Valley. The variables in such a program of experimentation, he points out, are immense, and it may take 200 years to determine which clones are best for Oregon's cool and misty climate. "The benefits will not be felt in my lifetime," he told a wine writer recently.

Most of TheEyrie Vineyards' wine is sold in Oregon, a lot of it during the Thanksgiving weekend open house. Despite the fuss made about his wines, however, David Lett is not trying to cash in on The Eyrie Vineyards' reputation; he is genuinely interested in making better wines. The confident single-mindedness of his efforts has already accorded him a place of honor in the roll call of Oregon's great winemakers. He is held in the highest esteem by many colleagues; David and Ginny Adelsheim honored the

Letts' contribution to Oregon winemaking by putting a picture of Diana Lett on the label of their 1981 Pinot Noir.

There is no permanent staff at The Eyrie Vineyards other than the Letts and their vineyard manager, Joel Myers, and there are no regular tasting-room hours. But small groups of visitors can make appointments for a tour. Lett understands, after all, that while wine can be made in private, it must be sold in public.

# *Hidden Springs*

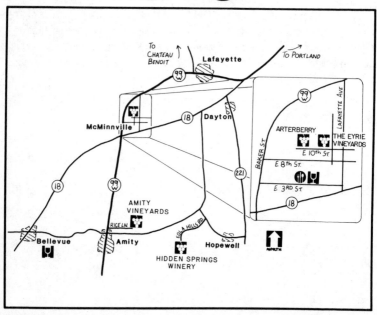

From the converted prune drying shed which houses the Hidden Springs winery atop the Eola Hills, you look down into two valleys: the broad and fertile plain of the Willamette, extending eastward to the foothills of the snow-capped Cascades in the hazy distance, and, to the west, the productive basin of the Yamhill River. Winemaker Don Byard admires the view with his visitors, and enthusiastically shows you the hillside acreage he owns himself: cherry trees, holly trees, Italian plum trees, vineyards. A little spring bubbles up from a swale on the property line. Before you can ask Byard about the vineyards, he tells you about the plums, which are dried to make Brooks prunes, famous throughout the region for their size and sweetness.

Byard, a tall man with an infectious smile and easy manner, works as a highway department planner in Salem. His partner, Al Alexanderson, is an energy lawyer in Portland. They began planting their vineyards in 1972, on this warm hillside of Jory loam, selling the grapes to home winemakers, selling the prunes, selling the cherries and holly branches.

Standing among the Pinot Noir, Riesling, and Chardonnay vines in the vineyard is a thermograph, a weather station that records temperature,

## ⚘ HIDDEN SPRINGS

Winery:
Eola Hills Road
Box 252-B
Amity, OR 97101
835-2782
Mail & Byards:
2400 Cottage Street S.E.
Salem, OR 97302
363-1295
Alexandersons: 635-8741

| | |
|---|---|
| Open to the public | weekends, March-Nov. |
| Tour groups | by appointment |
| Charge for tour groups | $1 per person |
| Picnic facilities at the winery | 3 tables in orchard next to winery or on winery dock |
| Festivals/special events | both the Yamhill County. Thanksgiving wine tour and the Salem area Tastevin tour |
| Wines available (1984) | 1982 White Rieslings (dry and sweet) 1981 Pinot Noir 1981 Reserve Pinot Noir 1981 Chardonnay 1983 Zinfandel Blanc 1982 Cabernet Sauvignon |

humidity, and sunlight intensity. "There's plenty of data for airports," Byard explains, "but not much for higher elevations. Oregon State University is trying to figure out why the growers are having such trouble getting the fruit to set on Gewurztraminer."

No such problems with Pinot Noir. "I think we've got the right site here," Byard told us. Ironically, it wasn't until 1980, a poor growing season, that Hidden Springs had its first commercial crush. The big question was how that first Pinot Noir would turn out. It wasn't released until the summer of 1983; it wasn't entered in competition until the Pacific Northwest Enological Society in August. The wait was a long one.

Byard acknowledges that his lack of formal training in enology makes it difficult for him to evaluate, now, what a wine will be like in a year or more.

**HIDDEN SPRINGS**

| | |
|---|---|
| Owners | Don & Carolyn Byard |
| | Al & Jo Alexanderson |
| Winemakers | Don Byard and Al Alexanderson |
| Year bonded | 1980 |
| Year first planted | 1972 |
| Vineyard acreage | 23 |
| Principal varieties | Pinot Noir |
| | White Riesling |
| | Chardonnay |
| | Muller Thurgau |
| Year of first crush | 1980 |
| Production capacity | 8,000 gallons |
| Production in 1983 | 5,077 gallons |
| Awards, 1983 | |
| 1980 Pinot Noir: | Gold, Seattle |
| | Silver, Oregon State Fair |
| | Silver, New York |

He knows what he'd *like* it to taste like: the great wines of Europe, for which he developed an appreciation during his travels.

He must have done it right, though. The 1980 Pinot Noir is smooth and velvety, and exhibits a true Pinot aroma. Its clean yet earthy varietal texture is reminiscent of the best Burgundies. It has been greeted with a cavalcade of honors: it was the only Pinot to win a gold medal in Seattle, and it went on to win silvers at the Oregon State Fair and the American Wine Competition in New York. (What about Dick Erath's 1980 Knudsen Erath Pinot Noir, the one recently named America's best? It wasn't entered in Seattle. Nor was Oak Knoll's Pinot.) Ask Don Byard who consistently makes the best Pinot Noir in Oregon and he'll tell you, without hesitating, Dick Erath. Yet he's unabashedly jubilant about the honors his own Pinot has won, especially since he planted the vines personally. "Imagine," he exclaimed, "reaching the ultimate in the first year!"

There's much more to come. We tasted the 1983 Pinot Noir from the barrel on a recent visit; what an enormous wine it is! Deep-colored and full-flavored, a wine that Byard believes will put Oregon on the world wine map once and for all.

He also believes in a strong future for sparkling wines in Oregon, using Pinot Noir and Chardonnay grapes produced in relatively poor growing seasons. (Grapes used for sparkling wine don't have to get as ripe as those used in still wines.) The 1981 Chardonnay is a fine example of balance, restraint, and classical flavors. Byard also thinks Riesling is a good grape for Oregon and Washington, and makes two types: a dry Riesling to be enjoyed with food, and a sweeter "sipping wine" with lemon and honey flavors. "The 1982's were the best Rieslings in five or six years," Byard points out, "but how do we convince the public?"

Well, as many a winemaker has found out, the way to convince the public is to make the wine as best you can, put it on the counter in the tasting room, and let the public discover for itself.

# Knudsen Erath

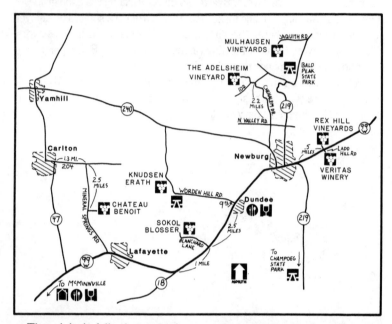

There it is, in full color on the front cover of the *Wine Buying Guide*, the American Wine Champion Pick-of-the-Best issue: a bottle of Knudsen Erath's 1980 Vintage Select (Yamhill County) Pinot Noir. We'd already seen that wine win a gold medal at the San Francisco Fair, a gold at the Oregon State Fair, and a gold at the American Wine Competition in New York. Now, American Champion! Best in the country!

Actually, this sort of recognition for Dick Erath's wines has been going on for some time. He's one of Oregon's best-known and most honored winemakers.

Erath's view of medals is that they're meaningful only in a "general" sense: a winery that consistently wins medals is a winery to watch. Erath has been winning medals ever since he settled in the Red Hills of Dundee in the late 1960s, a long time ago by Oregon standards; he has produced dozens of top-flight wines, and won over fifty awards in regional and national competitions.

"There's a tendency [among judges] to choose the most aggressive, distinctive wines when judging—without food," Erath comments. But most people drink wine *with* food, and that's the audience Erath is trying to

| **KNUDSEN ERATH**<br>Worden Hill Road<br>Route 1, Box 368<br>Dundee, OR 97115<br>538-3318 | |
|---|---|
| Open to the public | 10-3 weekdays, 12-5 weekends<br>(closed major holidays) |
| Tour groups | by appointment |
| Charge for tour groups | $1 per person (over 10 people) |
| Picnic facilities at the winery | small patio at winery; Crabtree<br>Park is adjacent to winery |
| Festivals/special events | Harvest Festival, Aug. 25-26 |
| Wines available (1984) | Pinot Noir<br>White Riesling<br>Chardonnay<br>Merlot<br>Gewurztraminer<br>Sparkling |

impress. We've enjoyed the award-winning Pinot with several fine meals, and tend to agree with Erath: it's an exceptional food wine.

There are those who say, with smugness and envy, that Knudsen Erath is a successful winery today because of its financial backing. These critics should remember that when Dick Erath's vineyards were first planted, in 1969, there was no guarantee of success, and that it wasn't until three years later that lumberman Calvert Knudsen became financially involved. (Knudsen was a senior vice-president of Weyerhaeuser; he went on to head the giant Canadian wood-products firm of MacMillan-Bloedel and has since retired to Seattle, but remains active in the winery's business affairs.) The original arrangement was for Dick Erath to run his own vineyard *and* Knudsen's separate property, five miles away; when it turned out that the agreement couldn't be carried out because of Oregon's Byzantine liquor laws, the two vineyards merged. Thus the credit for Knudsen Erath's success must be given to Dick Erath, the resident partner, full-time winemaker, and self-assured pioneer in the Willamette Valley vineyards.

Although he was trained as an electronics engineer, Erath comes by his interest in wine quite legitimately: both his father, Charles, and his grandfather before him were winemakers in the Rheinland of Germany. Charles Erath, who now lives in California, also learned the craft of barrel making,

**KNUDSEN ERATH**

| | |
|---|---|
| Owners | Dick Erath, Cal Knudsen |
| Winemaker | Dick Erath |
| Cellarmaster | Dr. Richard Nunes |
| Year bonded | 1972 |
| Year first planted | 1969 |
| Vineyard acreage | 111 (93 producing) |
| Principal varieties, acres | Chardonnay, 37 |
| | Pinot Noir, 32 |
| | White Riesling, 17 |
| Year of first crush | 1972 |
| Production capacity | 103,000 gallons |
| Production in 1983 | 51,000 gallons |
| Expansion plans | 8 more acres of Riesling |

Awards, 1983
1980 Yamhill County Vintage

| | |
|---|---|
| Select Pinot Noir: | American Wine Championship |
| | Gold, San Francisco |
| | Gold, Oregon State Fair |
| | Gold, New York |
| 1981 Merlot: | Gold, Tacoma |
| | Gold, Seattle |
| 1981 Chardonnay: | Silver, Oregon State Fair |

and applies that skill to Dick Erath's cooperage when he visits Oregon. Still, it was the prospect of an electronics job in Oregon that brought Dick Erath from California to the Portland suburbs, and an encounter during that trip with Richard Sommer, whom he had met at a short course at the University of California at Davis, that sold him on the quality of Oregon-grown grapes. So it happened that Erath moved to Oregon, a self-confessed "electrical engineer gone berserk" to start his vineyard.

Since then, Erath has travelled extensively in Europe (Burgundy, Chablis, Champagne, and Alsace in France; the Moselle, Rheingau, and Pfalz in Germany), and continues to approach his work with dedication. He has planted virus-free cuttings from the University of California at Davis in order to assure grapes which ripen a week or so earlier, before the rains set in and interrupt the harvest.

Knudsen Erath today is a 265-acre property, with 111 acres planted in vinifera, principally Chardonnay, Pinot Noir, and White Riesling. One "secret," Erath told a group of wine writers, is that his vineyard is planted *off* the valley floor, with a southern-southeastern exposure. The winery bottled 51,000 gallons of wine last year, and over 87,000 gallons the year before, more than any other Oregon winery. (Knudsen Erath, Tualatin, and Sokol Blosser share the distinction of being the state's largest producers in terms of volume, but it's not a "race" in any sense; it's a question of who bought how many grapes, not how much any of them will sell, and certainly not a measure of how much profit they make.)

There's no mistaking the fact that you are in wine country as you make the sharp turn just past Crabtree Park, just outside of Dundee, and start up the hill toward the Knudsen Erath winery: the soil is the characteristic orange clay of the Red Hills of Dundee, and the grape-laden vines grow to the very edge of the road.

Visitors to the winery will find Pinot Noir, Chardonnay, and White Riesling, as well as Coastal Mist, a proprietary blend of Pinot Noir, Chardonnay, and Riesling that smells a bit like Pinot Noir with a blush of orange and 3-percent residual sugar. Prices are quite moderate for most bottles. Erath is also making a sparkling wine with Chardonnay and Pinot Noir. The tasting room, which adjoins Dick and Kina Erath's home, looks back down the road bordering the vineyards; a painting of the scene by Robert Hudson hangs above the counter. A second tasting room is down in Dundee.

And what has Dick Erath learned in his years of making good wines? "I have become aware," he writes, "that wines, good wines, are the product of their total environment." With that in mind, Erath continues with his intention of producing world class wines.

# Rex Hill Vineyards

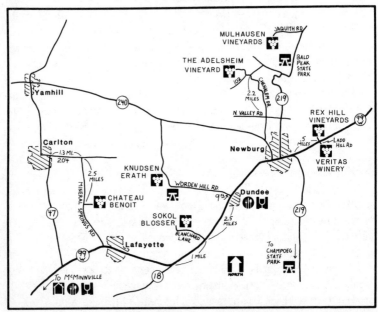

The rows of vines are easy to spot, on this hillside outside of Newberg. Eighteen acres of Pinot Noir, Chardonnay, and Riesling grapes wave across a slope that overlooks the Yamhill Valley, each plant protected by a plastic milk carton. It makes the vineyard look like a contour map, a dot-to-dot drawing.

The winery is built around a nut-and-prune-drying facility. It is huge: 8,400 square feet. Its stemmer-crusher can handle eight tons of grapes an hour, the basket press is enormous, and the boiler space below the old drying tunnels is being converted to "champagne cellars."

Clearly, Rex Hill intends to start out on the right foot, with operations big enough to sustain commercial production. The owners are Paul Hart, a financial consultant, and his wife, Jan Jacobsen, an artist. To run the winery they hired David Wirtz, a vineyard owner near Forest Grove and winemaking consultant.

Wirtz bought grapes from several growers in the area in the fall of 1983 and made 12,000 gallons of wine, half Pinot Noir, half Chardonnay, so that the winery will have wine to sell when it opens in the spring of 1985.

## REX HILL VINEYARDS
Highway 99 at Ladd Hill Road
Route 2, Box 338
Newberg, OR 97132
538-3793

| | |
|---|---|
| Open to the public | spring, 1985: 12-5 Wed.-Sun. |
| Tour groups | yes |
| Charge for tour groups | yes |
| Picnic facilities at the winery | will be near winery |
| Owners | Paul Hart & Jan Jacobsen |
| Winemaker | David R. Wirtz |
| Year bonded | 1983 |
| Year first planted | 1983 |
| Vineyard acreage | 18 |
| Principal varieties | Pinot Noir |
| | Chardonnay |
| | Riesling |
| Year of first crush | 1983 |
| Production capacity | 12,000 gallons |
| Production in 1983 | 12,000 gallons |

It's being aged in nearly new Nevers barrels, and from what we tasted, it promises to be excellent wine. Wirtz will be making some Gewurztraminer, too, a wine he thinks has unrealized potential. Wirtz's family has been involved in the wine industry for a long time; David himself was the cellarmaster for Charles Coury and winemaker for Reuter's Hill Vineyards before both went out of business in the late 1970s. "I think it's very important for a winemaker to be 'worldly' in terms of wine knowledge," Wirtz tells us. "The problem arises of a winemaker only tasting his own wines, and thus making false judgments and assessments of his wines because he has nothing to compare them to."

The hardest part for him, Wirtz says, is waiting for changes in the weather during harvest. We're waiting to retaste the 1983 Rex Hill Pinot Noir (it was made with grapes from Maresh Vineyards, owned by Fred Arterberry's father-in-law) to see whether the concentrated effort that went into its production makes a difference. We suspect that Wirtz's effort and experience will pay off.

# Sokol Blosser Winery

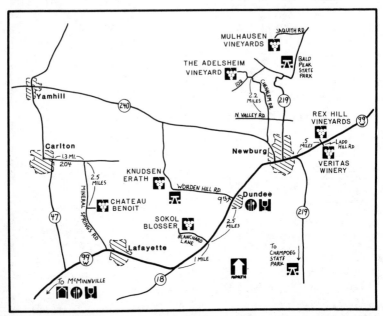

Bill Blosser was an urban planner, his wife Susan Sokol Blosser a professor of history. They both graduated from Stanford; he has a master's from the University of North Carolina, she has one from Reed. There's virtually nothing in their personal or academic upbringing to presage that today—barely half a dozen years since they established Sokol Blosser—they would be owners and managers of a winery with a production capacity of 60,000 gallons a year, one of Oregon's "big three" (with Tualatin Vineyards and Knudsen Erath). This remarkable accomplishment is based as much on expert enology as on a combination of astute planning and access to capital.

By the Blossers' own account, the venture started as an adventure: a romantic notion of planting a vineyard on weekends in the Red Hills of Dundee in the Willamette Valley southwest of Portland. The property's 125 acres of fruit trees were supposed to guarantee a cash crop (a processor of maraschino cherries being one purchaser). But the Blossers' determination to do more than just till the soil, grow grapes, and make wine came soon enough, and with this vision came bold but meticulous planning.

The single most important step was the decision to hire a full-time, pro-

---

### 🍇 SOKOL BLOSSER WINERY

Blanchard Lane
P.O. Box 199
Dundee, OR 97115
864-3342

| | |
|---|---|
| Open to the public | 11-5 daily |
| Tour groups | yes (appointments for groups larger than 15) |
| Charge for tour groups | $1 per person, refunded with purchase |
| Picnic facilities at the winery | 6 picnic tables in landscaped area adjacent to tasting room |
| Wines available (1984) | White Riesling |
| | Sauvignon Blanc |
| | Pinot Noir |
| | Chardonnay |
| | Gewurztraminer |
| | Muller Thurgau |
| | Merlot |
| | Bouquet Blanc |
| | Bouquet Rouge |
| | Bouquet Rose |

---

fessional winemaker—a virtual heresy among owners of mom-and-pop wineries. Generating enough cash flow to pay the winemaker's salary necessitated a high volume of production from the start, which in turn required an investment in large-scale facilities, not to mention more grapes than the Blossers' own vines could provide.

By 1977, Sokol Blosser was ready for its first crush. Financial backers (members of the Sokol family and sympathetic bankers) had contributed some $1.5 million; Dr. Robert McRitchie, a chemist from Franciscan Vineyards in the Napa Valley, had been hired as winemaker; the winery itself had been built.

From the beginning, the Blossers understood that attracting tourists to their vineyard and winery would be essential to create a market for their wine, so they commissioned a first-rank architect, John Storrs, to design their tasting room. (The Knights of the Vine have just presented Storrs with an award for outstanding service to the wine industry for the Sokol Blosser project.) The Blossers also understood that awards and medals impress wine buyers, so they entered competitions as far away as London;

**SOKOL BLOSSER WINERY**

| | |
|---|---|
| Owners | Sokol & Blosser families |
| Winemaker | Dr. Robert McRitchie |
| Year bonded | 1977 |

| | |
|---|---|
| Year first planted | 1971 |
| Vineyard acreage | 45 |
| Principal varieties, acres | Chardonnay, 15 |
| | White Riesling, 13 |
| | Pinot Noir, 13 |

| | |
|---|---|
| Year of first crush | 1977 |
| Production capacity | 60,000 gallons |
| Production in 1983 | 50,000 gallons |
| Expansion plans | more vineyard plantings |

| Awards, 1983 | |
|---|---|
| 1980 Chardonnay: | Gold, New York |
| | Gold, Oregon State Fair |
| | Silver, London |
| 1982 Sauvignon Blanc: | Gold, Tri-Cities |
| | Gold, Reno |
| | Silver, Seattle |
| | Silver, Oregon State Fair |
| 1978 Pinot Noir | Silver, New York |
| | Silver, Oregon State Fair |

their wines were rewarded handsomely with a panoply of regional and international honors.

The first of the new state signs directs travelers along Highway 99 outside of Dundee up Blanchard Lane. You follow the gravel road, encouraged by a series of small arrows as the road meanders through peach and cherry orchards, and finally reach the fringe of the vineyard. Rows upon rows of grapes—forty-five acres at this point, planted mostly in Chardonnay, White Riesling, and Pinot Noir—extend up the hill until they disappear into the stands of fruit trees. The old walnut orchard below the winery is being converted to a vineyard this year; some cherry trees were taken out a year ago. Grapes are better cash crops now.

Facing this scene from a shaded knoll is the striking, angular stucco shelter where visitors can picnic, taste wines, hold club meetings or small banquets, and buy souvenirs. A few feet away, bunkered into the hillside, is the cast-concrete winery itself, whose stainless steel fermentation tanks and huge oak barrels are watched over by winemaker Bob McRitchie.

Susan Sokol Blosser tended the vines while holding down a job teaching American history at nearby Linfield College. She gave up the classroom early in 1981, but not her seat on the tractor.

Bill Blosser continued to work full-time as a consultant, doing environmental planning for industrial clients, until November, 1980. He also plotted the winery's marketing strategy, recognizing that three factors were converging upon American winemakers. First, the rising cost of grapes, which were going up again after several years of overplanting; second, the rising cost of money, which was making it increasingly expensive for winemakers to keep an inventory of wines in their own cellars for aging; and third, the increasing demand of American wine consumers for white wines, which need less aging, and are thus less expensive to produce. Elementary only in retrospect.

"In France," Blosser points out, "the *negociants* withhold wines from the market until the wines are ready to be drunk. No one is willing to take that risk in the U.S. today." Thus the wines being sold to American consumers are *made* to be drunk "young," and it's no accident that American tastes are shifting to "younger" wines.

One of Sokol Blosser's best wines to date is the 1982 Sauvignon Blanc, made from Washington grapes, a fine wine to accompany the Northwest's seafood bounty. Dry, acidic, yet lightly perfumed, it is a very versatile table wine, showing almost patrician restraint in aroma and taste. All the Sokol Blosser wines, medal-winners and ordinary wines alike, are very well priced. Oregon consumes 80 percent of Sokol Blosser's output, but Sokol Blosser wines are also being marketed in some distinguished European settings: Spurrier's in Paris and l'Escargot in London, for example. Articles about Sokol Blosser are appearing in wine journals and wine columns, and the Sokol Blosser label is on an increasing number of wine lists, particularly in tenths, a popular size many wineries unjustly avoid.

Back at the winery, there's an occasional newsletter ("The Sokol Blosser Infrequent"), informative pamphlets for visitors, detailed write-ups on each of the handsome wine labels, a gift shop selling souvenir glasses, wine in boxed sets, and Sokol Blosser T-shirts.

"We want to make the finest wines in the world," the Blossers say in their newsletter. They know it's a heady ambition, and one shared by many Northwest winemakers. Unlike many of their colleagues, though, they also know the value of marketing. Not just to sell the product, but to create a demand. Fortunately, they also make wines that meet the buyer's expectations.

# *Veritas Vineyard*

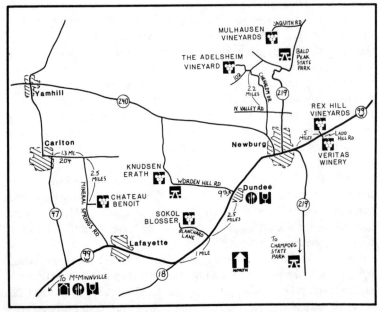

In wine there is truth. *In vino veritas.*

And the truth is, 1983 was a fortunate year to begin making Pinot Noir, with fruit of exceptional quality that yielded dark, richly flavored wine.

And the truth is, 600 gallons is probably the smallest reported crush of any winery in Oregon.

We're talking about Veritas Vineyard, just across the highway from Rex Hill; the two new wineries will anchor the northeastern corner of the Yamhill Valley. The first grapes, from Hyland Vineyards, were crushed in 1983 at Sokol Blosser's facilities and will be moved to the new winery as soon as it's built and federal approval is received.

The principal owners of Veritas are a longtime amateur winemaker, John Howieson and his wife, Diane. Jack Myers, an advertising-agency art director and graphic-design teacher, and his wife, Miki, are also owners; they are well known in Oregon winemaking circles as the owners of Champoeg Vineyards.

John Howieson is currently a professor of diagnostic radiology and associate professor of neurology at the Oregon Health Science University in Port-

## VERITAS VINEYARD

Highway 99 at Ladd Hill Road
Route 4, Box 337
Newberg, OR 97132
(no phone at winery;
John Howieson's business
phone is 225-7576)

| | |
|---|---|
| Open to the public | spring, 1985 |
| Tour groups | yes, by appointment |
| Picnic facilities at the winery | 2 picnic tables at end of trail through wooded area beside vineyard; viewpoint overlooks valley (planned for 1985) |
| Anticipated wines available (1985) | 1983 Pinot Noir<br>1983 Chardonnay<br>1984 Riesling<br>1984 Chardonnay<br>1984 Semillon |
| Owners | John & Diane Howieson; Jack & Miki Myers |
| Winemakers | John Howieson (with Jack Myers) |
| Year bonded | 1984 (anticipated) |
| Year first planted | 1983 |
| Vineyard acreage | 20 |
| Principal varieties, acres | Pinot Noir, 5.5<br>Chardonnay, 5.5<br>Riesling, 5.5<br>Gamay, 1 |
| Year of first crush | 1983 |
| Production capacity | 2,000 gallons |
| Production in 1983 | 600 gallons |

land. His work requires him to deal with sickness and suffering. "After nearly thirty years of this," he tells us, "I want to be associated with a source of pleasure rather than pain."

For Howieson, then, winemaking is "the perfect combination of agriculture, chemistry, and esthetics." Come 1985, we will be able to share it. And that's the truth.

# *Lodging*

## *McMinnville*

### *College Inn*
1102 S. Baker Street
472-2221

This is a modest, one-story motel adjacent to the Linfield College campus, with kitchens. Prices are very low.

### *Old Oak Bed & Breakfast Inn*
246-8366

This fine old home, decorated with American antiques, is close to McMinnville's beautiful city park, and within walking distance to Nick's Italian Cafe. Alice Cooper, who runs the place, has listed it with Northwest Bed & Breakfast, a registry service headquartered in Portland; more information on all the registries toward the back of this book.

### *Safari Motel*
345 N. Highway 99W
472-5187

John Jankowski built this motel and restaurant, and has added to it over the years. His personal attention shows in the spacious, comfortable rooms, and in the well-run restaurant, which is open for three meals a day. Deep-fried French toast is a morning specialty. A heated pool, moderate prices, and quick access to the wine country make this a fine place to stay.

## *Yamhill*

### *Flying M Ranch*
Route 1, Box 95C
362-3222

This is a rustic dude ranch tucked away in the rolling foothills of the Cascade Range. You can fly in by chartered plane, or drive through twenty miles of spectacular woods with nothing but little "Flying M" signs to guide you. The winding county roads will get you within about five miles of the ranch, but even if you've called ahead for directions, you'll probably think you're lost as you navigate the final stretch of dusty, unpaved dirt and gravel. The scenery is worth it, though.

What you'll find when you get here isn't bad, either; in approximate order, you'll see the airplane runway, the horse corral, a swimming hole as large as a city block, and the remains of the log cabin lodge. Built in the early 1970s overlooking the north fork of the Yamhill River, the lodge burned down a year ago, but the Bryce Mitchell family, which owns this 200-acre spread, plans to rebuild.

Meantime, the horses are still here (you can rent one, or bring your own), and the ranch still sponsors overnight horsepacking trips across the Coast Range. There are half a dozen large campsites, several pleasant cabins that sleep up to eight people, and "motel rooms" in an old-fashioned bunkhouse. The rooms have private baths, two queen-size beds, and, to help you really get away from it all, no television or telephone.

# *Restaurants*

## *Bellevue*

### *Augustine's*
Upstairs at the Lawrence Gallery
Highway 18
843-3225

Rodney Augustine and Susan Hope have installed an airy, elegant restaurant at treetop level, using fresh ingredients for fancy soups and salads at lunch, classically prepared seafood and steaks at dinner. Some light dishes are featured at dinner also, such as stir-fried chicken, stuffed artichoke, pasta al pesto. And there's an a la carte Sunday brunch. The food is tasty and attractively presented, and the wine list, not surprisingly, offers a wide range of local bottlings.

## *Dundee*

### *Alfie's Wayside Country Inn*
139 S.W. Highway 99W (at 11th)
538-9407

Alfie Tahan, who made his way to Dundee from Portland a couple of

---

years ago, has moved his restaurant to a large, attractive house on the highway. Soup-and-sandwich combinations are featured at lunch; in the evening, a blackboard at the entrance announces special dinner offerings. The wine list emphasizes Oregon wines (fifteen labels at last count).

## McMinnville

### Alf's
1250 S. Baker

When was last time you saw a green Hamilton Beach milkshake machine? 1950? Alf's still has one. Alf's also makes hamburgers that taste the way they used to taste back then. And homemade ice cream, too. Gadzooks! It's on the southern end of Highway 99 as it passes through town, and is well worth a stop.

### Blue Moon
300 E. Third Street
No phone

A small-town tavern, but only in the small town of McMinville; good hamburgers, loud music, and a stock of The Eyrie Vineyards Pinot Noir behind the bar. The staff from Nick's sometimes comes in late at night.

### La Maison Surette
729 E. Third Street
472-6666

John Surett is in the kitchen, cooking bistro lunches and formal dinners; Carol Surett is at the door, welcoming guests from all over the valley to this lovingly restored house next to the old railroad depot. The garden has been manicured; the interior decorated with genuine antiques. The wine list emphasizes Oregon bottlings. The overall effect might remind you of one of Vancouver's house restaurants: very elegant.

### Nick's Italian Cafe
521 E. Third Street
472-7919

We've come here often, sometimes alone, sometimes with a group of friends, and we've always been welcomed by an atmosphere of genuine caring. We sometimes wish we could plant clones of Nick's in every wine-touring region of the state!

This almost legendary place, founded eight years ago by Nick Peirano, is an Italian trattoria masquerading as a conventional storefront cafe. It has become a wonderful, informal, good-humored gathering place, hardly fancy, hardly expensive, that many consider the best Italian restaurant in Oregon.

Dinner begins with an antipasto (prosciutto with melon, perhaps, or stuffed clams, or marinated fava beans), accompanied by Ken Piontek's bread. Then comes a big tureen of superb minestrone topped with a dollop of pesto, followed by a fresh salad. Then a pasta course (ravioli stuffed with spinach, or canelloni). That's enough for many diners, but the truly hungry continue for a selection of main courses (steak with caper sauce, or scallops, or chicken in lemon sauce). Then incredible desserts (a chocolate velvet cake, for instance) made by Nick's wife.

The wine list is particularly good. Nick's house wines, named for his daughters Carmen and Aida, come from the nearby Sokol Blosser winery, but lots of local wines are available for only a dollar or two above retail.

There's an early seating between 6:00 and 6:30, and a second between 8:00 and 8:30, except Sunday, when the doors open at 5:00 to catch the traffic coming home from the beach. Children are welcome, and are served at half price. Reservations are essential on weekends.

## Roger's
2121 E. 27th Street
472-0917

This seafood restaurant is a welcome addition to McMinnville's restaurant scene. The owners, Roger and Shirley Newton, began with a wholesale poultry business, added retail seafood and custom smoking of game, and now emphasize seafood in their restaurant. The view from the windows is of a small creek, and a covered patio is available for outdoor dining. The seafood is excellent and very fresh; it's also available for sale at the restaurant's retail store. The wine list is very good, too.

## Umberto's
828 N. Adams
472-1717

A new Italian restaurant with moderately priced spaghetti dinners, weekly specials, and a children's menu.

# Wine Shops & Delicatessens

## Bellevue

### Lawrence Gallery
843-3787

Amity Vineyards operates the back of this attractive gallery as a tasting room and retail outlet for almost all Oregon wines. The tastings are free, of course, and make a splendid introduction to Oregon wines for visitors in a hurry. It's also a good starting point for travelers who want to get an idea of wineries they might want to visit. When Amity's Myron Redford started this tasting room, it was the only one in the state promoting the product of other wineries, a most commendable effort.

## Dundee

### Knudsen Erath Satellite Tasting Room
691 S.W. Highway 99W
538-9407

An outlet for Knudsen Erath wines on Dundee's main drag. (It's in the same building as Nut World, making this an attractive stop for filbert lovers as well as wine connoisseurs.) As we pointed out in our profile, Dick Erath makes some of the best wines in the state, and this little tasting room provides a sales opportunity to travelers who don't have the time to visit the winery itself.

## McMinnville

### Wheyside Cheese Company
701 E. Third Street
472-8819

This quaintly named establishment is the perfect place to assemble the makings of a picnic: over a hundred kinds of cheese, an assortment of sausages, Ken Piontek's bread, bagels from the Beaverton Bakery.

There's a fine stock of beer, and dozens upon dozens of Oregon wines, many of which are available by the glass. The Wheyside also sells sandwiches from the deli counter, and there's sit-down service, too. So if the weather happens to be hostile to your notion of a picnic in the vineyards, you can take your bottle from the wine shop at the front to the tables at the back, and, for a modest corkage fee, enjoy it on the spot.

## Jake's Deli
1208 S. Baker
  Good family fare, deli sandwiches, and lovely people.

## Cafe Rue
705 E. Third Street
472-2517
  Kathleen Spencer is gone, but her influence lingers: hearty breakfasts, nice little lunches, an atmosphere of charm and love.

## Newberg

## Unicorn Garden
607 E. First
538-5900
  A very pretty place in a house beside the highway. The prospect of a good delicatessen in Newberg is cause for celebration.

## Willamina

## Piontek Bread Works
212 N.E. D Street
876-4351
  Ken Piontek got his start only a couple of years ago baking bread—thick, crunchy bread in the tradition of that baked by his Alsatian grandmother—in the ovens at Nick's, then driving it around to restaurants and delicatessens in the neighborhood. Now he and Peggi Lilly have established a retail outlet in Willamina, ten miles down the road from McMinnville, in addition to his wholesale business. If you can't stop in McMinnville for a meal, you owe it to yourself to buy a loaf of his bread: it's unlike any French bread we've tasted.

# *Picnic Spots*

## *Champoeg*

### *Champoeg State Park*

To cross the Willamette, take Highway 219 southbound from Newberg toward St. Paul; the park is on the river's southern bank, at a site where Indians once gathered because of its easy river access. That same access devastated the first town of Champoeg, built on this site by early settlers. A museum and the historic Newell House are on the grounds, as well as extensive facilities: picnic tables, bike trails, river fishing and boating. A cabin called Pioneer Mother's Home stands nearby; it's filled with artifacts from the 1850s. A tour of French Prairie settlements runs along here, too; pick up a map at the visitor center.

## *Dundee*

### *Crabtree Park*

Warden Hill Road

A small but very pleasant park just below the entrance to Knudsen Erath's vineyards. Softball fields as well as picnic tables.

## *Hopewell*

### *Maud Williamson State Park*

Highway 221

One of the prettiest approaches into the Yamhill County wine country is from the east: take the Wheatland ferry twelve miles north of Salem across the Willamette. The park is in a grove of tall, shady trees looking across the Yamhill Valley to the Chehalem Mountains. (Willamette Mission State Park, which has fishing, boating, bicycling, and a nature trail, is on the other side of the ferry crossing.)

## Lafayette

### Yamhill Locks
Locks Road
   The Yamhill River meanders through this unassuming, out-of-the-way and peaceful county park.

## McMinnville

### City Park
Third & Adams
   There are several picnic sites on the grounds of this hilly, wooded, flowered, shady park: grassy spots, barbecues, covered areas, a stream. Downtown parks like this make you feel that the city fathers care about their citizens as well as their visitors.

## Newberg

### Bald Peak State Park
   Nine miles northwest of Newberg on Highway 219, this little park overlooks the valley through a stand of Douglas firs. There's no water, but the view is simply splendid.

### Herbert Hoover Park
   A very pleasant spot at the northern end of Newberg, insulated from the highway traffic by leafy trees.

### Dr. Henry John Minthorn House
115 River Street, one block off Highway 99W
   Herbert Hoover grew up here, in the home of his pioneer Quaker uncle. There's an admission charge to the home itself; no charge to use the grounds.

# Salem Area

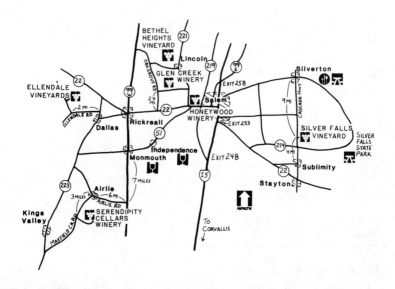

Almost a score of new wineries have been established in Oregon since the publication in 1982 of the first edition of this book, and some of the most interesting are clustered around Salem. In fact, the winegrowers here foresee the eventual establishment of a new viticultural appellation for this region, midway along the Willamette Valley between Portland and Eugene.

The specific geography and climate they have discovered is in the Eola Hills, a twenty-mile trail of knobs and knuckles rising no higher than 1,000 feet above the flat and fertile valley floor north and west of Salem. The Eola Hills lie south and east of the Red Hills of Dundee, Yamhill County's principal winegrowing slope, with a similar soil of jory clay loam and a few more heat units to warm the vines.

Two established wineries on the northern end of the Eola Hills—Amity Vineyards and Hidden Springs Winery—could be included in this chapter on the basis of their topographical location, although we have put them in Yamhill County, which claims their political allegiance. For visitors touring the wine country by car, the distinction is virtually irrelevant.

100

Salem, Oregon's capital city, makes a fine home base for wine touring. Accommodations are plentiful, restaurants are numerous. But the principal attraction is still the land, the incredibly bountiful Willamette Valley. The settlers who arrived here a century ago found a land of plenty, and to celebrate their discovery they gave their towns and villages names from a Biblical past to describe their joy. Names like Sublimity, Bethel, Aurora, Damascus, New Era, Amity. Those ancient rhythms complement the Indian names like Molalla, Chemeketa, Mehama, Waconda, which also mark the maps of the valley.

It's all in the imagination, of course, but the sky seems broader here, as the road traverses the softly rolling hills. It happens when you leave the freeway, with its flat, high-speed monotony. The roads go up and down the hills, and the change in elevation, perhaps only a hundred feet, produces a new perspective, new vistas: an agglomeration of farm buildings, a combine cutting a wide swath through a field of grass seed, a lone tree silhouetted against the horizon. And everywhere the broad, pastel expanse of sky.

*Notes:*

*The wineries in the Salem area, including Hidden Springs, stage a wine-tasting event called the Tastevin Tour on Memorial Day weekend. Some of the wineries have live music. Because all the wineries participate, we have not included the Tastevin Tour among the special events, but visitors should keep it in mind.*

*There's also a Salem Wine Festival in early November (the 3rd and 4th in 1984) which draws some 10,000 people for a weekend of food, wine, arts, and crafts. Two dozen wineries from Oregon and Washington participated last year.*

*Finally, the Oregon Museums Association has produced an illustrated guide to the historic buildings of this area, available by writing to the Marion County Historical Society, P.O. Box 847, Salem, Oregon 97308.*

# *Bethel Heights Vineyard*

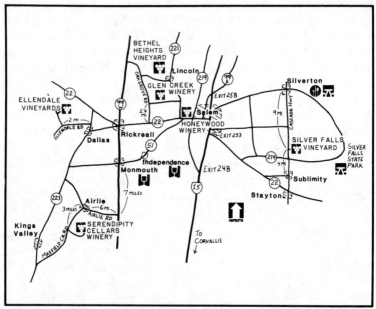

As the strange and wonderful tales of childhood (and contemporary news reports) remind us, common experiences frequently befall identical twins, though they may be separated by barriers of distance and even culture. The common experience that befell twin brothers Ted and Terry Casteel was their excited discovery of, and ever-growing appreciation for, the wines of France.

Ted and his wife, Patricia Dudley, were at the time pursuing graduate studies in history in Nimes, France. Quite naturally, they were enjoying the relatively inexpensive meals of Provence as well as the wines of that sweet country. Especially the wines.

Meantime, Terry and his wife, Marilyn Webb, practicing psychologists in Seattle, were beginning to experience the fascination and quality of inexpensive Bordeaux wines.

The two couples discovered their mutual passion, and in the best storytelling tradition gave up their individual professional careers and turned to wine. They bought a large vineyard in the Eola Hills that had been planted in 1978 on the site of a walnut grove. (The seller, not to get too far afield

## 🍇 BETHEL HEIGHTS VINEYARD

6060 Bethel Heights Road N.W.
Salem, OR 97304
378-0565 or 585-5630

| | |
|---|---|
| Open to the public | spring, 1985 |
| Owners | Patricia Dudley & Theodore Casteel |
| | Marilyn Webb & Terrence Casteel |
| Winemaker | Terry Casteel |
| Year bonded | 1984 (anticipated) |
| Year first planted | 1977 |
| Vineyard acreage | 48 |
| Principal varieties, acres | Pinot Noir, 21 |
| | Chardonnay, 14 |
| | Gewurztraminer, 6.5 |
| | Riesling, 4 |
| | Chenin Blanc, 2 |
| Year of first crush | 1984 (anticipated) |
| Production capacity | 7,000 gallons (anticipated) |

from our story, was Vic Winquist, who had planned his own winery, Stonewood, for the property; he remains in the neighborhood, managing vineyard property for several investors.) Ted and Pat spent a year at the University of California at Davis studying viticulture, then set to work.

Bethel Heights is a remarkable property. From the moment you arrive at the estate, one glorious view follows another as the road winds through the high-trellised, double-curtain vineyard. Ted Casteel's home is at the end of one aisle, looking as appropriate to its setting as does Chateau Margaux; Terry Casteel's home stands at the very end of the drive, overlooking the grand vistas from the heights of the Eola Hills.

As an amateur winemaker using grapes from Bethel Heights vines, Terry Casteel won a gold medal, two silvers, and a bronze in the 1982 Oregon State Fair amateur division. We tasted some of his three-month-old Pinot Noir from the barrel; it was remarkably clean and fruity. The 1982 Gewurztraminer, sampled with lunch, was well balanced and delicately spicy. Come 1984, the Casteels will crush 7,000 gallons of Gewurztraminer, Chardonnay, Chenin Blanc, and, no doubt, Pinot Noir, which Terry Casteel describes as "the" Oregon grape.

Bethel Heights Vineyard is totally irrigated with a drip system, allowing the Casteels to control moisture to the vines with great precision. This is particularly important on a property as large as theirs, where the distance from one end of the estate to the other—some 3,700 feet—would get you clear across many famous Burgundy vineyards, with attendant changes in microclimate and quality.

The winery and tasting room for Bethel Heights Vineyard will be built on a knoll at the top of Spring Valley, looking across the Willamette to Mount Jefferson, and the outlook for the winery is as bright as the view is expansive. The Casteels have a high level of intellectual curiosity coupled with an extraordinary energy, and their desire to succeed has distilled and revealed their strengths. The ecstasy of their love affair with wine has been tempered by the discovery of individual talents. Marilyn, already an important figure in the Oregon Winegrowers Association and editor of the O.W.A.'s current manual on viticulture, will be the winery's administrative officer; Ted, author of a chapter in the O.W.A. manual on vineyard economics, will grow the grapes; enologist Terry will make the wine; and Pat, while involving herself also in the politics of the industry, will see that the wine gets sold. Come 1985, given all the requisite approvals by state and federal authorites, the winery will be on its way.

# *Ellendale Vineyards*

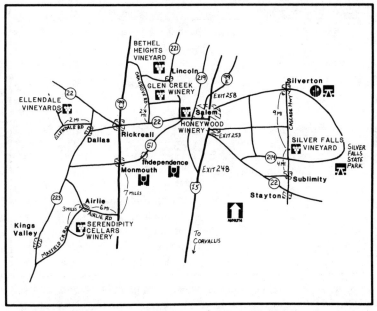

Some fifteen years ago, when Robert Hudson was still an Air Force navigator, he purchased a piece of property in Polk County for his retirement. By 1979, he had begun planting vineyards. And by 1981, after a twenty-three-year Air Force career and thirty years of amateur winemaking, Hudson had opened his retirement dream: a winery where he could be his own master. Now Hudson and his wife, Ella Mae, set their own rules and live by them.

The Hudsons regret that many citizens of Dallas, a bedroom community ten miles west of Salem, remain unaware of the presence of a winery on the outskirts of their town. But there it is, with an enthusiastic welcome for anyone who drives up. "If the gate is open, we're open," says Ella Mae Hudson. The structure itself—a bit like a country store with a peaked roof and a wide front porch—sits at the end of a curved driveway. Ella Mae promises to give you one of the most "fun" wine tours you'll ever take, peppered with local information, tales, goings-on. You know that anyone who can produce and sell a wine named "Woolly Booger" is going to have a sense of adventure, fun, and an abundance of theater.

---

### ❖ ELLENDALE VINEYARDS
300 Reuben Boise Road
Dallas, OR 97338
623-5617

| | |
|---|---|
| Open to the public | 12-6 daily |
| Tour groups | by appointment |
| Charge for tour groups | none |
| Picnic facilities at the winery | 8 fir tables in fir grove near winery; 2 tables on winery veranda |
| Festivals/special events | Oregon Trail Days, July 4; Wine & Art Fair, first full week of Dec. |
| Wines available (1984) | Riesling |
| | Merlot |
| | Cabernet Sauvignon |
| | Gewurztraminer |
| | Pinot Noir |
| | Chardonnay |
| | 15 fruit, berry, honey wines |

---

Robert Hudson set out to make wines from premium grapes, and still produces 6,000 gallons a year of varietal wines, but he has found another line: fruit and berry wines. He retraced the Oregon Trail a couple of seasons ago, checking on wine sales along the way, and came to the conclusion that there was no fruit wine industry west of the Mississippi. So he plunged right in, making 20,000 gallons of wine from over a dozen varieties of fruit and berries.

The grape wines remain; the winery won a silver medal at the Oregon State Fair for its 1982 Merlot, and more varietal wines will be released soon. In the underground barrel room, reached by a steep set of stairs, we tried some promising reds, including a 1982 Cabernet Sauvignon with a young varietal aroma of bell peppers.

Among the fruit wines, the plum and raspberry were particularly true to their fresh-fruit aroma and taste. Hudson finishes his wines with about 4 percent sugar, balanced by a pleasing acidity.

Robert Hudson's creativity is further demonstrated by his zeal for landscape painting, with examples of his oils (mountain scenes, deserts) proudly covering the walls of the tasting room. But it is as a maverick (in an industry of mavericks) that Hudson seems to draw the most pleasure and

**ELLENDALE VINEYARDS**

| | |
|---|---|
| Owners | Robert & Ella Mae Hudson |
| Winemaker | Robert Hudson |
| Year bonded | 1981 |
| Year first planted | 1979 |
| Vineyard acreage | 13 |
| Principal varieties, acres | Pinot Noir, 7 |
| | White Riesling, 2 |
| | Chardonnay, 2 |
| | Cabernet Franc, 1 |
| Year of first crush | 1981 |
| Production capacity | 8,000 gallons grape wine |
| | 20,000 gallons fruit wine |
| Production in 1983 | 20,000 gallons |
| Expansion plans | 2 acres vinifera plantings |
| | 3,000 gallons of tanks |
| Recent awards | |
| 1981 Merlot: | Silver, Oregon State Fair |

energy, a nonconformist and iconoclast who takes a puckish delight in pointing out the foibles of Oregon's wine industry.

As we sampled Ellendale's wines, Hudson led us from the tasting room to the winery behind it, full of tanks and cold-storage lockers, to a concrete slab out back where an expansion of the winery will soon be built, to a cellar filled with oak barrels. Each sample was accompanied by Hudson's detailed discussions of winemaking techniques and jabs at various sacred cows of the industry, including the infallability and impartiality of competition judges.

Hudson believes sparkling wines will become increasingly important in the Willamette Valley, a view shared by many colleagues. In the meantime, however, he still makes Woolly Booger. Turns out it's a relatively sweet fruit wine made from blackberries, loganberries, and cherries, which Ellendale sells in gallon jugs to taverns.

# Glen Creek Winery

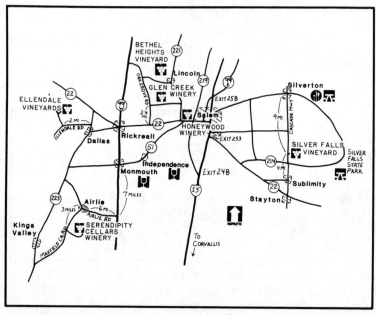

Tom Dumm is a rare find: an authentic gentleman. In voice and gesture, he is caring, attentive, confident. He also drives a pickup truck whose license plate reads "CHRDNY". Chardonnay is one of three white wines Dumm makes at Glen Creek Winery, but it's clearly his favorite.

Dumm moved to his quiet, fifteen-acre property of forest and pastureland near Salem in 1976 after living in Long Beach, California, where he owned the city's leading wine shop, Le Grand Cru. For a while, he managed stock and bond portfolios, built a gabled house and swimming pool, and made some Cabernet Sauvignon at home. A methodical man, he wanted to erect a garage big enough for the cars his children would one day drive (they're 17 and 14 now) and to house his pool equipment. Before long, the "shed" he set out to build turned into the beginnings one of Oregon's most modern commercial wineries.

Visitors driving out from Salem on Highway 22 play peekaboo with the winding river for several miles, then turn north through orchards and farmland before arriving at the yellow ochre house, the picnic pergola, and the striking winery itself. What's different here is that half of the "works" are

## 🍇 GLEN CREEK WINERY
6057 Orchard Heights Road N.W.
Salem, OR 97304
371-9463

| | |
|---|---|
| Open to the public | 12-5 weekends, holidays |
| Tour groups | yes, by appointment |
| Charge for tour groups | $1 per person |
| Picnic facilities at the winery | 4 wooden tables on grass adjacent to the winery |
| Festivals/special events | Memorial Day Weekend festival with bluegrass and Cajun music |
| Wines available (1984) | 1982 & 1983 Sauvignon Blanc |
| | 1982 & 1983 Gewurztraminer |
| | 1982 Chardonnay |

outside. During crush, when the grapes arrive at the winery in totes and lugs, you'd expect to find the stemmer-crusher and press outside, but Glen Creek Winery also keeps its five stainless steel fermenting tanks on a concrete slab outdoors, and pumps the wine indoors only for barrel aging and bottling.

Glen Creek's first release was a 1982 Sauvignon Blanc made from Yakima Valley grapes. What Tom Dumm did with those grapes was remarkable, considering that with this variety "less [varietal character] is more": the wine was pale in color, with a refined nose hinting of black currants and bursting with mouth-filling flavors. As a brand-new wine from a brand new winery, it was the most talked-about wine at Summerfest, an Oregon Winegrowers event in May, 1983; the wine took a silver medal at the Oregon Wineries Showcase later in the season, and by August had matured enough to win a gold medal at the Enological Society competition in Seattle.

Dumm didn't enter any of the Reserve Sauvignon Blanc he'd aged in oak barrels (there wasn't very much of it, anyway); we thought it was even better, with the oak giving the wine additional smoothness and complexity. What's significant is that all the Glen Creek Sauvignon Blanc to be sold in 1984 will be aged in those oak barrels, which come from the Nevers forest in France.

Also coming up in 1984 will be Glen Creek's first Chardonnay, a wine with a lovely, medium straw color, a nose that's fruity and slightly oaky, and a silky-soft texture. Dumm, who enjoys the "big" Chardonnays produced by David Bruce and Chalone, thinks his own wine will have a similar char-

## GLEN CREEK WINERY

| | |
|---|---|
| Owners | Thomas & Sylvia Dumm |
| Winemaker | Thomas Dumm |
| Year bonded | 1982 |
| Year first planted | 1983 |
| Vineyard acreage | 9 |
| Principal varieties, acres | Gewurztraminer, 4.5 |
| | Chardonnay, 4.5 |
| Year of first crush | 1982 |
| Production capacity | 6,000 gallons |
| Production in 1983 | 6,000 gallons |
| Expansion plans | new tasting room adjacent to barrel room; additional 3,000 gallons fermenting capacity |
| Awards, 1983 1982 Sauvignon Blanc: | Gold, Seattle |
| | Silver, Oregon Wineries Showcase |

acter and be able to "stand up to anything, even curry!"

What makes the difference in Dumm's wines? Perhaps it's the liquid yeast cultures he uses. Certainly there's great attention to detail, to planning, to design. Dumm spent several years in sales, production control, and forecasting for an industrial company; the experience shows in every corner of the winery. It also shows in Dumm's awareness of marketing as a crucial factor for wineries. "One of the benefits of having owned a wine shop is knowing what sells and what doesn't," he points out. "The truth is, packaging sells."

Dumm realizes that nothing can happen in the marketing continuum of wine until a consumer removes a bottle from the shelf. Hence his disappointment at people's reluctance to buy and taste new wines. "It tries my patience," Dumm wrote to us, "to see so many Americans not enjoying such wonderful wines available to them at pretty reasonable prices. I guess they just don't know what they're missing, and it's too bad."

# *Honeywood Winery*

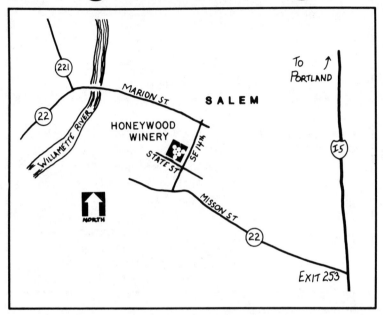

"Fruit wines aren't second-class citizens any more," Paul Gallick says with conviction. Three out of every ten bottles of Oregon wine are made from Willamette Valley fruit and berries, and Gallick's Honeywood Winery in downtown Salem is the largest producer, turning out nineteen "flavors" as well as a line of varietal wines.

He has a professional winemaker, Bill Wrey, on hand to run the winemaking; Gallick concentrates on management. "We have to convert the skeptical," he says. "We have to prove that fruit wine can be real wine, too."

Honeywood has a luxury of space unheard of in most Oregon wineries; it covers 23,000 square feet, ten times as much as, say, Alpine's facility. But then, Honeywood has been around for fifty years, brought to life by Ron Honeyman and John Wood as a brandy-making operation shortly after Repeal, when space was cheap. The marks of huge, long-gone brandy stills remain on the concrete floor of a room now used only for weddings. Today, Honeywood is a thriving enterprise, Oregon's largest winery in both space and production. Gallick, a former bank president in Minneapolis and originally one of several investors who bought the winery in 1972, moved to

---

### ◼◼ HONEYWOOD WINERY

501 14th Street S.E.
P.O. Box 12278
Salem, OR 97309
362-4111

| | |
|---|---|
| Open to the public | 9-5 Mon.-Fri. |
| | 10-5 Sat. |
| | 1-5 Sun. |
| Tour groups | yes, with reservations |
| Charge for tour groups | none |
| Wines available (1984) | 1982 Pinot Noir |
| | 1983 Riesling |
| | 1983 Chardonnay |
| | 1982 Pinot noir Blanc |
| | 1983 Niagara |
| | Fruit & Berry: Loganberry, |
| | Blackberry, Red Currant, Concord, |
| | Raspberry, Apricot, Apple, |
| | Cherry, Gooseberry, |
| | Boysenberry, Mead, Plum |

---

Salem three years ago and took over.

So now it is Gallick's tread that echoes down the wide hallways as he manages the business side of the winery. The dilemma that faces many Oregon winery owners—whether to give up their former professions—has not befallen Gallick: business management is his profession. It is Gallick who eagerly and expertly acts as administrator, manager, policy-maker, marketing director, and financial planner. (Another banker, Baker Ferguson, does much the same at Lowden Schoolhouse Winery near Walla Walla.) Gallick's wife, Marlene, is responsible for the winery's spacious tasting room; her parents, Don and Mary Brown, run Honeywood's tasting room, Oceans West, at Lincoln City.

It may be fifty years old and in need of methodical updating, but what a magnificent facility Gallick has inherited! The tasting room alone is double the size of many complete wineries and offers a dazzling array of wines and wine-related gifts.

One room, given over to the aging tanks, houses twenty giant redwood vats that reach to the ceiling, each tank holding 5,000 to 6,000 gallons of wine. A network of sturdy catwalks connects them.

**HONEYWOOD WINERY**

| | |
|---|---|
| Owners | Paul & Marlene Gallick |
| Winemaker | William Wrey |
| Year bonded | 1934 |
| Year of first crush | 1982 (grape wines) |
| Production capacity | 62,000 gallons fermenting |
| | 150,000 gallons storage |
| Production in 1983 | 31,220 gallons fruit & berry |
| | 6,000 gallons varietal wines |
| Expansion plans | garden court for picnics |
| | satellite tasting room in Salem |
| Awards, 1983 | |
| Blackberry: | Gold, Oregon State Fair |
| Raspberry: | Silver, Oregon State Fair |
| Apricot: | Silver, Oregon State Fair |
| Raspberry: | Silver, Tri-Cities |

Behind a fire wall next door stands the winery's rumbling boiler, used to heat the fruit puilp to 100 degrees to intensify the natural flavors, and used again (after the wines have been aged in those big tanks, just before bottling), to heat the wine briefly to 143 degrees and eliminate the need to add spoilage-retarding sorbates to the bottles.

Honeywood's wines are finished with high levels of sugar and acidity. "What's the point," Gallick asks, "of making raspberry wine that tastes like Chenin Blanc?" At their most successful, they are redolent of the fresh, ripe fruit: Loganberry, Blackberry, even exotic tropical flavors. We think the piquant Red Currant could be tried with poultry dishes, for instance, and anyone with a sweet tooth would relish many of the Honeywood wines as an aperitif or at dessert. Their flavors are so intense that they could also be topped with soda water (Perrier, for princess-and-pea palates) to make a refreshing, low-alcohol, summer cooler.

Honeywood's first varietal wines, a Riesling and a Pinot Noir, will be on the market in 1984. They will be made from purchased grapes ("that way, you only buy the best"), and will be sold under the "Gallico" label.

Gallick is concerned that Oregon's fruit wine industry has fewer and fewer places to show off its products. Three of the major festivals have dropped their fruit wine categories; only the Oregon State Fair remains. Gallick's point: "The public doesn't have a snob attitude about fruit wines."

# *Serendipity Cellars*

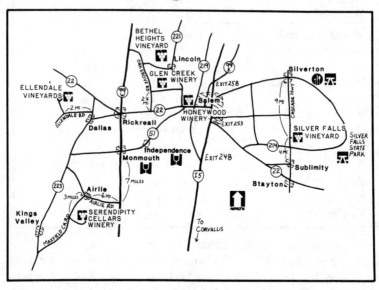

Once you turn off the main road (Highway 99 W) and head west toward Serendipity Cellars Winery, you feel a growing sense of peace and wonder. The soft, overlapping curves of the blue and green hills ripple down from the horizon like falling pillows. Whatever lies ahead, you know you it will be friendly; you don't expect your intellect and senses to be challenged.

The gentle couple who have built their home and Polk County's first winery at the end of the road, overlooking a twenty-acre property of vineyards and forestland, turn out to be far from simple or complacent folk. Glen Longshore holds two master's degrees, and for the past ten years has been a media specialist at Chemeketa Community College in Salem; Cheryl Longshore has earned a master's degree in library science. Indeed, Glen Longshore's winery began with a question. A deep curiosity about the winemaking process prompted him to ask Amity's Myron Redford, one day in early fall, "But where do you learn how to do it?" The next morning, he found himself at Redford's elbow, helping with the crush, listening, learning, doing.

Although three of the Serendipity Cellars wines are made from Pinot Noir grapes, it's a grape called Marechal Foch that makes Glen Longshore's

---

### ☙ SERENDIPITY CELLARS WINERY
15275 Dunn Forest Road
Monmouth, OR 97361
838-4284

| | |
|---|---|
| Open to the public | 12-6 weekends |
| | 12-6 Fridays from May to Dec. |
| | and by appointment |
| Tour groups | yes; call ahead |
| Charge for tour groups | $1 per person for groups of more than 10 people; refundable with purchase |
| Picnic facilities at the winery | 3 tables on the terrace overlooking the Dunn Forest Valley; wine by the bottle or glass for picnics |
| Festivals/special events | Midsummer Eve Festival, Aug. 4-5 |
| | (evening stargazing and wine); Year-end Sale, week after Christmas |
| Wines available (1984) | 1983 Chenin Blanc |
| | 1983 Pinot Noir Blanc de Noir |
| | 1983 Muller Thurgau |
| | 1981 Pinot Noir |
| | 1982 Marechal Foch |
| | 1982 Pinot Noir Fruite |
| | 1982 Chardonnay |
| | 1982 Cabernet Sauvignon |
| | 1982 Muller Thurgau/Riesling |

---

eyes light up with conviction and pleasure. Longshore believes there's a niche in the market awaiting this wine, a niche that Washington's Lemberger grape is also trying to establish: a good red wine at a reasonable price, made with a relatively unfamiliar grape variety that grows well in its region. In California, the Petite Syrah has already done this. In Oregon, the Marechal Foch grape produces a deep red wine with a rich, fruity nose; the 1982 that we tried had a somewhat bitter finish, but time and Glen Longshore's patience may well bring this grape to its potential.

Serendipity uses the "traditional" varieties, too. From the Pinot Noir grape, Longshore uses the free-run juice to produce a Blanc. He also uses

---

**SERENDIPITY CELLARS WINERY**

| | |
|---|---|
| Owners | Glen & Cheryl Longshore |
| Winemaker | Glen A. Longshore |
| Year bonded | 1981 |
| Year first planted | 1980 |
| Vineyard acreage | 3 |
| Principal varieties, acres | Pinot Noir, 2 |
| | Chardonnay, 1 |
| Year of first crush | 1981 |
| Production in 1983 | 2,500 gallons |
| Expansion plans | to 10,000-gallon capacity |
| | eventually |
| Awards, 1983 | |
| Marechal Foch: | Bronze, Oregon State Fair |
| Chenin Blanc: | Bronze, Oregon State Fair |
| Pinot Noir Rose: | Bronze, Oregon State Fair |

---

Pinot Noir to make a very light red table wine (which he has also called Fruite), where the grapes are given three days of skin contact, then put into American oak for six months; the resulting wine has a fresh, appealing aroma. And there's a third wine: the classic form of Pinot Noir as it is treated in Burgundy. In 1981, his Pinot Noir produced a pleasant, varietal aroma and a lemony acidity in the mouth.

Longshore feels he has a responsibility to experiment with wine styles during these early years of grape growing and winemaking. Just as his curiosity prompted him to ask Myron Redford that fateful question a decade ago, his ardent curiosity (rebelliousness, even) has prompted him to go beyond what everyone else is doing. "Very few winemakers are trying anything new," he told us. So he's going beyond the "Burgundy" and "Chardonnay" stage, trying different styles, trying different grapes. He's fiercely loyal to Oregon and doesn't buy any of his grapes from out-of-state.

Because Serendipity is such a small winery, the Longshores promise to explain their philosophy and production methods to visitors and answer individual questions fully. And from the balcony of their home, with nothing in view except the deep green trees of the Coast Range, pastureland, and vineyards of Pinot Noir and Chardonnay, they will take the time to direct their fortunate visitors along scenic side roads past the region's country stores, county parks, and covered bridges.

# Silver Falls Vineyard

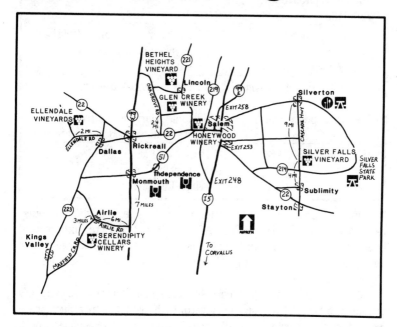

"We're mavericks here on the east side," says Jim Palmquist, owner with his wife, Joyce, of Silver Falls Winery, which stands on a 100-acre parcel planted with grapes, wheat, oats, and grass seed. Though Silver Falls is the only winery to locate on the east side so far, quite a few growers are nearby, and Palmquist contends that the east side is more productive than the west. Palmquist speaks with the pride of a native; he was born and raised in the area around Silverton and once worked on the property where he now farms and grows grapes. From his hilltop, he surveys the vineyards and points to the fields where he will plant four more acres of Pinot Noir and another four of Pinot Gris, a grape he believes has a great future.

Most of the farmers in the central Willamette Valley, however, produce nothing but grass seed; it's big business in these parts, with enormous farms that produce the seed for lawns around the country. After harvest, the farmers burn the stubble, partly because it's easier to burn it than to rake it up, partly because the heat makes the grass germinate better in the following season. The disadvantage is the columns of dark smoke that the

---

**■ SILVER FALLS WINERY**
4972 Cascade Highway S.E.
Sublimity, OR 97305
769-9463

| | |
|---|---|
| Open to the public | 10-6 weekends (summer, 1984) |
| Tour groups | yes; appointment preferred |
| Charge for tour groups | none |
| Picnic facilities at the winery | 2 tables under oak trees near the winery |
| Festivals/special events | Sublimity Harvest Festival and Tractor Pull, second week of Sept. |
| Wines available (1984) | Pinot Noir Blanc<br>Red Table Wine<br>White Table Wine |

---

burning causes. "Oregon takes its grass seed seriously," Palmquist reminds us. There's only one Wine Advisory Board, and a recently created board at that, but there are at least two important state commissions to deal with grass seed issues: a Red Fescue Commission and a Bent Fescue Commission.

Palmquist's neighbors can't conceive of the kind of intense farming he's putting into his relatively small vineyard. It almost takes that much space just to turn their tractors around! Ironically, the zoning in Palmquist's neck of the woods makes it difficult to cultivate grapes. The minimum size for a parcel is 400 to 600 acres; established farmers aren't interested in grapes, and newcomers can't afford to plant a 400-acre vineyard.

Jim Palmquist left the land for a time, getting a degree in food technology from Oregon State University. One of his professors was enologist Hoya Yang, and that contact sparked a life-long interest in wine. But professional responsibilities came first, with positions as a research chemist for Carnation and a quality control technologist for Diamond Fruit. He currently sells food processing equipment for Beatrice Foods and travels throughout the Northwest; fortunately, his family shares his enthusiasm for grapes and winemaking.

Joyce Palmquist, a neurological nurse at Salem Memorial Hospital, chairs the Oregon State Fair's winejudging committee, and is responsible for the winery's public relations and tasting room. Young Mike Palmquist, a student in agri-business and nursery management at Chemeketa Junior College, is co-winemaker with his father, and will have full responsibility for the

**SILVER FALLS WINERY**

| | |
|---|---|
| Owners | Jim & Joyce Palmquist |
| Winemaker | Jim Palmquist, Mike Palmquist |
| Year bonded | 1983 |
| Year first planted | 1974 |
| Vineyard acreage | 17 |
| Principal varieties, acres | Pinot Noir, 9 |
| | Chardonnay, 7 |
| | White Riesling, 1 |
| | Muscat Ottonel, 1 |
| Year of first crush | 1983 |
| Production capacity | 10,000 gallons |
| Production in 1983 | 5,000 gallons |
| Expansion plans | more plantings |

vineyard.

Silver Falls crushed about 40 tons of grapes in 1983 and fermented the wine at Honeywood Winery in Salem. The Palmquists intend to bottle some of the Chardonnay as White Table Wine, and the Pinot Noir (which hasn't seen oak) as Red Table Wine, in order to have a product available to tourists. Their intention is to emphasize the red wines, and to explore the possibility of sparkling wines. Most wines will be dry, but the Riesling, when it's made, will be a bit sweeter. The winery itself will be built at the foot of the Pinot Noir vineyard, where a large metal building, once used for farm animals and tractors, is already in place. By the time 1984's harvest rolls around, you can be sure that fermenting tanks will have replaced the tractors.

# *Lodging*

## *Salem*

### *Murlin's Bed & Breakfast*
2491 Gray Oak Lane S., Salem 97302
585-1476

Five miles from town, surrounded by fields of horses and grazing cattle, stands a farmhouse styled like a Swiss chalet. In its annex is a self-contained guest room with a double bed and a hide-a-bed, yours (with three days' notice) for under $30 a night, continental breakfast included. A full breakfast, including eggs and homemade muffins, costs $1 per person extra. Your alarm clock will be the farm's crowing rooster.

### *City Center Motel*
510 Liberty Street S.E.
364-0121

A family-run, thirty-unit motel, small and inexpensive, with a nice personal touch: free coffee and rolls in the morning. There's a coin-operated laundry on the premises, and color TV with Showtime. Pets are welcome. Easy walking distance to Pringle Creek and to Bush's Pasture, two of Salem's nicest parks.

## *Corvallis*

### *Madison Inn*
660 Madison Avenue, Corvallis 97330
757-1274

Kathryn Brandis has firmly established her bed-and-breakfast inn here, the first in Corvallis. It's on a quiet street only two blocks from the Oregon State University campus in a big house overlooking the rose gardens of Corvallis's Central Park. The Madison was built in 1903 as a private home, and eventually passed into the hands of Brandis and her family, who decided to convert it into a "lodging alternative" for overnight guests. There are five bedrooms, furnished with Queen Anne reproductions and handmade quilts; guests share bathroom facilities and are welcome to use the library and living rooms downstairs. Rates are $35 to $40 per couple, including a lavish continental breakfast (home-baked bread, homemade jams, fresh fruit, "Dutch babies" with real maple syrup).

Not surprisingly, O.S.U. sends a lot of visiting professors to stay at the Madison Inn, and the after-dinner conversation in the drawing room, beneath the carved Victorian staircase, can be quite stimulating. "It's better than sitting in bars," Kathryn Brandis thinks. You said it!

### Corvallis Hotel
205 S.W. Second Street
753-7349

Fifty low-priced rooms available here, without any frills.

### Benton Plaza
408 S.W. Monroe
753-4411

The TV is black-and-white, and there's no pool or air conditioning, but this is what "downtown" hotels were like before chain motels started siphoning away the business. Rooms start at $13!

# Restaurants

## Salem

### The Terrarium
156 Church Street
363-1611

Jeff Isaacson has created in this simple space a restaurant where you can find the fresh, the exotic, the unexpected. Isaacson trained in Hawaii, so his dishes have intriguing names as well as exotic ingredients: Mahoganny Chicken (an appetizer of chicken wings marinated in hoisin and plum sauce), a Kahala Burger based on a burger created at the Kahala Hilton, omelets with water chestnuts, scrupulously fresh fish.

His wine list, carefully thought out, offers many of the very best Northwest wines and is updated every three or four months. Isaacson's understanding of the restaurant business is both broad and refreshing. Footnotes: the tropical sauces are also sold for take out, banquet rooms are available upstairs, and Barbara Isaacson does catering, too.

### Old Europe Inn
2460 Commercial Street S.E.
371-1850

Walter Hausermann was trained in the finest culinary tradition of his native Switzerland: to do it absolutely right, every time. From stockpot to garnish, he lavishes full attention on his dishes. Some are well-worn favorites (veal schnitzels, steak Diane), some are specials (osso buco), but it is as if you were eating them for the very first time. One recent meal included a cream of sauerkraut soup; it boasted a complexity of flavors that would make a fine wine blush. Most of the dinners cost less than $10—an Old World bargain.

### D'Alessio's
1128 Edgewater N.W.
378-1780

Colleague and countryman of Walter Hausermann, Hans D'Alessio prepares his classical menu with professional care. Leave time for a more leisurely and formal service, and try one of the specialties, like abalone with shrimp and scallops. By 1985, D'Alessio hopes to move to a house further up West Salem's hill.

### Boon's Treasury
888 Liberty Street N.E.
399-9062

This is a casual "read the paper on Sunday, check out who's there" kind of place that's evolved from an ordinary tavern to a more important place for the regulars; they call themselves "Boonies." It's a little like a village pub, but with good, lighter foods, darker beers, and Northwest wines. Open every day, frequently with easygoing live music.

### Off-Center Cafe
1742 Center N.E.
363-9245

It's at the back of a commercial building off Center Street, and it's really just a cafe: a counter up front, a few tables, and a kitchen pass-through at the back. But you might hear Mozart's Prague Symphony playing on the stereo, find a baby napping in the crib in one corner, and watch a college professor in a three-piece suit correcting papers. The coffee beans are kept frozen until they're needed to make a fresh pot, and the walls are covered with vaguely anti-establishment sentiments ("Jane Wyman Was Right").

Breakfasts, served from 7 to 11, are wonderful: toasted orange date bread; an omelet of green chiles, onions, and sour cream; a grilled rainbow trout. All very inexpensive.

## Via Florencia Pasta Factory
3838-C River Road N. (Keizer)
390-6673

It's in a shopping center north of Salem, and shares an entrance with a well-regarded deli called Chicken John's. The Via Florencia makes a lot of pasta for takeout, but the real treat is in the back of the shop, where Pilar Thompson has set up a cafe and serves the freshest of pasta dishes on heirloom china. A remarkable woman (born in Spain, she fled from Franco to Argentina, where she earned a doctorate in music at the age of 18, then pursued a second career as a successful jewelry designer in Southern California and Seattle before moving to Salem early in 1984), Pilar Thompson cooks with a zeal that borders on religious devotion. She comes up with tastes that are inspired: a split-pea soup as smooth as cream; raviolis that melt in your mouth, covered with a tomato sauce that's been sweetened with carrots; linguine with pesto, fresh walnuts, and garlic. And prices that are almost embarrassingly low.

## Old Town Pizza
180 S.E. High Street
588-8822

Funky antique decor and good value make this a favorite spot for inexpensive lunches. The espresso drinks, produced at the bar, are terrific, but the wine list is limited to Paul Masson. For shame!

## Ram Pub
1170 Bellevue S.E.
363-1904

A pleasant place on the fringes of Willamette University's campus, with pool tables and a blazing fireplace. Monday is fish and chips night, Tuesday offers delicious two-for-one burgers. The house wine is Sebastiani, and the list includes Ellendale and Hillcrest bottlings. Kids are welcome here until 9 p.m.

## Dallas

### Ponderosa Joe's

880 Church Street
623-2249

The Ponderosa is a down-home honky-tonk, but the dining room in back, operated by Paula Leifritz, aspires to better things. Six-course Italian dinners (antipasto, soup, salad, pasta, choice of entrees—steak, calzoni, scallops—dessert, coffee) cost less than $10. The room is dimly lit, the tables are brightly napped, and the concept of a big Italian meal, pioneered in the wine country by Nick's Italian Restaurant in McMinnville, is certainly valid.

## Silverton

### Town House Cafe

203 Main Street
873-9971

The biggest cinnamon roll you ever saw (outside of Rose's in Portland, perhaps) costs eighty-five cents here, and the prime rib dinner on Sunday night (with a baked potato, soup, and salad) is $6.95. This unassuming place, next to the hardware store, serves as Silverton's village square and back fence, where everybody meets everybody.

## Albany

### De Naro Noodle Company

619 S.E. Ninth
926-0343

They make their own pasta here, as you'd expect, and serve Oregon wine by the glass besides. What more could one want?

## *Corvallis*

### Class Reunion
777 N.W. Ninth
757-1700

Upstairs in a modern shopping complex, this place achieves instant campus nostalgia with photos of campus life and prime rib choices called Bachelor Cut, Master's Cut, and The Ph.D. There's fresh seafood, too. Ownership is the same as the Oregon Electric Station in Eugene, and the commitment to Oregon wines is, if anything, even stronger. Three-quarters of the wine list is Oregon bottlings, ten of which are available by the glass at all times.

### Gables
1121 N.W. Ninth
752-3364

A roadside cottage, looking somewhat out of place on this busy street, but comfortable inside, with plush carpets and flocked wallpaper. Prime rib and steaks are the favorites.

# *Wine Shops &*
# *Delicatessens*

## *Salem*

### Reed Wine & Cheese Co.
189 Liberty Street N.E.
585-9463

A fine wine shop (as well as restaurant) inside the restored Reed Opera House. Rob Boaz has commissioned a new work of art for each of the nine years he's been in business here, a nice touch. Soups and sandwiches are served at lunch, with a dozen wines available by the glass. Monthly specials give good value on the bottled wines.

---

### La Tricia's Deli
4908 River Road N. (Keizer)
393-1138

A deli-restaurant in the Keizer Plaza, specializing in German-style smoked meats and sausages, along with other top quality deli items.

### Sally's Market Basket
110 Hansen Street
399-1657

There's a wide array of deli items in this grocery-deli setting, with wine and beer to take out or enjoy on the premises.

### Roth's Vista IGA
3045 Commercial S.E.
364-8449

A Los Angeles-style grocery, with an uncommonly good selection of cheeses, sausages, wine, beer, and a very good in-house bakery.

### The Wine Rack
2671 Commercial Street S.E.
370-9663

Nathan Allen, proprietor of this distinguished wine shop in the Candelaria Plaza shopping complex, is a home winemaker and friend of most of the winemakers in the vicinity. He's also superintendent of the wine judging at the State Fair for 1984. A reliable guide to Northwest wines.

---

## Independence

---

### Wine Peddler
329 S. Main Street
838-5577

A small wine shop in a very pretty town, which sells the better varietal wines and ordinary jugs, too, no doubt because of the town's proximity to Monmouth, one of Oregon's few remaining "dry" communities. Coffee, too.

## Monmouth

### The Brown Bagger
113 E. Main
838-5405

Get your picnic lunch here, then drive out to Serendipity Cellars Winery or over to Independence for your bottle of wine; the sandwiches are very good.

## Corvallis

### Rube's Deli
777 N.W. Ninth Street
754-0100

This attractive deli in the Cannery Mall carries a full line of local wines along with delicatessen staples. Two more Corvallis delis are The Wine Man, and International Foods, with an emphasis on beers.

# Picnic Spots

### Salem

### Bush's Pasture Park
600 Mission Street S.E.

An eighty-nine acre park behind a restored Victorian mansion with gardens, hiking paths, and picnic spots.

### Pringle Creek
This little body of water runs just south of Salem's Willamette University, and makes a cool spot for a picnic in summer. Walking distance from downtown.

### Wallace Marine Park
Musgrave Lane

Facilities for boating, swimming, and picnicking in the most popular of Salem's parks.

---

## Cascade Gateway Park

Turner Road, southeast of Salem

Family-oriented recreation, including picnics, on a hundred acres.

## Silver Falls State Park

On Highway 214, twenty-six miles east of Salem

Don't let the distance from Salem put you off; this is one of the most beautiful parks in the state, and the drive is well worth it.

Whispering waterfalls (nine of them accessible to the public) and wooded canyons are the park's attractions. There's a well-maintained trail connecting all of the falls, and parking areas along the way for those who'd rather drive. Several attractive day lodges provide shelter and cooking facilities in case the weather gets drizzly. Oregon grape and ferns cover the ground except for the clearings and trails. Dozens of picnic tables, a bike path, nature trails, swimming, extensive group facilities, and parking for 3,000 cars. Even so, the park fills up on summer weekends. Stop at the new Silver Falls winery along the way to pick up a bottle of wine for your picnic.

---

## Silverton

---

## Coolidge-McClaine Municipal Park

Silverton is a tiny town settled by Scandinavians 100 years ago. Many of the homes have been restored, and the town is full of churches. The pleasant park adjoins Silver Creek, where there's good fishing; picnic tables stand in a grove of trees.

---

## Polk County, near Monmouth

---

## Sarah Helmich Wayside

Off Hwy, 99, six miles south of Monmouth

Picnic tables and fishing in the quiet countryside southwest of Salem. The Buena Vista ferry is nearby, and there's a park at the ferry landing, too.

## Ritner Creek

Highway 223, south of Pedee

A small picnic area sits beside the creek, which is spanned by a landmark covered bridge.

# *Eugene Area*

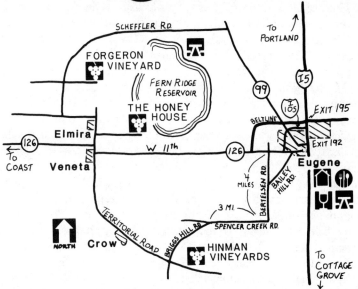

Oregon's agricultural heartland is in the Willamette Valley. Now several modern vineyards and wineries are adding viticulture (and even apiculture) to this countryside of historic covered bridges, old timber, traditional row crops, orchards, grass seed, and pastureland.

Although wine touring in the Eugene area offers fewer wineries than the Yamhill or Tualatin valleys, visitors will find this part of the state no less rewarding: the pleasures of bosky byways along the Willamette, the cultural life of Eugene, the pioneer festivals.

Eugene, Oregon's second-largest city, lies in the heart of this region, known as the Emerald Empire. The Lane County "Empire" stretches from the ocean to the Cascades, whose forested hillsides provide the timber on which much of the region's economy is based. The Willamette Valley is covered with orchards and grassland, with stands of lichen-draped alder; fields are dotted with Christmas tree farms, acres of row crops and a sprinkling of fundamentalist churches.

Eugene itself is prosperous and well educated. The University of Oregon brings some 17,000 students to the city; their influence no doubt helps the city's two public markets thrive. The Fifth Street Market (at High St.) attracts shopper interested in local crafts and produce; it's a place to stock up on picnic supplies, too. And the Saturday Market, open from April until Christmas, is an informal bazaar held on Saturdays atop a parking lot at Eighth and Oak. (If you find yourself in a long line at the Saturday Market, chances are that it's leading to Ritta's, a much-admired burrito stand; Ritta will be back again this year.) Eugene is also a city enamored of bicycles, and has provided 150 miles of bike trails in an excellent system of public parks to accommodate this passion.

Most of the people who visit wineries do so by car, not bicycle, however. And for these visitors, one of the chief attractions, apart from the pure joy of driving along the country roads, is to discover the dozens of covered bridges that still span the streams and tributaries of the Willamette. The bridges (well over two dozen in the Linn-Benton-Lane-Lincoln county area) are reminders that automobiles did not always carry travelers at high speeds along well-paved roads. There were times, not all that long ago, that these "quaint" roads were used by wagons to transport hay, produce, and logs to market. Bridges played stragetic roles in the rural economy; many were built with roofs, to protect the timbers below from Oregon's moist weather. Some of the bridges are still in use today, although most have fallen under the watchful protection of local historical societies.

Also of interest to automobile travelers in the valley are the three remaining ferry rides across the Willamette River. (They used to be free; now they cost less than a dollar.) There's a handy crossing at Buena Vista (pronounced "Byoo-na Vista" by the locals) midway between Salem and Albany, near the Willamette's confluence with the Santiam; two other ferries cross the Willamette further north, at Wheatland and at Canby. The century-old Buena Vista ferry fits only six cars; it's a modest barge, really, guided across the river by cables. But once the vessel starts to move, it creates the same magic, restful effect you experience in boats of all sizes.

For the more adventurous, over a dozen outfitters offer trips down rivers such as the Rogue, the McKenzie, the Umpqua, the Owyhee, the Klamath, and the Deschutes. River runs vary from placid day trips to three-day, white-water adventures; there's a trip for almost any level of personal participation and excitement (from suntan-lazy to paddle-for-your-life) and every price range ($25 for a day trip and up). Many outfitters are headquartered in the Eugene-Springfield area, so it's possible to make contact with a company here, and join a Rogue River trip later on in Grants Pass or Roseburg.

Finally, if the water's too cold or you're just plain wined-out, consider the possibility of a nice soak in a hot tub. You can do just that at Onsen's Hot Tubs, 1883 Garden Street; phone 349-9048 to reserve yourselves a spot.

# *Alpine Vineyards*

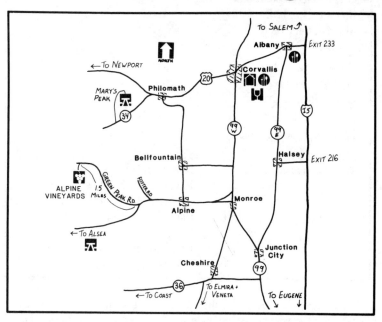

Dan and Christine Jepsen have built a success story here, on their green, sixty-acre hillside planted with White Riesling, Gewurztraminer, Chardonnay, Cabernet Sauvignon, and Pinot Noir. The very first wine they made commercially, a 1980 White Riesling, won a silver medal at the Enological Society festival in Seattle in 1981; they were unable to enter the rest of their first year's production, a blended white and a Gewurztraminer, because they had already sold out.

Their prize-winning Riesling was hardly the first wine the Jepsens had ever made; they were enthusiastic home winemakers before taking the big step and bonding their own 5,000-gallon commercial winery. But since their first crush, they have gone on to even greater successes, among them the Best of Show designation at the 1983 Tri-Cities wine festival for their estate-bottled 1982 White Riesling.

Dan Jepsen prepared for this particular career by studying chemistry at Carleton College and traveling extensively in the wine regions of Europe. He also earned an M.D. at the University of California, San Francisco, and continues to work part-time as a physician at the University of Oregon.

131

---

### 🍇 ALPINE VINEYARDS

Green Peak Road, Alpine
Route 2, Box 173D
Monroe, OR 97456
424-5851

| | |
|---|---|
| Open to the public | 12-5 Sun. |
| Tour groups | by appointment |
| Charge for tour groups | $1 |
| Picnic facilities at the winery | tables overlooking vineyard |
| Festivals/special events | release of new wines, March and Sept. |
| Wines available (1984) | 1980 & 1981 Pinot Noir |
| | 1982 Pinot Noir (late summer) |
| | 1980 & 1981 Cabernet Sauvignon |
| | 1982 Blanc de Blanc |
| | 1982 Chardonnay |
| | 1983 Riesling |
| | 1983 Gewurztraminer |

---

The vineyard is beautifully situated on the eastern slope of the Coast Range, with the winery tucked underneath the Jepsens' multi-level brick home. On a recent sunny morning we sat down to talk to Dan and Christine Jepsen about wine, but our first discussion centered around music. Dan—a competent cellist—related his difficult early decision to choose between music and medicine as a career. His choice of medicine reflected the calm and thorough thinking that distinguishes the Jepsens' lifestyle today and has led to honors in the modern winemaking arena. After four years of service in the Peace Corps, the Jepsens returned to the United States and Dan Jepsen decided to locate his medical practice in an area where vineyard acreage was available.

The acreage he found couldn't be better. We sat indoors beneath the heat-trapping solar panels, observing the sun-drenched vineyards which abut the driveway.

Jepsen feels strongly about the importance of retaining control over the grapes that go into his wines. "Eighty percent of wine quality is established in the vineyard," he maintains, explaining why the wines of Alpine Vineyards will remain estate-bottled. He also believes in a long and cool fermentation process to keep prevent oxygen from spoiling his Rieslings.

**ALPINE VINEYARDS**

| | |
|---|---|
| Owners | Dan & Christine Jepsen |
| Winemaker | Dan Jepsen |
| Year bonded | 1980 |
| Year first planted | 1976 |
| Vineyard acreage | 20 |
| Principal varieties | Riesling, 6 |
| | Cabernet Sauvignon, 4.5 |
| | Pinot Noir, 4.5 |
| | Chardonnay, 1.5 |
| | Gewurztraminer, .5 |
| Year of first crush | 1980 |
| Production capacity | 14,000 gallons |
| Production in 1983 | 7,857 gallons |
| Awards, 1983 | |
| 1982 White Riesling | Gold & Best of Show, Tri-Cities |
| | Gold, Seattle |
| | Silver, Oregon State Fair |

Among the wines being released in the coming months are a 1981 Blanc de Blanc, whose high proportion of Chardonnay gives it a wonderful, apple-like aroma. It has a clean and satisfying finish. There's also a 1982 Chardonnay, a very pleasing, medium-bodied wine with good fruit flavors and a silkiness in the mouth. Its acid backbone should render this a complex and interesting wine in a year or two.

The 1982 Pinot Noir will be a very fine wine, with that elusive, warm, varietal nose that one looks for in a memorable Pinot. Alpine will release this wine in the summer of 1984. The 1980 Pinot was judged sixth best in the country in the first American Wine Championship sponsored by *Wine & Spirits Guide*.

And the 1982 Cabernet Sauvignon, which Dan Jepsen offered to us from the tank with a proud twinkle in his eye: rounded, fruity, fresh, a superb accompaniment to smoked salmon (yes!). This splendid wine won't be ready for a couple of years, but it's one to look for.

There is no full-time staff, however, so tours are limited to Sunday afternoons and appointments. A visit to Alpine Vineyards represents the best elements of wine touring: a lovely drive, dedicated owners, superb wines, and a sense of discovery and exploration.

# *Forgeron Vineyard*

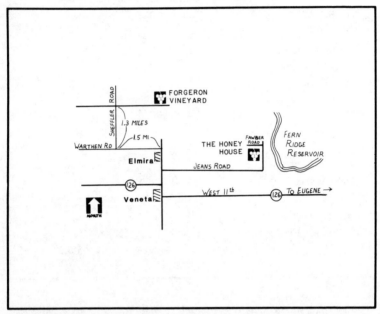

The French word for Smith (as in blacksmith) is "forgeron." Hence the name Forgeron Vineyard for the twenty-six-acre vineyard owned by Lee and Linda Smith near Elmira. Lee's fascination with wine began while he was studying in Europe, and stayed with him while he worked as a driver/salesman for Royal Crown Cola. He always felt he wanted to be part of Oregon's wine industry and, as he describes it, "to produce and manufacture the complete product from start to finish." Now he's able to do that.

The site is the southernmost in the Willamette Valley to be used for growing vinifera grapes, and is unusually warm for the area. Lee Smith has recorded over 2,300 heat units a year at the vineyard; summer days get quite warm, with fifty days more sunshine a year than nearby Eugene. Yet the nights stay cool, which keeps the acid levels in the grapes high. The peculiarities of site and climate allow him to ripen his Cabernet Sauvignon regularly; he planted Cabernet here as early as 1970, and feels he was an influence in Dan Jepsen's decision to plant Cabernet grapes at Alpine, some fifteen miles further north.

We tasted some of Forgeron's 1979 Cabernet when we visited the winery recently. Still darkly youthful, it showed off a rich coffee nose at first, and

## 💐 FORGERON VINEYARD
89697 Sheffler Road
Elmira, OR 97437
935-1117 or 935-3520

| | |
|---|---|
| Open to the public | 12-5 daily, May-Sept. |
| | 12-5 weekends, Oct.-April |
| | closed Jan. |
| Tour groups | yes, with notice |
| Charge for tour groups | $1 per person (groups over 10) |
| Picnic facilities at the winery | wine garden with tables and |
| | fountain; additional picnic area |
| Festivals/special events | Bluegrass Festival, third week |
| | in July; Spring Releases, May |
| | (mailing list customers) |
| Wines available (1984) | 1982 & 1983 White Riesling |
| | 1980 Pinot Noir |
| | 1982 Blanc de Pinot Noir |
| | 1982 Rose |
| | 1983 Chenin Blanc |
| | 1980 Cabernet Sauvignon |

gradually, as it aired in the glass, it revealed itself as a complex and interesting wine showing the promise of a very fine maturity.

Smith has also had a good deal of success with his Pinot Noir. The 1979 Pinot, no longer available, is Smith's personal favorite, although the 1980 Pinot won a bronze medal at the International Wine Competition in Ithaca, New York. We appreciated its full varietal nose, clear toffee-apple color, and pleasant underlying tannin. With the free run juice of Pinot Noir grapes he makes a Blanc de Pinot Noir; the remaining grapes are further pressed to produce an off-dry Rose of Pinot Noir, a wine with a candy-apple aroma that's very popular in restaurants.

On the viticultural front, Forgeron Vineyard is actively involved in a series of experiments with Oregon State University to measure vineyard climate. Every fifteen minutes, remote sensors record temperature, moisture, and radiation (sunshine) conditions. Later, chemical analysis and sensory evaluation of the wine will be added to the computerized data. Five years from now, Smith says, scientists will have enough data to project crop and market value while the grapes are still in the field. "This will allow everyone to understand that this is going to be one of the premier wine

**FORGERON VINEYARDS**

| | |
|---|---|
| Owners | Lee & Linda Smith |
| Winemaker | Lee Smith |
| Consulting enologist | Bill Nelson |
| Year bonded | 1977 |
| Year first planted | 1971 |
| Vineyard acreage | 20 |
| Principal varieties | White Riesling, 9 |
| | Pinot Noir, 8 |
| | Cabernet Sauvignon, 2 |
| | Chenin Blanc, 1 |
| Year of first crush | 1978 |
| Production capacity | 13,425 gallons |
| Production in 1983 | 9,382 gallons |
| Expansion plans | 2 acres Chardonnay; |
| | total 25,000 gallons by 1990 |
| Awards, 1983 | |
| 1982 Oregon White Riesling: | Gold, Lane County Fair |
| 1982 Willamette White | |
| Riesling: | Silver, Oregon State Fair |
| 1980 Pinot Noir: | Gold, Lane County Fair |
| | Bronze, New York |
| 1982 Rose: | Silver, Lane County Fair |

growing areas of the world," Smith believes.

The Forgeron winery was moved from the basement of the Smith home to a spacious new building in time for the 1981 crush. The new winery, with a large tasting room out front, was built to handle current production levels as well as the grapes from an eventual twenty-five-acre expansion of the vineyards. The Smiths host a Bluegrass Festival in July that draws vast crowds, but picnic facilities are available for visitors any time except January. Linda Smith plants thousands of flowers around the property every spring to produce an enchanting setting for the winery; the tasting room itself is spacious, orderly, and welcoming. Upstairs, a cozy gallery features works by local artists. Altogether, there is a loving attention to detail.

Smith's philosophy is to make wines for the table, wines that are, as he puts it, "a reflection of the customers' good taste." In other words, he's making wines not for judgings but for people. That's the spirit.

# *Hinman Vineyards*

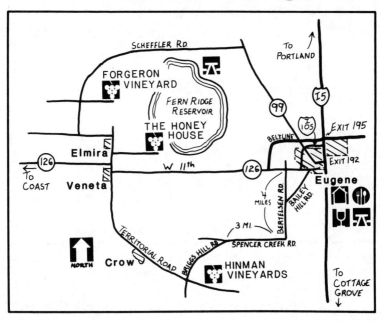

Doyle Hinman and David Smith, the partners who own Hinman Vine-yards, have taken advantage of the vineyard's splendid setting along Briggs Hill Road outside of Eugene: visitors arrive along a road that meanders through the thirty-acre property, past rows of Gewurztraminer and Ries-ling, and across a little bridge to the base of a wooded hill. The winery, sheltered by a stand of evergreens, is built of brick in order to keep the inside temperature uniformly cool; its architectural style is European, with great wooden gates at one side that open to a receiving area for the grapes, and a squared-off tower at the other side for the tasting room.

Doyle Hinmman, a high school teacher and former television producer, lives in a snappy A-frame tucked into the trees a few yards from the winery. His interest in wine was triggered by "curiosity," which he followed up with winemaking studies at Geisenheim in Germany and the University of California, Davis.

Partner David Smith, who shares winemaking duties and is responsible for much of the cellar work, is a soft-spoken, tactful man. Formerly a pur-chasing agent, Smith genuinely enjoys the country life made possible by his

---

### ♉ HINMAN VINEYARDS
27012 Briggs Hill Road
Eugene, OR 97405
345-1945

| | |
|---|---|
| Open to the public | 12-5 weekends & by appointment |
| Tour groups | yes |
| Charge for tour groups | $1 per person (groups over 30) |
| Picnic facilities at the winery | grassy amphitheater with stage; pond |
| Festivals/special events | Summer Jazz Festival, July |
| Wines available (1984) | White Pinot Noir |
| | Riesling |
| | Gewurztraminer |
| | Vintner's Special White Table |
| | Pinot Noir |
| | Cabernet Sauvignon |

---

new career. His calm speech quickens as he speaks of the new plantings going on his vineyard across Briggs Hill Road (eleven acres of Cabernet Sauvignon, Pinot Noir, and Gewurztraminer), and of his long-range plans to convert the old farmhouse at the top of the drive into a bed & breakfast hotel.

Hinman Vineyards was bonded in 1979 and reaped almost immediate success: the Consumer's Choice award for its 1980 Gewurztraminer at the 1981 Tri-Cities festival, and a silver medal at the Oregon State Fair for the same wine. The 1980 White Riesling won a silver at both the Lane County and Oregon State fairs.

Hinman wines are made in a German style, fermented to dryness, then brought to the desired sweetness by adding *Sussreserve* (a reserved quantity of unfermented grape juice at its original 20-percent sweetness). This results in a lower-alcohol wine, in which the fresh fruit flavors add complexity to the taste of the fermented juice.

Most of Hinman Vineyards' wines are sold through retail and wholesale distributors, but Hinman will again sell his highly regarded White Pinot Noir, Riesling, Gewurztraminer, Chardonnay, and Oregon White Table Wine to visitors at the tasting room. There are also plans to release two red wines this year. We particularly enjoyed the 1982 Oregon White Riesling, with its low alcohol, sweet-tart contrasts, and delicate aroma. The 1982 Oregon White Pinot Noir, made from free-run juice, has a fresh, plummy

**HINMAN VINEYARDS**

| | |
|---|---|
| Owners & Winemakers: | Doyle Hinman & David Smith |
| Year bonded | 1979 |
| Year first planted | 1972 |
| Vineyard acreage | 30 |
| Principal varieties | Riesling, 4 |
| | Gewurztraminer, 2 |
| | Pinot Noir, 2 |
| | Lemberger, 1 |
| Year of first crush | 1979 |
| Production in 1983 | 15,000 gallons |
| Expansion plans | additional 35,000 gallons; |
| | additional plantings of Cabernet |
| | and Pinot Noir on Smith's property |
| | across Briggs Hill Road |
| Recent awards | |
| 1982 White Riesling: | Bronze, Seattle |
| 1981 Gewurztraminer: | Silver, Seattle |

aroma, and leaves the mouth clean and fresh; the fine balance of sweetness and acidity will make this a very popular wine in restaurants.

The winery, which began with the capacity to produce 15,000 gallons, crushed enough grapes in 1983 for over 30,000 gallons. That sort of increase indicates a true commitment to the future of Oregon wine. The wines are delicious, but there's an additional reason to tour the winery: Hinman Vineyards provides a particularly lovely spot for a picnic, whether on a day trip from Eugene or for tourists passing through the Willamette Valley. The amphitheater on the grass below the winery tower is an ideal setting for weddings, small jazz groups, or romantic picnics.

# The Honey House

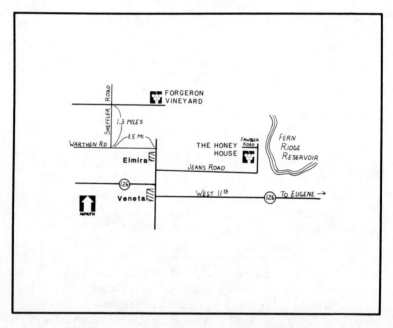

Mead is often described as the oldest fermented beverage known to man. According to Greek legend, it's said to have great curative and aphrodisiac powers; Bacchus was the god of mead long before he became god of wine.

Variations of mead are made with fruit juices, herbs, and grains, but the basic ingredient in all mead is freshly gathered honey. The key to good mead is thus the quality of the honey. You can buy commercial honey from various domestic and imported sources to put on your morning toast, but that's really no guarantee of quality. The only way to be sure, says Robert Saxton, is to produce your own, and that means keeping your own bees.

And so he does. His bees buzz around a patch of Marion blackberry bushes adjacent to The Honey House winery at blossom time, tens of thousands of them, and return by instinct to the hives in a grove of trees behind the Saxton home to deposit their honey. A well-managed colony is home to some 70,000 honeybees, and Robert Saxton has had as many as twenty-five colonies in that grove behind his house.

---

### 🐝 THE HONEY HOUSE WINERY
(Willamette Valley Homestead)
26202 Fawber Road
Veneta, OR 97487
935-2008

| | |
|---|---|
| Open to the public | by appointment |
| Wines available (1984) | Mead, dry |
| | Blackberry, dry |
| | Cherry |
| | Rhubarb |
| | Blueberry |
| | Plum |
| Owner & winemaker | Robert H. Saxton |
| Year bonded | 1976 |

---

Saxton is a quiet-spoken, silver-haired man in the Jimmy Stewart mold. He is just winding up a thirty-three-year career as a biology and chemistry teacher at Churchill High School in Eugene. He learned about beekeeping while studying entymology at Oregon State University thirty years ago, and has been making mead ever since. His approach to winemaking is rather professorial, intense, putting great value on the meticulous documentation of his technical information. He is also endlessly and fearlessly experimenting; most recently he produced tomato wine! He also makes several other fruit wines as they come in season (Blackberry, Plum, Sour Cherry, Rhubarb, Pear) and markets them under the Willamette Valley Homestead label.

It is as a producer of mead that Saxton has established his reputation. Mead is usually made to taste rather sweet, but Saxton's mead is quite dry, with a "honey" nose, as you'd expect, and with an unexpectedly good balance of its components. The quality is due in part to Saxton's care and skill, and in part to his raw materials: those thousands and thousands of bees, out there in the hives behind his house. No other mead-maker in Oregon (and there are several other commercial meads) has taken the extra step of "growing his own."

There's more to mead-making than the good honey, to be sure, but Saxton is reluctant to discuss the subtleties of his winemaking. He says it involves certain yeasts, certain fermentation temperatures, and the addition of certain acids. What we know is that he does it very well.

# Lodging

## Eugene

### Central Bed, Breakfast & Dessert
1327 Lawrence Street, Eugene 97401
343-9510, 484-5098

In the spring of 1984, this "inn" consisted of one comfortable room (with adjoining bath) in the home of Don Marsh, a fair-haired young man of apparently insatiable curiosity about everything from art to geology to mechanics. Marsh is an excellent source of information on what to see and do in Eugene; he's also co-owner of the Cafe Central around the corner and partner in the adjacent Volkswagen repair shop. In addition to fine company and an eclectic library, Marsh offers his guests a complimentary dessert at the Cafe (truffles are made fresh daily). The room is spacious: the inviting bed is covered with flannel sheets and a down comforter. There's cable TV for people who don't want to read. Breakfast consists of fruit, juice, cheese, fresh baked goods and coffee. All this for extremely modest rates.

Marsh hopes to expand his B&B operation in the near future by converting the upper story of the Cafe Central itself into a small guest house.

### Griswold Guest Homes
5361 Burnett Avenue, Eugene 97402
689-0680 or 688-9566

Phyllis Griswold places visitors to Eugene in private homes or condominiums through her registry for $25 to $45 a night. Some "country estates" are up to thirty minutes away, but most homes are within a couple of miles of downtown Eugene. Most serve a continental breakfast, and private baths are available.

### Valley River Inn
1000 Valley River Way, two miles north of Eugene
687-0123

A big, expensive motel complex overlooking the river. You can rent bikes and follow the jogging trail, board a jet boat, or swim in the outdoor pool. If you insist on luxurious lodging, this is the place.

# *Restaurants*

## *Eugene*

### *Cafe Central*
382 W. 13th
343-9510

Enter through the intimate cafe-bar setting; pass, if you can, the strategically placed dessert and chocolate display case. A little further on is the dining room, a pleasant mixture of opulence and restraint. Finely worked oak, subtle lighting, and exquisite pottery hint at the pleasures you can expect from the kitchen. Fortunately, the kitchen follows through with the same attention to detail: the herbed whipped-cream garnish on the soup, the vinegar redolent of fresh raspberries, the ginger-cilantro butter on a pork tenderloin, the puree of parsnips, the dense and crusty bread. Much of what Eugene is all about can be found in this restaurant, which is owned and inspired by Don Marsh and Richard Fulwiler, who are also proprietors of The Wagonworks garage next door.

### *Excelsior Cafe*
754 E. 13th
342-6963

A relaxed yet elegant restaurant in a Victorian house with seating on the greenhouse terrace, in the informal cafe, the dining room, or the bar. The French Provincial food is fresh and imaginatively prepared, and there's a good wine list. Open late on weeknights; Sunday brunch.

### *L'Auberge du Vieux Moulin*
770 W. Sixth
485-8000

French dinners from the freshest of ingredients, served (without haste) in a restored old home. There are no innovative enticements on this menu, but each item—escargots, pate, canard a l'orange—will have been prepared with the utmost care. Your table will be ready at the appointed time, and it is yours for the entire evening. Prices are accordingly high.

---

## Oregon Electric Station
27 E. Fifth
485-4444

It would be simplistic to call this a Spaghetti Factory for adults: part singles bar, part formula dining. There are a number of pricey appetizers to titillate those at the fabulous bar, and meals are served in rooms converted from old railroad cars. But the food is good (most dinners cost less than $10, with a soup and salad bar only $1.50 extra) and the wine list is admirable. At least twenty-nine Oregon wines are on the regular card, with half a dozen available nightly by the glass. A commendable commitment to the local wine industry.

## Cafe Zenon
898 Pearl Street
343-3005

An imaginative restaurant, with an eclectic, Greek-accented menu of salads, pasta, and seafood. Appetizers include ripe Calamata olives and pickled green beans; the lunch menu offers eggs sardou, beef vinaigrette salad, and boudin blanc sausage. At dinner, there's a spicy lamb curry or empanadas de pollo. Of particular merit is the beverage list, which includes a dozen soda waters, five brands of vermouth, and a full page (single-spaced) of wines from Oregon, California, France, and Greece. Another ten sparkling wines are listed elsewhre. Among the notable bottles: The Eyrie Vineyards 1974 Pinot Noir, at $24. There's a 10-percent discount on full bottles to go.

## Poppi's
675 E. 13th
343-0846

Poppi's is a friendly taverna, done up in a mellow Northwest style. Instead of facing onto a whitewashed square in a small Greek town, it opens onto its own pleasant, shaded garden: cool, green, laid back. A nice range of Greek dishes is available: baked lamb, fried squid, stuffed grape leaves, garlicky olives, good wine. If you can't decide, there's a sampler plate of seven different items, served with a liter of house wine. It's not at all expensive, either. Lots of traffic at the front door as people pick up orders to go.

### Country Inn
4100 County Farm Road, five miles north of Eugene
345-7344

A very odd place, but a great success. One seating only, at 7 p.m. for four tables only. Plan on waiting months for a reservation, then spending $100 for a meal for two. But the meal itself (perfectly prepared soups, salads, entrees, desserts), in an antique-filled setting, will be exquisite.

### Zoo Zoo's
454 Willamette
344-4764

This is it if you're seeking a place for breakfast. Fresh produce, and a commitment to quality. The huevos rancheros are particularly good.

### Emerald Valley Forrest Inn
83293 Kuni Road, Creswell
485-6796

The dining room overlooks a championship golf course. Fresh seafood on Mondays, and an excellent selection of Northwest wines.

# Wine Shops & Delicatessens

## Eugene

### Excelsior Charcuterie
901 Pearl
342-3110

A cold sweat of indecision breaks out as you face the choices available among the prepared salads. Their inspiration comes from around the world: Szechuan, Italian, Jewish. Your mouth waters. Finally you give in and order everything. Also, some bread, some cheese, a bottle of wine from the broad selection of Northwest bottlings. And don't forget dessert, from "mother" (the Excelsior Cafe).

### Of Grape & Grain

Three locations: 29th and Willamette, 686-9463
160 Oakway Road, 344-9463
260 Valley River Center, 345-9463

Roger and Karen Rutan have built up a small empire of wine shops, with some 800 varieties of wine and a most knowledgeable staff. There's also a good selection of deli items. The Oakway Road store is open Sundays.

### Northwest Wine & Cheese

296 Fifth
343-0536

Domestic as well as imported wines (and beers), with generous case discounts. A good selection of Northwest wine in half-bottles, too. Located in the Fifth Street Market complex, where you'll also find a good supply of bread and delicatessen items.

### Oregon Sampler

160 East Broadway
342-1111

Paula and Rod Evans manage this fine shop in Eugene's historic Quackenbush Building (look up as you come in to see the whirligig whose wires shuttled change from the mezzanine to the sales floor). In addition to local products and artifacts, and a complete library of books about Oregon, you'll find a fine selection of Oregon wines.

# Picnic Spots

### Benton County

### Alsea Falls

You have to work to get here from the Willamette Valley side, but the drive from Alpine Vineyards is worth the effort.

### Mary's Peak

Off Highway 34, southwest of Corvallis

This campground in the Siuslaw National Forest offers a panoramic view (on a clear day) from the Pacific Ocean to the Cascades; Mary's Peak, at 4,100 feet, is the highest elevation in the Coast Range.

## Lane County

### Fern Ridge Reservoir

Head toward Forgeron Vineyard (to Elmira), then follow signs to Fern Ridge Dam and head into the woods for seven miles. You wind up on the banks of the Long Tom River, where the trout fishing is first class. There are five parks on the reservoir: Zumwalt, Perkins, Orchard Point, Richardson Point, and Krugur. All have picnic facilities. On a sunny summer afternoon, sailboats dot the water.

### Willamette River Greenway

The greenway extends 250 miles from the Cottage Grove Reservoir to the Columbia, and provides opportunities for picnicking, hiking, and overnight camping. Most of the land along the greenway is private, but the Oregon State Parks Division publishes the *Willamette River Recreation Guide* showing points of public access to the river. Write to the Division at 525 Trade Street S.E., Salem, OR 97310, for a copy. Or contact the Lane County Parks and Recreation Division, 135 E. Sixth, Eugene, OR 97401, for their map, which locates all 157 parks in Lane County; most have picnic sites. The map also shows where the county's twenty-one covered bridges can be found.

## Eugene

### Alton Baker Park
Foot of Ferry Street

This park, part of the Willamette River Greenway, covers 425 acres of downtown Eugene riverfront and can be reached by pedestrian bridges. Canoes can be rented; bike paths wind through the park, and there's a four-mile jogging trail. As much as any aspect of Eugene, this park symbolizes the town's status as one of the nation's "most livable" smaller cities.

### Skinner's Butte Park
Access from High Street

This park overlooking downtown Eugene has eighty-four picnic sites, plus nature trails and playgrounds. A bike path connects the base of the bluff with Alton Baker park.

# Roseburg Area

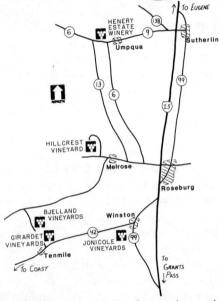

The Umpqua River has carved an impressive setting for this region: its northern fork cascades over gleaming ledges, swirls around shallow rocks, languishes in deep, clear pools. Here, fly-fishermen stand up to their waists in the cold, swirling water, casting their lines with patient repetition, waiting for a strike. It's one of the very best fishing streams in the country, if not the world. When the spring Chinook or summer steelhead are running, the license plates of the cars parked along Highway 138 indicate how far their occupants have traveled for the thrill of fishing the Umpqua; there's hardly an unoccupied foot of riverfront.

Gateway to this paradise is Roseburg, a timber town of 20,000, capital of Douglas County. Agriculture, lumber, and tourism have played important roles in the development of the region ever since travelers from California to the Oregon Territory made Roseburg a stopping point in the nineteenth century. There are several reminders of those days: Oregon's first territorial governor, General Joseph Lane, lived in Roseburg; his house is open to the public on weekends. More historical memorabilia are found in the excellent Douglas County Museum at the county fairgrounds (just south of Roseburg along Interstate 5): pioneer artifacts, tools, and early logging equipment are on display in an attractive modern complex.

History buffs will also enjoy a stop in Oakland, where much of the downtown recreates the town's Gold Rush heyday. For a generation after the arrival of the original Applegate wagon train, Oakland was a center of commerce and transportation. A walking tour of Old Town can be educational and entertaining.

Visitors to the Umpqua Valley who are not avid fishermen might nonetheless be interested in the fish ladders at Winchester Dam, five miles north of Roseburg. You can watch the migrating salmon and steelhead through underwater viewing windows.

The wineries lie in the hills west of I-5. Little brown creeks come rushing down creases in the sweeping mountainsides, between blankets of evergreen and lichen-draped deciduous trees. Barns, cows, sheep appear through the drifting mist that covers the valley floor. It is a cool climate, precisely what is recommended for the best grapes. Richard Sommer was the first to arrive with vinifera plantings, in 1961; many growers have since followed, and confirmed one of viticulture's basic lessons: the more marginal the growing season, the harder it is for the grapes to ripen, the better the wine.

And even as the region's wineries continue their contribution to enology, they are having a positive influence on tourism. Already (in some circles) the sunny Umpqua Valley, its golden hillsides laced with cool, clear streams and green vineyards, is as famous for its wine as it is (in other circles) for its fly-fishing.

# Bjelland Vineyards

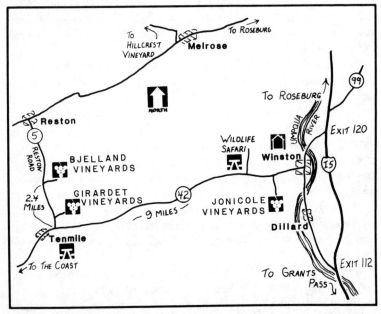

The drive from Roseburg to Bjelland Vineyards is simply gorgeous. If you head southwest from Roseburg, past the Wildlife Safari, and go about fifteen miles toward Coos Bay on Highway 42, you will see a rocky promontory jutting unexpectedly into the Southern Oregon landscape. Turn off the highway at a junction called Tenmile and follow the old Reston Road, once used as a wagon route to the coast, to reach the base of the rock and Bjelland Vineyards.

Here, amid the paraphernalia of a working 200-acre farm, complete with livestock, woodpiles, and assorted outbuildings, Paul and Mary Bjelland have also been tending nineteen acres of grapes and making wines since 1969. Paul Bjelland worked as a public relations representative for the California Teachers Association in Los Angeles before he moved to the Umpqua Valley seeking a total escape from urban life. The Bjellands bought their property for $74 an acre in 1968 (it's now worth about $5,000, he says), and bonded the second post-Repeal vinifera winery in Oregon some six years after Richard Sommer started Hillcrest. Paul founded the Oregon Winegrowers Association that same year, and started the annual Oregon Wine Festival and "Greatest of the Grape" awards in 1969.

## BJELLAND VINEYARDS
Bjelland Vineyard Lane
Roseburg, OR 97470
679-6950

| | |
|---|---|
| Open to the public | 10-5 daily, summer |
| | 11-5 daily, winter |
| Tour groups | yes |
| Charge for tour groups | none |
| Picnic facilities at the winery | table adjacent to winery |
| Wines available (1984) | Chardonnay |
| | Sparkling Chardonnay |
| | Semillon |
| | Johannisberg Riesling |
| | Sauvignon Blanc |
| | Gewurztraminer |
| | Cabernet Sauvignon |
| | Pinot Noir |
| | Rhubarb |
| | Boysenberry |
| | Blackberry |
| | Raspberry |
| | Brambleberry |

The production of Bjelland Vineyards remains modest; not more than 4,000 gallons in most years, although the winery could probably handle 20,000. The Bjellands have opened two satellite tasting rooms on the Oregon Coast to market their wine; these facilities, at Bandon and Gold Beach, allow the winery to sell almost all its production at retail. Still, there's no way even the most dedicated winemaker can make a living selling 4,000 gallons of wine a year; hence the farming. Paul Bjelland, whose OshKosh overalls have become his trademark, does his own butchering and makes his own sausages; surely there aren't many winemakers with that sort of experience. He has also developed a reputation as a very capable chef.

Mary Bjelland, a teacher at nearby Winston Junior High School, takes sole charge of making the fruit and berry wines, including a blackberry wine that won the Governor's Trophy at the 1981 Oregon State Fair.

Bjelland Vineyards' wines are priced in the $4 to $10 range, and include Chardonnay, Sauvignon Blanc, Johannisberg Riesling, a spicy Ge-

| BJELLAND VINEYARDS | |
|---|---|
| Owners | Paul & Mary Bjelland |
| Winemaker | Paul Bjelland |
| Year bonded | 1969 |
| Year first planted | 1968 |
| Vineyard acreage | 19 |
| Principal varieties | Riesling |
| | Chardonnay |
| | Gewurztraminer |
| | Semillon |
| | Cabernet Sauvignon |
| | Sauvignon Blanc |
| Year of first crush | 1969 |
| Production capacity | 20,000 gallons |
| Production in 1983 | 4,000 gallons |
| Expansion plans | 5 acres Semillon |
| Awards, 1983 | |
| Boysenberry: | Gold, Oregon State Fair |
| Cranberry Apple: | Silver, Oregon State Fair |
| Brambleberry: | Silver, Oregon State Fair |

wurztraminer, and a full Semillon, as well as Roses of Cabernet Sauvignon and Pinot Noir. The mention of a Johannisberg Riesling is no accident: Oregon has some of the most stringent labelling laws imaginable, requiring the term "White Riesling" for all Oregon-grown Riesling grapes, but because Bjelland Vineyards had been using the term before the laws were passed, it was permitted to retain the Johannisberg Riesling name on its label.

Somewhat more expensive are the Bjelland Sparkling Chardonnay and Sparkling Semillon; they are made in the traditional methode champenoise. These wines cost quite a bit to produce, too, but the Bjellands have always shunned outside financing to help them expand their plantings and production. Instead of borrowing from the bank, or from private investors, the Bjellands remain content with their independent lives, beholden to no outside interests save their dedication to Oregon's winemaking industry.

# Girardet Wine Cellars

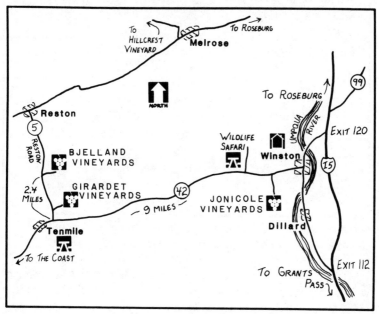

Every once in a while, we encounter a winemaking family with a remarkable inner peace, a spiritual calm that transcends their surroundings and the pressures of the winemaking business. We found these qualities in Philippe and Bonnie Girardet.

They began, as so often happens, with a vineyard. When they bought the property in 1972, just two miles from the Bjellands, they were looking for an alternative to the academic and technical life; Philippe, who grew up in Yverdon, Switzerland, had spent fifteen years at the California Institute of Technology in Pasadena. They built their home on a gentle slope in the hills south of Roseburg, surrounded by a sea of green.

By 1975, the vineyard had begun producing: Riesling, Gewurztraminer, Pinot Noir, Cabernet Sauvignon. Philippe's technical background also led him to experiment with some twenty hybrids developed by scientists in France. (The French call them American hybrids, the Americans call them French hybrids.) These newly developed grape varieties (called cultivars in modern terminology) are widely used in France, though the French don't advertise the fact. Girardet became interested in them because of their resistance to disease, which means that they require fewer chemicals and

---

**🍇 GIRARDET WINE CELLARS**
895 Reston Road
Roseburg, OR 97470
679-7252

| | |
|---|---|
| Open to the public | 12-5 daily, May-Sept. |
| | 12-5 Sat., Oct.-April, |
| | or by appointment |
| Tour groups | yes; prefer appointment |
| Charge for tour groups | 50 cents per person |
| Festivals/special events | Opening Celebration, June 16-17, 1984 |
| Wines available (1984) | 1983 White Riesling |
| | 1983 Blanc Maison |
| | 1983 Rouge Maison |

---

herbicides. (Ideally, Girardet would like to make wine entirely without chemicals, even without the sulphur dioxide that regularly doses most freshly crushed grapes.) He has planted five acres of red French cultivars— Baco Noir, Chancellor, Foch, Millot, among others—and two acres of whites— Seyval-Blanc, Verdelet, Aurora, Meuniere, Valerian, and a grape called Menu, which adds complexity to white wines. He has tried making wine entirely out of some of these new vines, with intriguing results; we think some of them will prove extremely interesting, and may soon share center stage with the older varieties.

The Girardet vineyard became well known for the high quality of its grapes, its Riesling and Gewurztraminer being especially sought-after. But the wineries buying grapes cannot be blamed for taking advantage of trends in the industry; the current trend is toward self-sufficiency in grapes. When the winery that had regularly contracted to buy Girardet's grapes didn't renew the contract, it was time to act.

The decision to start a winery was not taken lightly, but for Bonnie and Philippe Girardet it was inevitable. As the most recently bonded winery in Oregon, Girardet Wine Cellars has had the good fortune to hire an experienced consultant, Bill Nelson, to guide them through the thicket of early decisions. Nelson has been on hand to give advice on commercial winemaking technology and equipment, such as the purchase of a versatile three-phase variable speed pump. This may sound trivial, but small wineries need this sort of advice.

The Girardets expect their tasting and sales room to be open for the 1984

**GIRARDET WINE CELLARS**

| | |
|---|---|
| Owners | Philippe & Bonnie Girardet |
| Winemaker | Philippe Girardet |
| Consulting enologist | Bill Nelson |
| Year bonded | 1983 |
| Year first planted | 1972 |
| Vineyard acreage | 18 |
| Principal varieties | White Riesling |
| | Gewurztraminer |
| | Pinot Noir |
| | Gamay |
| | Cabernet Sauvignon |
| | Zinfandel |
| | Red French Cultivars |
| | White French Cultivars |
| Year of first crush | 1983 |
| Production capacity | 6,500 gallons |
| Production in 1983 | 4,350 gallons |
| Expansion plans | full production 1985-1986 |

season. Visitors will taste a red wine called, simply, Rouge Maison, that has been blended from Pinot Noir, Cabernet Sauvignon, Gamay, Zinfandel, and some of the hybrids. When we tasted a tank sample, the Cabernet was dominant, along with a hint of raspberries.

The Blanc Maison contains one-third Chardonnay, with the balance a blend of French hybrids; it showed a lemony, flowery nose. The 1983 Riesling is a pale-colored, brilliant wine with a pleasing, varietal aroma and well-balanced flavors.

The most interesting hybrid we tried was Girardet's home-made 1980 Baco Noir, with a lovely black currant nose suggestive of the Bordeaux wines. That's really not surprising, considering that Maurice Baco was a French enologist in Bordeaux who developed this grape as a hardy complement to Cabernet Sauvignon.

There's almost too much sun for Philippe Girardet's taste. "I long for Swiss summers," he mentioned to us in passing. No doubt; Lake Geneva can be very appealing. But the Girardets have found contentment where they are and with the bounty of their land. Their security is deeply rooted, not in the clay and shale soil of the vineyard, but in the tenacity and optimism their family has shown through the years.

# Henry Estate Winery

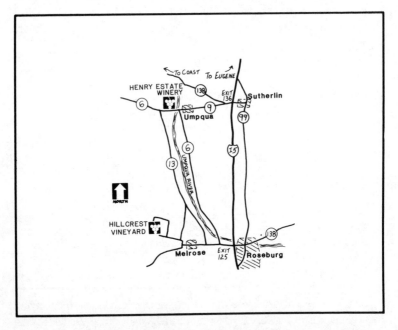

The road toward the Henry Winery meanders from Sutherlin, on Interstate 5 north of Roseburg, westward through golden farmland and orchards, past patrician homes set in the trees, to the settlement of Umpqua itself. The place appears modest, given the importance of the river valley whose name it bears: a gas station and a store. The road passes a little girder bridge spanning Calapooya Creek and crosses the north fork of the Umpqua on a cement bridge. And there, somewhat forlornly beside the highway, sits the winery, "Home of Henry Estate Wines."

But appearances are quite deceiving, and Henry's is yet another testament to the essential spirit of individualism that marks winemaking in Oregon.

Scott Henry, quick to smile, carefully spoken, is a scientist by training, a former aeronautical engineer who was working for Aeroject General in Sacramento when two of his colleagues started a winery and needed help on a few design problems. (One of them was Gino Zepponi, now vice president of Domaine Chandon in the Napa Valley; he is also a consultant to the Henry Winery.) When Scott was summoned home to run the family farm a dozen

---

**HENRY WINERY**
(Henry Estate Wines)
687 Hubbard Creek Road
P.O. Box 26
Umpqua, OR 97486
459-5120 (winery) or 459-3614 (home)

| | |
|---|---|
| Open to the public | 11-5 daily |
| Tour groups | yes, by appointment |
| Charge for tour groups | $1 per person |
| Picnic facilities at the winery | beside the winery under fruit trees |
| Wines available (1984) | 1980 Pinot Noir |
| | 1980 Chardonnay |
| | 1983 Gewurztraminer |
| | Umpqua Red Table Wine |
| | Umpqua White Table Wine |

---

years ago, he brought along some cuttings, and planted a few marginal acres of bottomland with grapes. Now he's in a quandary that faces few of his fellow winemakers: his Pinot Noir vineyards, planted on the wide-open floor of the Umpqua River Valley, are too productive.

In a state where most vineyards are struggling to produce three tons of Pinot Noir grapes per acre, and in many cases barely reached 1.5 tons to the acre in 1983, Scott Henry's vines readily produce up to 9 tons! If he prunes his vines to reduce the yield to three tons, the quality of the grapes actually suffers; the vines generate too many secondary buds, resulting in degraded berries. Of course, wine made from overly-productive vines isn't fabulous, either, but Scott Henry reaches a golden mean of quality and quantity at about six tons to the acre —double the best yield in the Willamette Valley! Double what the Grand Cru vineyards of Burgundy allow!

Scott Henry is proud of the fact that his releases tend to run a year or two behind the rest of the Oregon market. This has allowed him to wait until 1984 to release the 1980 Vintage Select Pinot Noir, which has a rich nose, a full, fruity taste, and a youthful, tannic finish. The 1980 Chardonnay, not released until early 1984, had time to develop a graceful bouquet of oak and fruit and a complexity of flavors that make this a memorable wine.

In all, the winery has very few bottlings on the market: Pinot Noir, Chardonnay, Gewurztraminer, and two table wines. Because he is limiting his product line so severely, Scott Henry is developing some options to contend with the vagaries of weather and the unpredictabilities of the market.

**HENRY WINERY**

| | |
|---|---|
| Owners | Scott & Sylvia Henry |
| Winemaker | Scott Henry |
| Consulting enologist | Gino Zepponi |
| Year bonded | 1978 |
| Year first planted | 1972 |
| Vineyard acreage | 31 |
| Principal varieties, acres | Pinot Noir, 12 |
| | Chardonnay, 12 |
| | Gewurztraminer, 4 |
| | Riesling, 3 |
| Year of first crush | 1978 |
| Production capacity | 30,000 gallons |
| Production in 1983 | 13,000 gallons |
| Awards, 1983 | |
| 1978 Pinot Noir: | Silver, London |
| 1979 Pinot Noir: | Gold, Oregon State Fair |
| Umpqua Red Table Wine | Silver, Oregon State Fair |

For example, when it appears that the Pinot Noir and Chardonnay are having difficulty ripening, he can use those grapes, with their high acid content and low sugar, to make a cuvee for sparkling wine. To give himself another option, and to cover the lower end of the market, he makes Umpqua Red Table Wine, a real gift to the consumer. This is 100-percent estate-grown Pinot Noir, picked ten days before the full-bodied vintage Pinot; it finishes fermentation just in time to make room for the riper batch. It's a smooth and versatile wine with a strong hint of strawberries and oak, lighter-bodied than the vintage Pinot Noir but a terrific value at under $5. Joining it in 1984 will be an Umpqua White, made from 75-percent Chardonnay, and a blend of Riesling and Gewurztraminer.

That Gewurztraminer, incidentally, is a wonderful food wine, an elegant dinner wine. "We sell more Gewurztraminer out of this tasting room than we do in the rest of the state," reports Sylvia Henry, who is in charge of sales, the tasting room, and vineyard management during the harvest.

"We could easily make more varieties," Scott Henry points out, "and we could get bigger, too. The question is, how big do we have to be to make them economically?" Is it worth the cost of producing the sparkling wine, for example? On the basis of quality, certainly; the samples we tasted were crisp, classical champagnes. But it's expensive to produce only a thousand bottles of a handmade product. And it takes two years at least to establish a product line.                               •

Scott tempers his agricultural humility with scientific management. For the past two years he has hired a weather service in Bend, Oregon, to provide him with forecasts in October to help him make better decisions during the crucial week of harvest. (He also uses them during the hay harvest in May.) Seven-day forecasts are routine for commercial weather services, but Scott suggested they use computer correlations of past weather patterns to forecast the entire month. The resulting forecasts were accurate and invaluable: his crews were able to finish picking only hours before the rains began.

There's a treat in store for off-season visitors to the Henry Winery. After harvest, following the return of the green leaf nutrients to the vines, Scott Henry allows his sheep to graze on the weeds and grasses that spring up in the vine yard. There's nothing quite like the sight of a flock of peaceful sheep browsing between the rows of vines in a winter landscape.

How many sheep, for how long? He lets them have at it until bud break in early April. And two sheep per acre, no more. "You certainly don't want to have to *feed* the sheep," he says.

# Hillcrest Vineyard

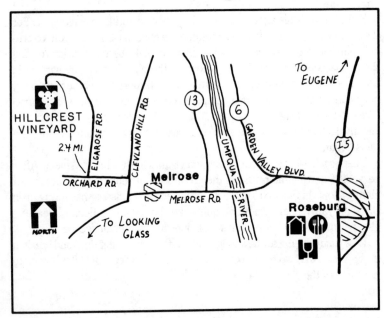

Richard Sommer is the pioneer, the grandfather and godfather of Oregon's modern table-wine industry.

He came north more than 25 years ago, migrating from the University of California at Davis, where he had been inspired by none other than the great professor of viticulture, Maynard Amerine, to search for a cool hillside and plant a vinifera vineyard. His quest led him to the Umpqua Valley, where he planted Napa Valley cuttings on five acres back in 1961, and bonded Hillcrest Vineyard in 1963.

It is hard to overemphasize the importance of Sommer's contribution to Oregon winemaking. Without his quixotic spirit, Oregon might have remained forever a state of labrusca plantings. Honeywood might have remained the largest influence on commercial winemaking.

Oregon had a flourishing table-winemaking industry before Prohibition, and quite a few wineries had started up after Repeal, but no one was growing vinifera when Sommer arrived in 1956. Sommer's grandparents had grown grapes in Oregon before World War II, in the Rogue River Valley

160

## ▓ HILLCREST VINEYARD

240 Vineyard Lane
Roseburg, OR 97470
673-3709

| | |
|---|---|
| Open to the public | 10-5 daily |
| Tour groups | yes; appointment for more than 10 |
| Charge for tour groups | $1 per person |
| Picnic facilities at the winery | 4 tables upstairs overlooking the vineyards; 1 table outside |
| Wines available (1984) | 1980 & 1981 White Riesling |
| | 1980 White Riesling (dry) |
| | 1982 Gewurztraminer |
| | 1977 Chardonnay |
| | 1978 & 1979 Cabernet Sauvignon |
| | 1978 & 1979 Pinot Noir |
| | 1980 Zinfandel |
| | 1982 Rose of Cabernet |
| | Oregon Mist (Sparkling Riesling) |

(Grants Pass was known then as the Tokay capital of Oregon), but Sommer found that location too dry, and ultimately settled on the Umpqua Valley in 1961 for his "ideal" cool climate.

He bought property for his vineyard at an elevation of 850 feet, in a valley ten miles west of Roseburg that was warm enough to avoid winter frosts but cool enough for the "marginal" conditions recommended by Professor Amerine for the finest wine grapes. To give his grapes as much sunlight as possible, Sommer trained them on high trellises, allowing the leaves to cascade down between rows. He began with White Riesling, and quickly demonstrated that a commercially viable vinifera wine could indeed be made in Oregon.

Sommer's success was a beacon to the winemakers who followed (and to whom Sommer gave valuable advice and inspiration), and an encouraging signal to the faculty at U.C. Davis who had been talking for years about the advantages of cool climates and difficult growing conditions. Today, thirty acres of the original farm are planted: twenty acres of Riesling, three each of Cabernet and Pinot Noir, and a four-acre plot of Gewurztraminer, Sauvignon Blanc, Semillon, Chardonnay, and Zinfandel. Sommer does much of the agricultural work himself: the pruning, training, applications of fertilizer; he has also taught many of the newcomers these hands-on aspects of

| HILLCREST VINEYARD | |
|---|---|
| Owner | Richard H. Sommer |
| Winemaker | Paul Vinciguerra |
| Consulting enologist | Bill Nelson |
| Year bonded | 1963 |
| Year first planted | 1961 |
| Vineyard acreage | 30 |
| Principal varieties | White Riesling, 20 |
| | Pinot Noir, 3 |
| | Cabernet Sauvignon, 3 |
| Year of first crush | 1963 |
| Production capacity | 20,000 gallons |
| Production in 1983 | 19,028 gallons |
| Expansion plans | to 30,000 gallons |
| Awards, 1983 | |
| 1979 Pinot Noir: | Silver, New York |

running a vineyard.

The wine business "was all here, it just had to be put together," Sommer says with characteristic understatement. Besides, he continues, "It's not the grapes, not the soil, not the winemaking. The climate is what makes the wine."

A very capable associate of Sommer's, Paul Vinciguerra, has the title of winemaker, with the highly regarded Bill Nelson serving as consulting enologist. Nelson, who consults for several wineries, feels that the 1978 Cabernet Sauvignon is similar to the St. Julien wines of Bordeaux, and considers it one of Oregon's best.

When the Salem Study Club, a winetasting group led by Nathan Allen of the Wine Rack in Salem, tasted French Burgundies in December, 1983, there was one extra wine. Since the group was tasting "blind," no one knew what it was until the scores were announced. A 1978 Richebourg won, a $40 wine. But beating all the others, the Echezeaux, the Beaune Clos Les Mouches, and a half-dozen other $25 bottles of prime French Burgundies was a 1979 Hillcrest Pinot Noir that sells for under $8.

The winery and tasting room are surrounded by vineyards. From the deck outside the upstairs picnic room there is a splendid view across the lush vines, growing in tall double Geneva curtains. And if you spot the tractor, there's a good chance that it's Richard Sommer at the wheel, his pruning shears at the ready, chugging through the vineyard like the spirit of Pan.

# *Jonicole Vineyards*

Jon and Laurie Marker want to have a road built from Highway 42 to their winery and five-acre vineyard half a mile away. Not that there isn't already a road; there is. And it has a terrific name, too: Vineyard Lane. But it's full of potholes and is almost impassable. The Markers want a new road that tourists can take without risking their transmissions to make that short detour from the highway to their tasting room.

Construction of the road depends on a financing package Jon is putting together, an investment that would reactivate Jonicole Winery, which has existed since 1975 as a partnership of three California couples. The Markers have now bought out the other investors, and hope to have their winery open to the public once again this summer.

---

**JONICOLE VINEYARDS**
491 Winery Lane
Roseburg, OR 97470
679-5771

| | |
|---|---|
| Open to the public | summer, 1984 |
| Tour groups | by appointment |
| Owners | Jon & Laurie Marker |
| Winemaker | Jon Marker |
| Year bonded | 1975 |
| Year first planted | 1969 |
| Vineyard acreage | 5 |
| Year of first crush | 1975 |
| Production capacity | 10,000 gallons |
| Production in 1983 | 5,000 gallons |

---

When we visited, Marker was busy building a new tasting room. The wine is already on hand, Pinot Noir and Cabernet Sauvignon from past vintages, still in barrels. To remain open, Jonicole will have to draw enough visitors and sell enough wine to make room for new production. It's not going to be easy for the Markers, but their venture might succeed—if the road gets built and the wine gets bottled.

Be sure to call ahead.

# Lodging

## *Idleyld Park*

### Steamboat Inn

Thirty-eight miles east of Roseburg on Highway 138
498-2411 or 496-3495

A much-admired fishing resort, Steamboat Inn at first appears to be little more than a gas station and coffee shop. Accommodations are typical of fishing resorts: eight unassuming cabins at modest prices from which fishermen can depart in the early hours without waking up their neighbors. A shaded veranda, with a view of the North Umpqua, links the cabins, and provides the setting for spontaneous, late-afternoon fellowship. No phones or TV in the cabins.

The big treat for guests is the Fisherman's Dinner, served on Saturdays and by request during the winter months, and nightly in summer. Half an hour after dark, the front door is locked to discourage passing motorists needing gas. Overnight guests and occasional outsiders who have managed to get a reservation then sip wine for an hour or so on the porch overlooking the river. Dinner, served at a single trestle table, begins with soup, followed by heaping dishes of vegetables, pasta, homemade breads, and several entrees (barbecued salmon, roast chicken). Then dessert. The cost, including wine, is moderate. One or both of the owners, Jim and Sharon Van Loam, is on hand every night to host the meal, underscoring the Steamboat Inn's motto: "You are a stranger here but once."

Plans for 1984 include remodeling the back porch to offer more seating for private parties, and a weekly program of special events such as wine tastings.

## *Roseburg*

### Windmill Inn

Garden Valley Boulevard at Mulholland (Exit 125)
673-0901

A better-than-average motel complex, with sauna and Jacuzzi, and a particularly agreeable outdoor courtyard and swimming pool. Cable TV. Some "executive suites."

## Winston

### Hill Side Court
101 N.E. Main
679-6736

A comfortable little motel not far from the Wildlife Safari with reasonable rates.

# Restaurants

## Roseburg

### Choo Choo Willy's
1370 N.W. Garden Valley Boulevard
673-7357

Yes, there's a choo-choo here, a model railroad that goes around on an elevated track. You can order hamburgers, seafood, steaks, and even wine from a decent wine list. The kids will love Choo Choo Willy's.

### P. B. Clayton's
968 N.E. Stephens
672-1142

This popular restaurant has more than done its duty with a wine list that includes almost a dozen Oregon wines. The "Roseburger" (we're in Roseburg, remember) is delicious and enough nourishment for a crowd. Evenings, the dining room goes fancy, with linen and silver, and tableside preparation of flambe items, a la carte steaks, and seafood. Complete dinners go for less than $8, and the service is friendly and capable.

### Duffy's
940 Garden Valley Road
672-4752

You won't find any surprises here; it's a straightforward American menu. But a number of local folks think it's the best place in Roseburg. Renovation should be complete by late spring of 1984.

---

## Oakland

---

### La Hacienda
114 Locust
459-5366

A tiny place on Oakland's charmingly restored main street. The Mexican food is well prepared and inexpensive. The same folks now have another restaurant in downtown Roseburg.

### Tolly's
35 Locust Street
459-3796

If you drop in during the day, Tolly's will appeal to you as an old-fashioned ice cream parlor. At night, the antique-filled dining room serves a full menu; on Wednesdays and Thursdays chef George Ioaninedes prepares Greek entrees (stuffed grape leaves, lamb chops with feta, spanikopita) accompanied by local wines.

# Wine Shops & Delicatessens

---

### Roseburg

---

### Cellar 100
100 Garden Valley Shopping Center
673-1670

The deli is run by Cheryl Anderson, the wine section by her husband Wayne, and together they have built The Cellar into the region's best combination wine shop and deli. Wayne's shelves hold hundreds of labels, including at least one wine from every Oregon winery. But the Northwest wines aren't segregated into a single section; instead, the bottles are placed among wines of similar varieties from California, France, and Germany. The result is a truly integrated wine shop. As for the deli, the sandwiches and salads are fresh and are ideal for a picnic on the Umpqua. Try one of the many unusual specialty foods, too. Plans are afoot to add a few tables for in-store eating.

# *Picnic Spots*

## *Roseburg*

### *Twin Rivers Vacation Park*
673-3811

One of the most popular campgrounds in the area. Go five miles west on the Garden Valley Road exit, then 1.5 miles south on county road 6. There are fifty campsites with picnic tables, plus a laundry, showers, a playground, and an adult rec room.

## *North Umpqua*

Along Highway 138, almost every bend of the road has room for a parking space and a picnic table or two. The Umpqua's rushing waters can usually overcome the traffic noise. Be sure to have a proper permit before fishing, and remember that the North Umpqua is limited to fly-fishing in most places.

## *Winston*

### *Ben Irvin Reservoir*
The turn is 500 feet from the Tenmile store. You'll find a boat ramp, swimming, fishing, water skiing, and picnic grounds.

### *Wildlife Safari*
Highway 42, five miles from Exit 115 from Interstate 5
679-6761

Here's a fascinating tourist attraction oriented toward exotic wildlife: some 600 animals roam freely across a 250-acre preserve. Visitors drive along a paved road in their own cars or escorted mini-buses. There's literally too much to see in one "safari" because many of the animals avoid the midday heat; a one-day ticket lets you drive through twice. Small-animal exhibits and a children's petting zoo can be visited on foot, and in summer there are educational presentations with endangered species of exotic animals and birds of prey, plus elephant rides. Everything else, restaurant, picnic tables, RV park, gift shop included, is open daily year round.

# Southern Oregon

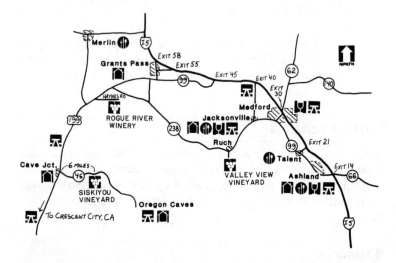

One-third of the tourists traveling in Oregon, be they natives or out-of-state travelers, spend a portion of their time in southern Oregon, taking advantage of the area's wide range of recreational opportunities and pleasant climate: wonderful, warm springs and summers, the glorious Shakespeare Festival, historic Jacksonville, the exciting Rogue River Trail, the pear blossoms along Medford's Bear Creek, the mysterious Oregon Caves, and even the southernmost wineries in the state.

The Rogue River loops through this region, a 215-mile aquatic trail ranging in character from smooth and tame to roaring white water. Variously designated a recreational river, a wild river, and a scenic river as it flows from Grants Pass to the ocean, the Rogue is well known for its trout fishing. In summer, its banks make a great hiking trail, and raft trips on jet boats are a popular attraction.

Highway 199, the Redwood Highway, travels a majestic path through the cathedral-like canopies of towering trees as it crosses the Siskiyou Mountains. The road levels out in the Illinois Valley; the Illinois River is one of the Rogue's principal tributaries. This valley, it turns out, has the right climate for growing premium grapes. At Cave Junction, there's a turnoff to the Oregon Caves National Monument, whose maze of corridors connects spectacular marble caverns.

The Applegate is another major tributary of the Rogue, and its valley, too, fosters good grape-growing. The pioneer town of Jacksonville, now designated a National Historic Landmark, offers quiet, tree-lined streets and older brick buildings that house banks, hotels, and restaurants; the town's residential sections feature carefully restored clapboard houses surrounded by wooden balustrades. The former county courthouse is now a museum, and the jail is a pioneer museum especially for children.

Pioneer Day in June celebrates Jacksonville's heritage; the Peter Britt Music Festival, named for an early settler and widely admired photographer, includes two weeks of open-air concerts and chamber music in August. For ticket information, write to Box 1124, Medford, OR 97501. There's a new event, too: a two-day Vintage Festival in late July, sponsored by the Southern Oregon Winegrowers Association, to celebrate the region's wines. The event includes a gala dinner, lectures, and tastings; the Jacksonville Inn Wine Shop has more specific information.

The town of Ashland has changed over the past years from sleepy college town (Southern Oregon State) to major cultural center thanks to the Oregon Shakespearean Festival, a nationally recognized program of classical and modern drama. Founded by a visionary theatrical producer, Angus Bowmer, in 1935, the festival has grown from a few ambitious amateur productions to a six-month season staged by a huge, and thouroghly professional, cast and crew. The Oregon Shakespearean Festival has developed into one of the nation's top repertory companies, with performances at two indoor theaters as well as the "original" outdoor theater patterned after a typical Elizabethan stage, the Globe Theatre in London. Performances are usually sold out well in advance, and are popular with group tours; write to the Oregon Shakespearean Festival, Ashland, OR 97250 for the current schedule and ticket information. Information on tour packages is available from the Southern Oregon Reservation Center, Box 1048, Ashland, OR 97250; telephone 488-1011.

Despite the tourist influx, Ashland has managed to remain almost breathtakingly beautiful. Set on a hillside overlooking a dark green and golden valley, the town offers stunning views; its main street offers a small-town folksiness with tempting tourist attractions, fine restaurants, quaint Bed & Breakfast inns, bookstores, and boutiques. And Ashland's Lithia Park is surely one of Oregon's most charming public parks.

# *Rogue River Vineyards*

The most northerly stretch of the Redwood Highway (U.S. 199 between Crescent City and Grants Pass) makes a rather swift transition, seven miles outside Grants Pass, from a picturesque, two-lane corridor through the Siskiyous to a four-lane highway through the outskirts of the city. At just that point, a turn onto Helms Road will put you firmly back in the country; the setting at Rogue River Vineyards is almost typically rural. From the hillside where four acres of young Chardonnay vines are growing, you can see a baronial white homestead and dairy farm just down the road, fields of grazing livestock, and snow-capped peaks in the distance.

Rogue River's property is home to the four families that own the winery. Winemaker Bill Jiron and his partners spend their workweeks at Lost Hills Vineyards in California, six hours away, but they return on weekends to cultivate the vineyard and develop the winery itself.

| ROGUE RIVER VINEYARDS 3145 Helms Road Grants Pass, OR 97527 476-1051 | |
|---|---|
| Open to the public | by appointment |
| Owners | Albert Luingo, Dan Solawy, John David, Bill Jiron |
| Winemaker | Bill Jiron |
| Year bonded | 1984 |
| Year first planted | 1983 |
| Vineyard acreage | 4 |
| Principal variety | Chardonnay |
| Year of first crush | 1984 |
| Production capacity | 10,770 gallons |

Jiron intends to sell the production of Rogue River Vineyards directly to markets in northern California. That's understandable, given his experience in those markets, but we suspect that there could also be a lot of local interest in a wine called Rogue River.

As we went to press, the winery's production plans were uncertain, but will eventually include Chardonnay from the vineyard. Plans for tourist facilities at the winery were also uncertain, although there was talk of a tasting room in Grants Pass.

# Siskiyou Vineyard

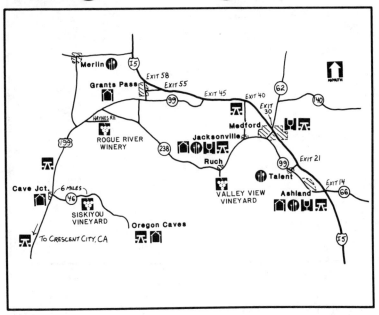

"If you're going to open a bottle of wine," says Suzi David, the owner of Siskiyou Vineyards in Oregon's far southwestern corner, "you should make it fun."

There's no doubt that she enjoys life. You won't have any trouble finding her when you reach the winery; she's the one with the fine black sheep trotting at her heels. His name is Jonathan—Jonathan Lambington Sheep, to be exact—and he thinks he's a dog. He comes when called, runs behind the truck, and swims in the lake with her three dark poodles.

But C. J. "Suzi" David cannot be put down as an eccentric country matron. Far from it. She has a great deal of savvy and business acumen, coupled with unceasing energy, resourcefulness, and altruism.

She is, when it comes down to it, a business owner with wild dreams and the energy to make them come true. It is a legitimately inherited trait; her father's sister is Merle Norman, owner and developer of her own cosmetics business. When Suzi's husband died unexpectedly in early 1983 she didn't fold up the winery, she went ahead with plans for a brand-new building, a two-story winery. Within a few months, the building was in place, the tast-

---

**SISKIYOU VINEYARDS**
6220 Oregon Caves Highway
Cave Junction, OR 97523
592-3727

| | |
|---|---|
| Open to the public | 11-5 daily |
| Tour groups | yes; prefer appointment |
| Picnic facilities at the winery | 2-acre trout lake; nature trails; picnic area |
| Festivals/special events | Annual Wine Festival, June 9-10 |
| Wines available (1984) | 1981 Cabernet Sauvignon |
| | 1981 Pinot Noir |
| | 1982 Rose of Cabernet |
| | 1982 White Riesling |
| | 1982 Gewurztraminer |
| | 1982 Chenin Blanc |
| | 1982 Sauvignon Blanc |
| | 1982 Semillon |

---

ing room was open (complete with a hand-carved bar and balustrades), and a new set of labels was designed for the wines themselves. And she had made 14,000 gallons of wine.

Siskiyou's vineyards, six miles outside of Cave Junction, cover twelve acres of the 100-acre property; the rest is wooded. The highway to the famous Oregon Caves, visited by over l00,000 tourists every year, passes right in front of the winery.

Suzi David is very involved with a number of community events, and is confident that the good will she shows will be returned. Her annual wine festival promotes arts and crafts as well as music; looms are brought in to demonstrate weaving, pottery wheels are set up to throw clay pots. The festival, now in its fifth year, takes place on the grassy banks of the trout lake on her property. Among the treats served are traditional Greek dolmas, made with Siskiyou's own grape leaves.

And Suzi knows how to use community resources to promote her own product, her own wine. She helped organize a wine tasting in Ashland at Southern Oregon College, and she has invited all the Oregon winemakers to pour their wine at a Recreation and Pleasure Extravaganza sponsored by a radio station in Grants Pass. The area's annual Moon Tree Run counts Suzi David as a co-sponsor, and she is always ready to make a radio or television appearance to help promote the Oregon wine industry.

| SISKIYOU VINEYARDS | |
| --- | --- |
| Owner | C. J. "Suzi" David |
| Winemaker | Donna Devine |
| Year bonded | 1978 |
| Year first planted | 1974 |
| Vineyard acreage | 12 |
| Principal varieties, acres | Pinot Noir, 4 |
| | Gamay, 2.5 |
| | Gewurztraminer, 2 |
| | Cabernet Sauvignon, 1 |
| | Merlot, 1 |
| | Chenin Blanc, .5 |
| Year of first crush | 1978 |
| Production capacity | 25,000 gallons |
| Production in 1983 | 13,800 gallons |

The wines of Siskiyou Vineyards are made by Donna Devine, whose first encounter with the winery came when she was a reporter for the *Grants Pass Courier* and the *Southern Oregon Weekly Review*. She wrote a story, came back to pick grapes, and ended up staying, in 1980. "I had no previous winery experience," she told us, "but I was curious."

Devine's curiosity, patience, and perseverance have taken her a long way. She is producing a wide spectrum of varietal wines, including a blend of Sauvignon Blanc and Semillon that has a flowery nose and a rich, herbal taste. Her 1980 Cabernet Sauvignon has a deep color and a racy, green pepper nose, a well-balanced wine that will age well.

The Pinot Noirs grown here in the Illinois Valley don't show the early softness and subtlety of flavors frequently found in Willamette Valley Pinots. Instead, the grape produces a more robust, fruity wine, with a very clean taste and a more tannic finish.

Suzi David and her crew aren't finished yet. By the summer of 1984, the area in front of the winery will be landscaped, and a more splendid entrance to the Siskiyou Vineyards complex will have been fashioned by woodcarver Faron Steele. A nature path lined with azaleas, ferns, and various indigenous plants will wind its way through the property for the pleasure of visitors. Adding further romance to the scene are two great Belgian draft horses that help bring in the grapes at harvest.

Some people use their time just dreaming; Suzi David keeps some for getting the job done.

# *Valley View Vineyard*

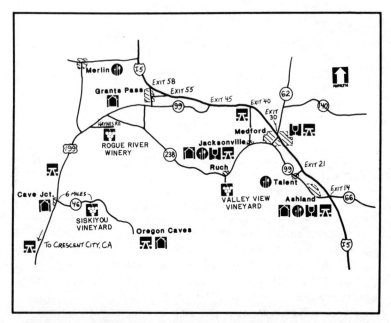

Never heard of Valley View Vineyard? It's the site of an orchard planted by pioneer photographer Peter Britt alongside the Applegate River. Not too many people outside the wine industry were familiar with Valley View until recently. Valley View wasn't trying to hide, but it hadn't had that "big break" either.

Many fine wineries operate for years in relative obscurity. Their wines make no big splash, they win no medals; beyond the support of local friends and buyers, they don't achieve wide recognition. Now, you don't have to win a gold medal to know you're a good winemaker, and some of the most successful wineries we know have no use for competitions or medals. Still, favorable publicity helps sell wine, and no winemaker minds if the winery gets favorable mention in print.

The big break for Valley View Vineyards came on September 23, 1983, in the form of an article by wine columnist Mike Lonsford in the *Houston Chronicle*. Lonsford pulled a trick on a friend of his; he used a 1978 Valley View Cabernet Sauvignon as a "ringer" in a blind tasting of world-class 1975 Bordeaux. Valley View's wine came in second, beaten only by a 1975

---

**🍇 VALLEY VIEW VINEYARD**
1000 Applegate Road
Jacksonville (Ruch), OR 97530
899-8468

| | |
|---|---|
| Open to the public | Fri., Sat., Sun.: |
| | 11-5 summer |
| | 12-5 winter |
| Tour groups | yes; please notify |
| Charge for tour groups | none |
| Wines available (1984) | Jefferson State Brand: |
| | Rogue Red, White, Rose |
| | 1982 Chardonnay |
| | 1982 Gewurztraminer |
| | 1980 Pinot Noir |
| | 1980 Cabernet |
| | Merlot |
| | Oregon Perry |

---

Chateau Mouton-Rothschild. When he unveiled the bottles, his guests were stunned. Lonsford, too, confessed to some surprise; he liked the Valley View wine, but he didn't know he liked it that much!

Cabernet Sauvignon has always been Valley View's most popular wine and the Houston article was gratefully received. The Cabernet comes almost entirely from grapes grown on Valley View's picturesque, eighty-acre vineyard on the Applegate River, eight miles south of historic Jacksonville.

Valley View's generic wines are distributed under the label "Jackson State Brand" Rogue White, Rose, and Red. The white contains 80 percent Chardonnay; the rose is all Cabernet Sauvignon; the red is 40 percent Cabernet, 30 percent Pinot Noir, and 30 percent California Gamay. These wines sell in many Northwest markets for under $3 a bottle. With a slight change of proportions, the wine is also being marketed in Washington as a privately labeled wine called Cougar Red.

Valley View's winemaker is John Eagle, who started out in California training to be an actor. Among his assistants is production manager Rob Stuart, whose enthusiasm has helped get the winery a wider following. Valley View's owner, Ann Wisnovsky, who began planting the vineyard in 1972, is very active in day-to-day operations; her son Robert pitches in frequently as marketing director when his studies permit.

**VALLEY VIEW VINEYARD**

| | |
|---|---|
| Owner | Anne Wisnovsky |
| Winemaker | John Eagle |
| Year bonded | 1978 |
| Year first planted | 1972 |
| Vineyard acreage | 25 |
| Principal varieties, acres | Cabernet Sauvignon, 11 |
| | Chardonnay, 6 |
| | Merlot, 2 |
| | Gewurztraminer, 1 |
| Year of first crush | 1978 |
| Production capacity | 20,000 gallons |
| Production in 1983 | 19,000 gallons |
| Awards, 1983 | |
| 1980 Chardonnay: | Silver, Oregon State Fair |
| Oregon Perry | Bronze, Oregon State Fair |
| Rogue White | Bronze, Oregon State Fair |

The winery has won honors for other wines, too, including a silver medal for its Jackson County Chardonnay at the Oregon State Fair. And winemaker John Eagle feels his Gewurztraminer is pretty good, too.

Valley View's location in the Applegate Valley and its proximity to the restored town of Jacksonville make a visit here a perfect excursion from Medford or Ashland. And remember the name: these are good wines indeed.

# *Lodging*

## *Wolf Creek*

### *Wolf Creek Tavern*
Exit 76 from Interstate 5

This stately stage-coach hostelry, the oldest active hotel in Oregon, was acquired by the State Parks Department in 1975 and restored to its 1870s condition. The eight bedrooms are comfortable and furnished with Victorian antiques and claw-footed tubs in the bathrooms. The public parlors have crackling fires. Rates are very reasonable.

Meals are served by a "costumed wench" throughout the day. Pot roast and gravy was the special one night in winter, and the $8 price tag included crab bisque, salad, dessert, and coffee. Oak Knoll wines were featured.

Vernon and Donna Wiard are retiring as concessionaires here at the end of 1984, but they expect that their successors will maintain the standards they have set. Just to have survived is no mean feat; of the sixty "taverns" originally on the Portland-to-Sacramento stage-coach route, the Wolf Creek is the only one to have survived.

## *Grants Pass*

### *Riverside Motel*
971 S.E. Sixth Street
476-6873 or toll-free 800-528-1234

This is a lovely spot for lunch overlooking the Rogue River. It's also the starting point for many of the excursions that take you through spectacular white water on jet boats. If you stay overnight, be sure to get a room with a balcony and a view of the river.

## *Ashland*

### *Columbia Hotel*
262-1/2 E. Main Street
482-3726

Owners Roxanne and Owen Jones apprenticed in Austrian hotels and know their business from the ground up. And that's where they are now, a flight above Ashland's bustling Main Street, with a delightful, European-style hotel: twenty-two very moderately priced rooms.

The lobby is a comfortable salon, with inviting chairs and books, a place where tea is served and chamber music groups occasionally perform. The bedrooms are large and freshly painted, furnished with fluffy new comforters. Some of the rooms have adjoining baths, others share a bath down the hall.

### *Ashland Hills Inn*
Interstate 5 at Highway 66 (Exit 14)
482-8310

A large, well-appointed motel complex, easily the fanciest place in town, with a fine restaurant to match. The wine card offers many Oregon bottlings. Plenty of amenities (swimming pool, tennis courts, putting green) and some terrific views of the mountains. Shuttle service to the theater is available. This is also the starting point for the Rogue River Valley balloon flights.

### *Stratford Inn*
555 Siskiyou Boulevard
488-2151

Here's a comfortable new motel, just four blocks from the theaters, with a heated indoor pool, a spa, and family units that include a kitchen.

### *Ashland Bed & Breakfast Inns*
The increasing popularity of Ashland's Shakespearean Festival has brought to this once-sleepy college town a new sense of its natural beauty as well as an understanding that people who travel any sort of distance to see professional live theater probably won't be satisfied with Motel Six accommodations. Within the past few years, there's been a surge of interest in Bed & Breakfast lodgings in and around Ashland; some are the old-fashioned kind, with a spare room or two converted for travelers, others are essentially small hotels. Make reservations directly with the establishment you select, or call *Bed & Breakfast Central,* a telephone registry provided by the inns, at 488-0338, for information on available rooms.

*Chanticleer,* 120 Gresham Street, 482-1919, is the largest, with six rooms (all with private bath) and an elaborate breakfast for $59 per couple in summer. *Winchester Inn,* whose restaurant is described below, also has six rooms, private baths, and full breakfast, for $60 per couple per night. *Edinburgh Lodge,* 586 E. Main Street, 488-1050, also offers six rooms, private baths, and a hearty breakfast, for $56 for two; a light afternoon tea is served in the parlor. *Coach House Inn,* 70 Coolidge, 482-2257, has six rooms. *Morical House,* 668 N. Main Street, 482-2254, has five rooms, private baths, and a full breakfast. *Ashland Guest Villa* (Lamb's), 634 Iowa, 488-1508, has four rooms and sumptuous breakfasts. *Romeo Inn,* 295 Idaho Street, 488-0884, has a swimming pool and whirlpool in addition to guest rooms. Sourdough pancakes are the specialty at *Miner's Addition,* 737 Siskiyou Boulevard, 482-0562, a B & B with two rooms and somewhat lower prices than the previous entries. The *B Street House,* 111 B Street, 482-4217, has three rooms sleeping a total of 8 guests, with 1-1/2 baths and a large kitchen; the entire house rents for $85 a day, with guests doing their own cooking. *RoyAl Carter House,* 514 Siskiyou Boulevard, 482-5623, will have three rooms and private baths by summer. *McCall House,* 153 Oak Street, 482-9296, is in a historic Victorian home. *Neil Creek House,* two miles from downtown Ashland at 341 Mowetza Drive, 482-1334, offers two guest rooms on five acres, plus a Shakespearean library in both English and German; the rate is $65 per couple, with a two-day minimum stay. And more: *Scenic View,* 467 Scenic Dr., 482-2315; *Iris Inn,* 59 Manzanita, 488-2286; *Wisteria House,* 453 Allison, 488-2302.

The Ashland zip code, valid for all of the addresses above, is 97520.

## *Jacksonville*

## *Livingston Mansion*
4132 Livingston Road
899-7107

This rambling, shingled beauty, flanked by oak and madrona trees, offers six richly furnished guest rooms overlooking the Rogue River Valley. In summer, the hum of bees in the wisteria and the honking geese soothe you as you sit beside the sparkling pool. In winter, the crackle of a fire in the grate welcomes your return to the Regal Suite (with its freshly ironed sheets) at the end of the day; another friendly fireplace greets you at breakfast in the morning. And what a breakfast! Fresh orange juice, "breakfast cookies" of whole grain and fruit, eggs Benedict, lashings of freshly ground coffee. Sherry Lossing, in this memorable setting two miles outside Jacksonville, has breathed new life into the time-worn phrase, "You're welcome."

### *Jacksonville Inn*
175 E. California
899-1900

This hotel, restaurant, and wine shop are housed in one of the most successfully restored buildings in this town full of interesting restorations. Owners Jerry and Linda Evans have refurbished eight guest rooms with antiques appropriate to the 1890s, and the effect is rather like a refined boarding house: spare, but in excellent taste. The modern touch is individual air conditioning for each room and private baths; accommodations are moderately priced and very sought-after, so it's a good idea to book well in advance.

The restaurant in the lower level, styled like an elegant bistro, serves classic dinners with a selection of 500 wines, thanks to the superbly stocked shop upstairs. Entrees range from prime rib to veal and seafood dishes; half portions are available for children.

### *McCully House*
240 California
899-1942

One of Jacksonville's most significant mansions, lovingly restored, is now a Bed & Breakfast. Rates are comparable to other B & Bs, which is to say expensive, but it's such a treat to spend a night or two in a home whose Classic Revival architecture has earned it a place on the National Register of Historic Places. Under the new owners, there's a full breakfast, too.

Two other Jacksonville B & B inns are the *Judge Touvelle House* (899-8223) and the *Farm House* (899-8963).

The zip code for Jacksonville is 97530.

## *Oregon Caves*

### *Oregon Caves Chateau*
Highway 46, nineteen miles from Cave Junction
Caves Toll Station Number 1

This lodge, operated under concession over the summer months only, was built at roughly the same time as Timberline Lodge on Mount Hood, although with less artistry. Still, it's an impressive, six-story building, with a stream running through the dining room, comfortable chairs in front of the lobby fireplace, and moderately priced bedrooms. Cabins are also available near the entrance to the cave itself, with views of the Siskiyous. Write for reservations to Oregon Caves Company, Oregon Caves, OR 97523.

Tours of the cave are considered strenuous, and take about an hour. Eight species of bats live in the cave, incidentally, as do rodents and rabbits. There's a baby-sitting service for children under six, who are not permitted on the tour. A number of trails lead past mountain streams, wildlife, mossy cliff sides, and dense underbrush.

## Cave Junction

### Junction Inn Motel
Redwood Highway (U.S. 199) at Caves Highway
592-3106

A comfortable, modern, sixty-unit motel conveniently located within easy driving distance of the Oregon Caves. A playground for children and a heated pool are among the amenities.

# *Restaurants*

### Merlin

### Merlin Mining Company
330 Merlin Avenue
479-2849

How unexpected that this little community on the banks of Jumpoff Joe Creek northwest of Grants Pass should have a decent restaurant, let alone a restaurant with an all-Oregon wine list. In an old grange and community center, restaurateur Buzz Baldwin and attorney Mike Bird have put this together, a straightforward menu of steaks, chicken, seafood, and "Miner's Stew," with about twenty moderately priced bottlings. There's a theater in the building, too, where old-fashioned, boo-the-villain melodrama is performed on weekends.

### Jacksonville

### Bella Union
170 W. California
899-1856

This quaint and cozy cafe, once used as a location setting for a scene from

"The Great Northfield, Minnesota, Raid," has grown to include a large new dining area, two small private rooms, and an upstairs banquet facility. Local artists exhibit their work in the Arts Alliance dining room, while historically important photographs by pioneer Peter Britt are displayed in a banquet room upstairs.

In summer, there's a deck for outdoor seating, a veritable vine-clad bower.

Breakfast, lunch, weekend brunch, dinner, are all imaginatively prepared and professionally served. And at reasonable prices, too.

### Pioneer Village
725 N. Fifth Street
899-1683

Well, the food and the wine list have their ups and downs, but this place is lots of fun: two dozen historic buildings, horse-drawn carriages, mining equipment, old-time theater in summer.

## Talent

### Chata
1212 S. Pacific Highway
535-2575

Much of what we seek out and heartily recommend is embodied in this family-run restaurant. The names of the dishes trip off the tongue like assurances of a cossetting mother: *mamaliga, golabki, musaka.* The flavors and textures are exotic yet reassuringly healthful: pickled cabbage, caraway, smoked pork, tomato sour cream, buckwheat groats, custards. Even the restaurant's name, Chata, brings to mind the love and traditions of a thatched-roof cottage in a Polish village.

The dining rooms are bathed in a warm golden light illuminating stencilled walls and red-napped tables. From the bar, a vital yet comfortable hub of white-washed walls and crackling fire, Josef Slowkowski dispenses his unique welcome and philosophy; his wife Eileen's careful eye embraces the dining room and kitchen. Josef's ties to his native Poland are reflected in the profusion of folk art, the handmade gift items, and the weavings that cover the walls, all for sale, incidentally.

The wine list covers the world without slighting the local product, and in summer, there's a grape arbor where you can sit in the dappled sunlight to savor your wine, time, and *bigos.*

## Ashland

### Change of Heart
139 E. Main Street
488-0235

A fine, relaxed place for an early dinner before the theater. The sidewalk blackboard catches your eye, and a broad staircase leads to the handsomely restored second floor, where comfortable tables overlook the street.

Chef Jeff Keys directs the preparation of an elaborate and eclectic menu, with ingredients as fresh as possible.

### Chateaulin
50 E. Main Street
482-2264

A tiny restaurant with provincial decor, Chateaulin features a classic French menu put together by chef David Taub. The pates, sweetbreads, and veal dishes are particularly good. If you have theater tickets, let maitre d' Michael Donovan know, and he'll make sure you make your curtain. Some people come in at six o'clock for a full meal, others at 7:30 just for appetizers, others wait until the theater crowd has left and come in at nine. Actually, the theaters are only a block away, and the cozy bar is very inviting; the nicest time is after the theater, when cast and crew often stop by for a drink.

### Clark Cottage Restaurant
568 E. Main Street
482-2293

Vern Weiss, a transplanted Portlander, lived in Ashland for many years before getting into the restaurant business, but he's doing it right; the croissants, breads, quiches, cakes, and sweet rolls are all made from scratch in a bright cottage tucked behind a gallery and bookstore. Breakfasts include *Hoppelpoppel*, a dish we haven't seen in years (it's a sort of German fritatta). Two homemade soups and a variety of sandwiches are offered at lunch. Dinners (yes, dinners, too) include staples such as filet mignon, stuffed Cornish game hens, and fettuccine. Wine is on its way.

### Creperie at Banbury Cross

55 N. Main Street
482-3644

A delightful little place tucked into a basement corner of the plaza that overlooks Ashland Creek. The entree crepes are hearty, the dessert crepes delicious, and half portions are available. And there's sparkling cider, just like in Brittany. Open daily until 7:30.

### Winchester Inn

35 South Second Street
488-1115

This beautifully restored Victorian house—one of Ashland's Grand Old Ladies—has expanded from a Bed & Breakfast Inn to full-fledged restaurant. A good thing, too, because more people can enjoy it this way.

The dining rooms, overlooking a terraced garden, are elegantly simple: oak floors, blond bentwood chairs, white linen, beautiful china, spare but pleasing artwork on the walls. Great care is taken with the presentation of the dishes, but on our visit the flavors lacked intensity and interest. A cup of vegetable soup called The Cultivator was beautifully arranged: fresh leaf spinach, large slices of carrots, sliced celery, potato and turnip chunks, and melted cheese over the whole underseasoned arrangement. Moderately priced at both lunch and dinner.

# Wine Shops & Delicatessens

## Ashland

### Ashland Wine Cellar

38 C Street
488-2111

Underneath the state liquor store isn't the best possible location for a wine shop, but this one does just fine, with a good assortment of Oregon bottles and daily wine tastings.

## Brother's Restaurant & Delicatessen
95 N. Main Street
482-9671

This New York-style kosher deli will serve you a sit-down lunch, dinner, or hearty breakfast. But if you're in a hurry, you can buy a wonderful toasted bagel with cream cheese to go, or some sumptuous sandwich combination, and head for the hills.

## Wizard's Den
59 N. Main Street
482-4867

No Caliban or Ariel in this Wizard's Den, which is an antique shop, wine shop, and deli combined in a handsome installation right on Ashland's plaza. A good selection of Oregon wines, delicious French bread, and pastries, all sold alongside the antiques. Ready-made lunches are sold, or you can buy your own combinations to take on a stroll through Lithia Park.

## Jacksonville

## Jacksonville Inn Wine and Gift Shop
175 E. California
899-1900

The wine shop, part of the hotel described earlier, merits mention on its own, being particularly well stocked with wines of the Umpqua and Rogue valleys.

## Medford

## Harry & David's Bear Creek Store and Reject Fruit Stand
2836 S. Pacific Highway
776-2277

This famous mail-order house (they sent out eighty-million catalogs and brochures last year) also holds one of Oregon's currently valid licenses to make wine. It turns out that they make their own fruit vinegars. They ferment the juice before letting it change into vinegar, and their permit lets them make the alcoholic base for the vinegar.

The Bear Creek Store sells a wide range of Oregon-made products, including jams, jellies, gifts, and so on, as well as a large selection of Oregon wines. You can buy a bottle to consume with a light lunch at the little Cafe les 2 Bears, or have an English tea there in the afternoon. Ask Fred DeSimone, who runs the fruit stand, to help you pick some "reject" fruit for a picnic in one of Medford's parks.

# Picnic Spots

## In and around Ashland

### Lithia Park

This has to be one of the state's prettiest parks. You can picnic almost anywhere in this ninety-nine-acre complex: on green lawns, under shaded trees, amid bursts of flowers, or beside a cool pond. If you have any leftovers, you can feed them to the swans.

### Mount Ashland

In the Siskiyou Range eighteen miles south of Ashland, Mount Ashland is a well-known ski resort and a fine destination for summer picnics as well. There's a campground just below the summit, where wildflowers bloom in July, and the seventy-five-mile Loop Drive makes a beautiful excursion.

### Emigrant Lake

Just six miles south of downtown Ashland on Highway 66, the lake is a county park, and includes camping, picnic grounds, beaches, boat ramps, and swimming.

## In and around Jacksonville

The grounds of the Peter Britt Music Festival, with its tree-shaded garden, are open all year (First Street south of California). There's also a municipal park adjacent to the old courthouse (now the Jacksonville Museum) on Fifth Street; the museum has maps of the town for visitors. And Pioneer Village, a privately owned attraction at 725 N. Fifth, has picnic facilities.

## In and around Medford

### Bear Creek Park

Bear Creek, a tributary of the Upper Rogue, runs through Medford and provides five miles of biking, jogging, and nature trails, as well as picnic areas.

### Valley of the Rogue

Interstate 5, twelve miles east of Grants Pass

This state park at first appears to be a standard freeway rest area, but it's much more. There are well-appointed picnic sites, campgrounds, boating, fishing, all in a splendid setting on the shores of the Rogue River.

## Applegate Valley

### McKee Bridge Park

The bridge is south of Ruch, along Highway 238, in a lovely setting along the gently flowing Applegate.

### Cantrall Buckley Park

This is an attractive recreation area on the south side of the Applegate, opposite Valley View Vineyards.

## Siskiyou National Forest / Oregon Caves

The best place to picnic is at the Caves Monument itself. We've described it in some detail in the Lodging section, above.

### The Last Resort, Lake Selmac

597-4989

A rustic campground at Lake Selmac, ten miles northeast of Cave Junction. Campsites, picnic tables, and recreational facilities (boat and bike rentals, swimming, nature trails) are available.

### Woodland Deer Park

A tourist attraction one mile south of Cave Junction, the park has deer, sheep, bison, monkeys, and ostriches to look at, and picnic tables to sit at.

# Oregon Coast

This chapter is hardly a definitive guide to the Oregon coast, and covers only the coastline between Astoria and Florence. There are several guidebooks to the Oregon coast, which is the state's single most popular tourist attraction. Our objective is to show tourists how the two coastal wineries, at Astoria and Nehalem, fit in with the rest of the attractions along the coast.

A case in point is the Newport Seafood and Wine Festival, held annually on the last weekend in February. Another is the Tillamook County Cheese, Food & Wine Tour, a very informal tour that begins at the Nehalem Bay Winery and ends twenty-six miles further south along Highway 101 at the Blue Heron French Cheese Factory in Tillamook. (More about Pat McCoy and the winery in a moment.) The other stops on the tour include Phil & Joe's in Garibaldi (for crabs); Smith's on Fisherman's Wharf in Garibaldi (for shrimp); the Bay Front Bakery in Garibaldi (for fresh pastries and bread); Art & Dick's in Bay City (for sausages); and the Tillamook Cheese Factory north of Tillamook (for a self-guided tour of an enormous cheese factory). The Blue Heron also makes cheese, and sells picnic-makings, too.

The magnificent scenery of the Oregon coast transcends the drab commercialism of several coastal towns (and even raucous challenges to its beauty in places like Lincoln City). This is not to say that the coastline ought to be regarded as pristine; parts of it have always been associated with the country's shipping and logging. Astoria, for example, has retained much of its maritime flavor; the old lightship *Columbia* is accessible to visitors. Nearby, Fort Clatsop National Memorial recreates the living conditions that faced the Lewis and Clark Expedition a century ago. Yet, further south, Gearhart has retained a backwater calm: 800 year-round residents, one or two tennis courts, a golf course, a solitary traffic signal, and a single beach-front street of restored Victorian summer houses.

Tourist attractions of all sorts line the coastal highway. The Marine Science Center in Newport, run by Oregon State University, provides an educational look at undersea life; there's a good aquarium in Seaside, too. Museums depicting pioneer life are open to the public in Astoria and Tillamook. In Garibaldi, a logging locomotive stands on a siding for kids to climb over. The Sitka Center for Art and Ecology, a respected institute for concerts, talks, and workshops, is located at Cascade Head, north of Lincoln City.

Other cultural activities are not numerous, but they do exist (and are active in summer): the Nehalem Bay Players, for instance, perform "Shakespeare in the Park" in Manzanita Park; and the Coaster Theater players perform at a theater in Cannon Beach. Cannon Beach also sponsors an annual Sandcastle Day (in June) for would-be sculptors. And antique shops abound along the coast, from Astoria to Bay City.

Opportunities for outdoor recreation are almost everywhere. Deep-sea fishing is available (full- or half-day excursions) at Seaside, Depoe Bay, or Newport. For the landlubbers, there's clam digging, too.

But the greatest attractions of the coast are still its natural wonders. Haystack Rock is one of the world's largest coastal monoliths and literally looms over Cannon Beach. The surf has carved a swirling hollow out of coastal rock at Devil's Punchbowl. Time and again, the vistas from Highway 101 are nothing less than breathtaking. And fortunately, the actual beach is all in the public domain.

# Nehalem Bay

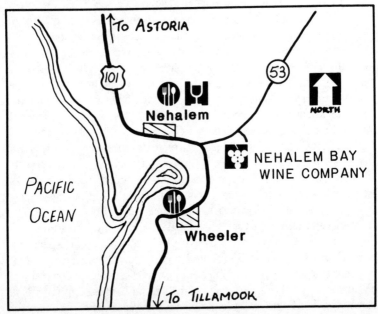

This lovely stretch of coast, outside the little village of Nehalem, is an unlikely site for a winery, but the man who runs it is an unlikely sort of fellow, too: big, jovial, outgoing, seriously committed to tourism on the Oregon coast. The winery is housed in a pretty building, a converted cheese factory with a Tudor facade and its own railroad siding.

Nehalem Bay Winery started out in 1973 as a fruit and berry operation. Grape wines have since been added, purchased mainly from wineries in the Tualatin and Willamette valleys. By 1981, half the winery's output was vinifera: Cabernet Sauvignon, Pinot Noir, White Riesling, and two blends, Nehalem White and Nehalem Red. And until just recently, everything was sold right at the winery.

The man behind this alluring roadside attraction is Pat McCoy, a talented, witty, iconoclastic promoter, who started the winery in 1973. With tens of thousands of visitors a year, Nehalem Bay Winery has much more tourist traffic than any of the "inland" wineries. His tasting room offers an array of wines "for all tastes," as well as an art gallery in the upstairs loft.

McCoy does not distribute Nehalem Bay's output through traditional

---

### ▓ NEHALEM BAY WINE CO.
34965 Highway 53
Route 1, Box 440
Nehalem, OR 97131
368-5300

| | |
|---|---|
| Open to the public | 10-5 daily |
| Tour groups | yes |
| Charge for tour groups | none |
| Wines available (1984) | Cabernet Sauvignon |
| | Pinot Noir |
| | Chardonnay |
| | Rose |
| | Blackberry |
| | Plum |
| Owner & winemaker | Patrick McCoy |
| Year bonded | 1973 |
| Production capacity | 30,000 gallons |
| Production in 1983 | 12,000 gallons |

---

wine shops or restaurants; instead, they are sold only at the winery's tasting room and at the tasting room of the Blue Heron French Cheese Factory, twenty-three miles down the coast at Tillamook. Nor does McCoy enter competitions. Nehalem Bay has recently added a $5 cork-finished Tillamook Blackberry wine, which is being shipped to distributors in Portland and Seattle. "Everybody expects blackberry," McCoy says, "but my grape wines are actually outselling the fruit wines. What's important is to get people to *taste* wine first. Nonvarietal wines are a better way to start." Indeed several wine writers over the past few years have praised the Nehalem Bay's Blackberry Wine in particular.

McCoy is a former broadcaster with a flair for the theatrical. A couple of years ago, he transported a pack of young pigs (Yorkshires and Berkshires from Seaside) to an island in the Columbia River, intending to harvest a regular crop of "wild boar" for gourmet restaurants and festivals at Nehalem Bay Winery. Looking for all the world like Orson Welles, McCoy solemnly assured the assembled reporters and TV cameras that he would "kill no swine before its time."

# *Shallon*

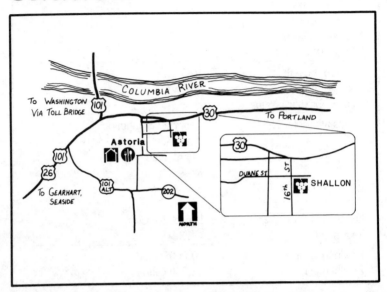

The name of the plant, an evergreen shrub related to wintergreen, with white flowers and edible black fruit that resembles large huckleberries, is *Gaultheria shallon*, commonly known as salal. The berries are dry and bland; birds like them.

So does Paul van der Veldt, Oregon's most unusual winemaker. Not only has he named his winery for the *Gaultheria* plant, he wants to make *wine* from salal as well. And why not? He's already making wine from peaches, blackberries, and cranberries. As soon as he solves a couple of problems (salal berries are dry, their flavor intense, but federal regulations won't permit him to dilute the juice because the acid level is too low), he'll be making salal wine as well. "Salal berries are the least utilized berries on the West Coast," van der Veldt points out. "They have a taste like no other berry. Intense and pungent, tangy. I've seen some salal jelly in gourmet shops, but nothing else."

A visit to Shallon will convince you that this is a winery like no other. The building formerly housed a freezer-locker business, and contained a ready-made lab, office, and well-insulated storage space when van der Veldt started up the winery in 1978. Among the improvements he made was to apply some paint. Today, the walls of the windowless "manufacturing room" are covered with bright pink plastic epoxy, and the floor is bright

---

**▓ SHALLON**
1598 Duane Street
Astoria, OR 97103
325-5978

| Open to the public | 12-6 daily |
| Tour groups | by appointment |

| Wines available (1984) | Peach |
| | Wild Evergreen Blackberry |
| | Cran du Lait |
| | Salal |

---

green. ("Pink, blue, and green are my favorite colors," van der Veldt explains.) To create the illusion of windows, he commissioned a *trompe l'oeil* mural; it depicts a scene from the Astoria harbor in 1811 in one of the four panels, and, in another, the airship *Akron* over Astoria in 1932. Van der Veldt's flights of whimsy aside, this is perhaps the most rigorously sanitary winery in the state.

He plays classical music when he's in the lab, observing the millions of yeast cells jostling in a drop of wine. "There's got to be some kind of consciousness there," van der Veldt told a visitor once. A consciousness that would respond to the "vibrations" of music. And so he plays music: trumpet music while mashing the fruit, Vivaldi's *Four Seasons* as it starts to ferment, chamber music for the duration of the fermentation process. And what's the result? The Blackberry wine, made from wild, handpicked berries, reminds you of the woods in which they were picked, rather than of syrup. Van der Veldt insists on using local products, preferably from the surrounding, Lower Columbia area. In addition to native berries, and peaches from Maryhill, Washington, those products include cranberries (shipped to Ocean Spray processing plants further north) and milk (used further south in Tillamook cheese). He is the first to combine the two.

Cran du Lait is the first wine ever made from cranberries and whey (the liquid portion of milk that remains after the manufacture of cheese). Until recently, cranberries were thought to be too acidic to make wine, and whey wasn't thought to have enough flavor (although a self-styled monk in Alaska produced some for a time). Van der Veldt has fermented the two together, producing a "breakthrough" that's neither a blend of cranberry wine and whey wine, nor whey wine flavored with cranberries. He suggests serving it in a punch, mixed with soda water, or in wine desserts in place of Marsala.

Another product of the winery is Gillnetter's Delight, a blended red table

| SHALLON | |
|---|---|
| Owner & winemaker | Paul C. van der Veldt |
| Year bonded | 1978 |
| Year of first crush | 1978 |
| Production capacity | 2,500 gallons |
| Production in 1983 | 1,006 gallons |
| Awards, 1983 | |
| Peach: | Gold, Oregon State Fair |

wine that commemorates the old fishing village of Clifton, Oregon; it was Paul's father, Ted Vanderveldt, who built the first road to the village.

One more project van der Veldt intends to develop: a lemon wine that recreates the flavor of the lemon meringue pies his mother, Esther, used to make. He's thinking about marketing the wine with a package of cookies that have the taste of meringue-topped crust. Don't wait for the next edition of this book to find out how van der Veldt is getting on; go see and taste for yourselves!

# *Lodging*

*Communities are listed from north to south*

## *Seaview, Washington*

### *Shelburne Inn*
Pacific Highway at J Street
(206) 642-2442

Only thirteen miles from the bridge that crosses the Columbia to Astoria, yet remote from other parts of Washington, the Shelburne is an integral part of the Lower Columbia area. It's a historic place to stay, with intimate, homey rooms and furnishings. Tony Kischner, the longtime manager of Rosellini's The Other Place in Seattle, has begun a program of renovating public rooms; he has already installed an innovative chef and a terrific wine list.

## *Astoria*

### *Rosebriar Inn*
636 14th Street
325-7427

A Bed & Breakfast inn that's in a renovated turn-of-the-century mansion, the Rosebriar has eight guest rooms. Buffet breakfast included.

## *Gearhart*

### *Eat Your Heart Inn*
601 Pacific Way
738-9691

This two-room B & B grew out of a catering service and deli in Portland called Eat Your Heart Out. The coastal outpost had a couple of extra rooms upstairs, which were remodeled to retain the charm of an old beach house (claw-footed tubs, for instance) while replacing the sagging furniture with new beds, couches, and chairs. Coffee from the deli is on the house, and we suspect you'll want to add some freshly baked bread or croissants for breakfast.

---

## *Seaside*

### *Riverside Inn*
430 S. Holladay Drive
738-8254

Those who remember Seaside's carnival atmosphere in an earlier day may be surprised to find the "new" Seaside, with a motel complex going in where the ferris wheel and amusement park once attracted teenagers of all ages. Seaside has gone up-scale, with a marathon, a Holiday Inn, and condominiums.

As an alternative to impersonal lodgings, the Riverside Inn offers "the warmth and charm of grandmother's house" and the hospitality of a family of innkeepers—Catherine Matthias, her daughter, Lisa Laser, and her mother, Kay Matthias. The inn encompasses seven guest rooms and cabins and overlooks the Necanicum River, which flows through Seaside to the ocean. Each unit has a separate entrance. Breakfast is included in the moderate price; there are excellent midweek and off-season specials (three nights for under $60).

## *Cannon Beach*

### *Seasprite Motel*
Tolovano Park Store
and
### *Hearthstone Inn*
Hemlock Street
436-2266

These two small inns are owned by Stephen Tuckman, who also owns the Riverside Inn in Seaside. The Seasprite has six units on the beach, with kitchens and fireplaces; the Hearthstone, with a less-favored location, is newer and more spacious.

---

## Gleneden Beach

---

### Salishan Lodge
Highway 101
764-2371

As a resort, Salishan has no equal on the coast, with beautifully appointed suites in low, cedar-sided buildings that blend into the landscape. Amenities include a superb golf course, an indoor swimming pool with sauna and Jacuzzi, tennis courts, access to a private beach, a pleasant bar, and a series of nature trails into the foliage around the golf course where deer and jackrabbits make regular appearances.

As a restaurant, Salishan's Gourmet Dining Room has won unprecedented accolades for its wine cellar. Assembled by Phil de Vito, the wine list was impressive enough to win one of only twelve Grand Awards from *Wine Spectator*, a national wine publication; thousands of bottles are in the restaurant's specially built wine cellar. Ask for a special tour of this unique facility.

---

## Depoe Bay

---

### The Inn at Otter Crest
Highway 101 Loop
765-2111

This resort has one of the most dramatic settings on the coast: a steep hillside overlooking Cape Foulweather. Cars are left at the top of the bluff, and a tramway or shuttle bus takes you down to your rooms, which are spacious, comfortable, and include a television set and a kitchen.

### Channel House
Highway 101
765-2140

The restaurant, specializing in seafood, overlooks the harbor and bay; you can sometimes see whales quite close by in the ocean. Seven rooms are also available, with fireplaces and kitchens, whirlpool baths, decks, and superb views of the channel. Continental breakfasts, too. Write to P.O. Box 49, Depoe Bay, OR 97341.

## Newport

### Embarcadero
1000 S.E. Bay Boulevard
265-8521

This large condominium and motel complex overlooks Yaquina Bay and its busy fishing fleet. The units are well appointed, and there's lots to do in the area: swimming, charter fishing, browsing in the shops along nearby Bayfront.

## Yachats

### Adobe Motel
Highway 101 one-half mile north of Yachats
547-3141

The fireplaces in the original, cliffside motel are made of adobe brick, just one of the reasons that this motel remains one of the classics on the coast. There's a good dining room, and a decent wine cellar, too.

### Shamrock Lodgettes
Highway 101
547-3312

Don't let the cutesy name put you off. The Shamrock is a (pardon the expression) real find: a conservative complex of housekeeping cabins with stone fireplaces and efficiency kitchens. Sheets are changed every three days on request, the newspaper is delivered daily, and well-behaved pets are welcome. Some cabins have ocean views, some overlook the river; all enjoy the peace and quiet of a four-acre park and a clean, sandy beach.

## Florence

### Johnson House
216 Maple Street
997-8000

A Bed & Breakfast inn at the oldest house in Florence. Double rooms cost $28 a night, which includes a full breakfast. A good place to stay while exploring Florence, which is one of the unsung treasures on the Oregon coast.

# *Restaurants*

## *Nahcotta, Washington*

### *The Ark*
Peninsula Road
(206)-665-4133
   Along with the nearby Shelburne Inn, the Ark is turning Washington's
isolated Long Beach Peninsula into an outpost of gastronomic achievement.
The owners, Jimella Lucas and Nanci Main, have been "discovered" by
James Beard, and have published an elegant cookbook. Their cooking is
innovative and imaginative, featuring combinations like prawns with feta
cheese and ouzo, or oysters baked with cheese and bacon. The wine list
emphasizes Northwest bottles.

## *Astoria*

### *The Columbian Cafe*
11th and Marine Drive
325-2233
   Here's a hole in the wall, mainly vegetarian until late afternoon, then a
terrific spot for fresh seafood, homemade pasta, and the best espresso bar
on the Lower Columbia.

### *Andrew & Steve's Cafe*
1196 Marine Drive
325-5762
   A family restaurant that's been here since 1916, this cafe offers the best
values for miles around. They cut and prepare their own meat and fish for a
demanding clientele of longshoremen and fishermen.

## *Seaside*

### *Norma's*
102 Broadway
738-6170
   The tourists line up early here for a cup of the clam chowder and a piece
of peanut-butter pie.

---

## Crab Broiler
Highway 101 at Route 26
738-5313

A very popular place, and consistently satisfying. The cracked crab and coleslaw plate is one of our favorites, but others enjoy the barbecued crab, or just the onion rings.

The gift shop here carries a good selection of Northwest wines.

---

## Cannon Beach

---

### Ron Martin's Bistro
263 N. Hemlock
436-2661

Come here on a rainy night for a quiet little dinner. The restaurant is tucked away at the back of a courtyard called the Weighing Station Shops, and features Italian specialties as well as fresh seafood.

### Cafe de la Mer
1287 S. Hemlock
436-1179

Located in the premises formerly occupied by the Bald Eagle, Cafe de la Mer retains the greenhouse-like patio, but upgrades the cuisine: pates, seafood, rich desserts.

---

## Nehalem

---

### The Kitchen Table
Highway 101
368-5538

Breakfast and lunch only here, in a little town lined with antique shops. The owners, Janet Bush and Cathy Clark, bake their own bread.

### River Sea Inn
380 Marine Drive, Wheeler (two miles south of Nehalem)
368-5789

The chef here, Nick Recio, is also the owner, and has allowed himself to cut loose with an eclectic menu that runs from standard steaks to Japanese dishes, Italian cioppino, and huevos rancheros.

## Tillamook

### McClaskey's
First Street at Pacific Avenue
842-5674

Tillamook Bay oysters are available here, and where could they be fresher? Seafood is offered at breakfast, too, with a seafood omelet and seafood Benedict on the menu.

## Newport

### Mo's
Bayfront

A classic place that serves the best clam chowder on the coast. The atmosphere is good natured, with communal benches, shrimp sandwiches on untoasted hamburger buns, and nothing stronger to drink than milk.

## Lincoln City

### Bay House
5911 S.W. Highway 101
996-3222

In a very soothing atmosphere on Siletz Bay, you are served fresh fish, or something a little more exotic, like scallops with a homemade chutney.

## Waldport

### The Experience
3750 Highway 34, three miles east of Waldport
563-4555

The cashew and kumquat pie produced by Janice Willinger and Betty Hoffmaster is the stuff of legend. They are back at the restaurant again, running the whole show all by themselves as far as anyone can tell, turning out a wide range of seafood dinners: fresh crab legs, oysters, clams, halibut, geoducks, plus unusual specials such as shrimp in black bean sauce.

# Wine Shops & Delicatessens

## Gearhart

### Eat Your Heart Out

601 Pacific Way

This wonderful delicatessen has no equal along the coast. Croissants and cinnamon rolls are snapped up by waiting summer people as soon as they come out of the oven, and six tables are set up for those who can't wait to get home.

## Cannon Beach

### The Wine Shack

Coaster Theater Square

436-1100

A good choice of Northwest wines here, along with specials on California bottles and imports.

### Laurel's Wine Shop

263 N. Hemlock

436-1666

Laurel Hood has set out to create the best wine shop on the coast, emphasizing Oregon wines but promoting other wine values (such as good jug wines, for instance).

## Nehalem

### Beverage Bin

Highway 101

368-5295

Nehalem itself is only a couple of blocks long, and it sometimes seems as if two dozen antique shops line the streets. The Beverage Bin, run by Ione Peters, is a serious shop that sells most of the wines produced by Oregon wineries.

## Garibaldi

### Phil & Joe's Crab Company
Highway 101
322-3410

A great spot to stock up on fresh crab and other seafood. There's a shaded picnic table alongside the store, in case you can't wait to find a spot on the beach.

### Smith's Pacific Shrimp Company
608 Commercial Street

You've never seen anything like this operation on Fisherman's Wharf: the shrimps go from the boat through peelers, cookers, separators, extractors, pickers, and packers, to the finished shrimp cocktail. Tours in summer, sales all year.

## Tillamook

### Blue Heron French Cheese Factory
Highway 101, at the northern city limits

The freshly made cheese is a straightforward Camembert. A number of delicatessen items are also stocked, as are some wines.

## Lincoln City

### Shipwreck Cellars
3521 S.W. Highway 101
996-3221

A delightful tasting room owned by Oak Knoll. The same wines are poured and sold here as at the winery outside of Hillsboro.

### Oceans West at Boatyard Village
30 S.E. Highway 101 (at the D River)
994-2755

A one-stop tourist complex, with an art gallery, gift shops, crafts display, grocery, all built around a tasting room for Honeywood winery.

# Picnic Spots

## Astoria

### Fort Stevens State Park
Off Highway 101
Ten miles west of Astoria

The site of a Civil War fort, whose bunkers are still in place, this is Oregon's largest state park. The wreck of the *Peter Iredale*, a British sailing ship, lies on the beach. There's a large, multi-purpose campground, with hiking trails, bike paths, picnic facilities, and an excellent visitor information center.

## Coastal Parks

The Oregon coastline is literally a public playground, thanks to legislation passed early in this century. Thus one doesn't have to look far for picnic spots. There are literally dozens of attractive viewpoints, waysides, and turnouts between Astoria and Florence, and they overlook some of the most magnificent pieces of coastline in Oregon. Almost all have picnic facilities, and many have nature trails as well. Following are some particular favorites.

### Ecola State Park
Cannon Beach

A quiet cove near the end of the Lewis and Clark Trail, with a view of Haystack Rock.

### Oswald West State Park
Manzanita

Ten miles south of Cannon Beach on Highway 101, this magnificent park is on a dramatic coastal headland. It's named for the Oregon governor whose foresight kept the entire coastline in the public domain. Thirty-six picnic tables, and trails into the park's own rain forest.

# Mount Hood Loop

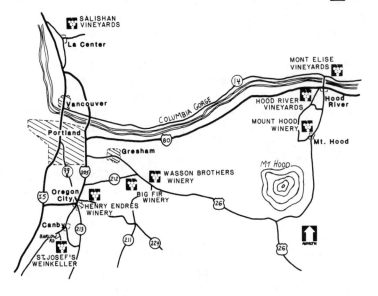

We consolidated the wineries east of Portland into a single chapter because of their proximity to the Mount Hood Loop, one of Oregon's prime scenic attractions. Throughout this developing wine country, which forms a large half-moon from the southeast Portland suburbs to the Columbia Gorge, "The Mountain" dominates the landscape, appearing unexpectedly from time to time as you travel along, its giant, friendly presence peering above the treetops and the fields.

The Mount Hood Highway, Route 26 eastbound from Portland, provides the axis for this chapter. As the highway leaves the pastures and enters the evergreen forests, you come upon a full-fledged resort complex at Welches, then a succession of smaller trailer camps and motels. The highway climbs and winds through the tall firs and little towns; you pass a string of gas stations, general stores, tourist cabins in Sandy, Wemme, Brightwood, Zig Zag, Rhododendron. At the highway's highest point, Government Camp, a wide range of slopes attract the day-skiers, while others proceed up a wind-

---

ing spur to Timberline Lodge. It's a side trip we heartily recommend for the view of the Cascades and a look at the lodge itself.

Followers of the wine trail will then head north on Highway 35 toward Hood River, stopping perhaps at the community of Mount Hood to visit the Mount Hood Winery before proceeding to the Columbia River.

The Columbia ranks fourth among North America's great rivers, behind the Mississippi, the Saint Lawrence, and the Mackenzie. It drains a basin that extends from the Rockies to the Pacific Ocean; it has twice the flow of the Nile, ten times as much as the Colorado. And much of that flow courses through the Columbia Gorge, a sixty-mile chasm of basalt between The Dalles and Portland that's one of the Northwest's most spectacular sights.

The great river, explored by Lewis and Clark in their expedition of 1804, has been tamed now by massive dams, from the Grand Coulee to Bonneville, and a scenic highway lines its banks. Around Hood River, on the sunny hillsides above the Columbia, it's possible to grow grapes; several vineyards have been planted, and there are two wineries. It's an area of unmatched natural beauty, wildlife, and recreation. The Columbia at Hood River also provides some of the continent's best windsurfing, with an international tournament scheduled for the summer of 1984.

The focal point of the region remains Mount Hood itself. As we drove from Oregon City toward Boring and Sandy recently, keeping the mountain in view as the road wound through the filbert groves and fields of blackcap raspberries (with their looping, rambunctious canes tied back for winter), we passed a Lutheran church called Christ the Vine, with—yes—three rows of grapevines planted out front. It seemed a fitting symbol for this rich agricultural land in the shadow of Oregon's highest mountain, an affirmation of the future of winemaking in this corner of the world.

# *Big Fir Winery*

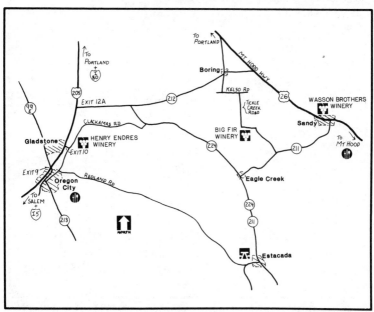

The Big Fir, though struck by lightning some twenty years ago, still towers proudly near the entrance to this 320-acre property; Big Fir Winery occupies a fine, sixty-year-old cow barn in its namesake's shadow. The wines produced here, berry wines made from the crop of the farm, are sold only at the winery itself and at the Saturday market in Portland. Winemaker Bill Miller, a jovial, hearty fellow who exudes equal parts of good will and good sense, is at home in both settings: the crowded bonhomie of the market or the tranquil activity of a long-established working farm.

The farm, at the end of a winding road that runs through the Clackamas County countryside south of Boring (yes, that's the name of the town), is owned by brothers Brinkley and Tony Schedeen; they are also partners with Miller and Sam Pengelly in the winery. One reason they decided to establish the winery was to help assure a market for the berries grown on the property.

For the moment, the farm's berry-picking machine, a huge lumbering device that replaced the crews of (often inebriated) pickers, stands ready to rumble through the fields, its prongs and belts only temporarily inactive. Five men ride this giant harvester, doing the work of twenty pickers; its

---

**BIG FIR WINERY**
17835 S.E. Tickle Creek Road
Boring, OR 97009
658-5769

| | |
|---|---|
| Open to the public | by appointment |
| Tour groups | by appointment |
| Charge for tour groups | none |
| Picnic facilities at the winery | grass, lawn, hillside; no tables |
| Owners | Brinkley, Tony, & Poly Schedeen; Bill Miller; Sam Pengelly |
| Winemakers | Bill Miller & Sam Pengelly |
| Year bonded | 1977 |
| Year of first crush | 1977 |
| Production capacity | 5,000 gallons |
| Production in 1983 | 0 |
| Expansion plans | New plantings; 20,000 gallons additional capacity; picnic and camping facilities; retail shop for all Oregon wines |

---

name, proclaimed by a metal plate fastened to the side of the mechanical monster, is Iron Wino.

The machine didn't pick any berries for Big Fir winery in 1983, however. Bill Miller concentrated instead on production from eighty acres of the farm: evergreen blackberries, marionberries, boysenberries. He hopes to resume winemaking in 1984. One wine we hope he makes again is his Sparkling Marion Blackberry, which won a bronze medal at the Oregon State Fair in 1982. Miller's winemaking technique calls for aging semisweet and dry wines in used whiskey barrels, racking them every two months. Miller used champagne yeasts in the past, but will switch to liquid yeasts when production resumes; he expects this will allow him to induce fermentation at lower temperatures.

The winery's tasting room is earmarked for conversion into a full-fledged retail outlet for all Oregon wines. Miller has been active in the Oregon Winegrowers Association and its marketing efforts; his commitment to the industry explains why he is eager to expand Big Fir's tasting room. The winery's setting is so idyllic, and the drive through the Clackamas County farmland leading here so splendid, that an outlet for all Oregon wines will make an excursion here even more worthwhile.

# *Henry Endres Winery*

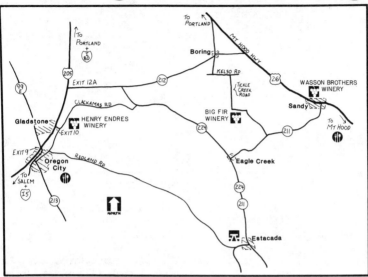

They look like a cascade of little green houses tumbling down a slope above the highway that runs alongside the Clackamas River. An Italian hill town of a winery, all by themselves. The big house at the top of the hill, where the original Henry Endres settled at the turn of the century, still holds most of the equipment, but as the winery has expanded over the years, the family has added a fermenting tank or two or three, and a new building when space ran out, and connected them like blocks.

The most recent addition is Winery D, and at the extremity of this building there's a covered porch for the combined tasting and sales area. A little parking lot at the end of the steep driveway holds the cars and pickups and motorcycles that arrive in a steady stream. The visitors stand at the porch window; they could be buying hot dogs or ice cream. They taste one or two samples from tiny paper cups, then they decide what they want: Loganberry or Niagara or Rhubarb or Elderberry. Everything comes in the same size, a 1.5-liter bottle with a screw cap, and everything costs the same, $7. The clerk wraps the bottles in a brown paper sack, which the customers take away in their cars and pickups and motorcycles.

This goes on all day long. Surveying the traffic, Henry Endres Jr. smiles and notes, "Everybody comes to the winery to buy."

Henry Jr. is a quiet, smiling, good-natured man, rather heavyset and

---

**❦ HENRY ENDRES WINERY**
13300 S. Clackamas River Drive
Oregon City, OR 97045
656-7239

| | |
|---|---|
| Open to the public | sales: 10-7 Mon.-Sat. |
| | winery: by appointment |
| Wines available (1984) | Loganberry |
| | Rhubarb |
| | Concord |
| | Niagara |
| | Mead |
| | Apple |
| Owner | Henry C. Endres |
| Year bonded | 1935 |
| Year of first crush | 1935 |
| Production capacity | 10,000 gallons |
| Production in 1983 | 6,000 gallons |

---

slow-moving, who took over the winery more than thirty years ago from his father, a German immigrant who established the business right after Repeal. Henry Jr., by training a zoologist and public health officer, actually retired from the winery not long ago, moving to an orchard a few miles away where he's planted an acre of vinifera among the fruit trees.

The original wine produced by Henry Endres was Loganberry, and it became famous in the local taverns as Henry's Lowball. It's still around, though it's no longer called Lowball. Henry Jr.'s specialty was Rhubarb, also very popular. For ease of "bookwork," everything has always been sold in one size, which used to be a half-gallon and is now 1.5 liters; everything's always had one price, too. "The Model T Ford theory of marketing: any color you want, as long as it's black." Henry Jr. quotes that with a chuckle.

There's a refreshing simplicity about this place. No competitions, no advertising, no pretensions. Just 6,000 gallons of wine annually, year-in, year-out. That's 12,000 half-gallon bottles. Even the tavern owners buy their cases from the window at the end of Winery D. And the Henry Endres winery sells every drop it makes, right on the premises. You don't tinker with that kind of operation, no sir.

# Hood River Vineyards

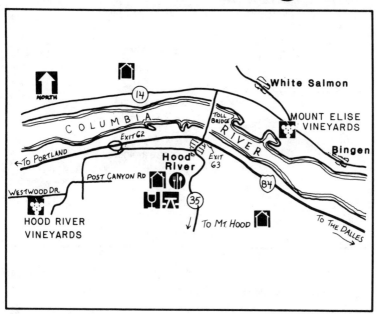

There's a feeling, at the end of this zigzagging road, of being on top of the world, on a high hillside backed by tall evergreens. Here, on a meadow overlooking the Columbia River, Cliff and Eileen Blanchette have converted an old lean-to, actually a cattle loafing barn, into a winery. Across the Gorge, they can see the vineyard in Washington where their grapes are grown; in the other direction, they can see Mount Hood.

Cliff Blanchette's family is from the Alsace region of France. His career has involved the fruit orchards, Post Canyon Farms, and a glass and glazing firm in Hood River. He started as a home winemaker, using fruit that would otherwise have gone to waste. But today, less than one-fifth of his output is fruit wine; the rest is vinifera. He is an unpretentious man, industrious, determined, with high goals. Eileen is welcoming, energetic, and communicative. Together, they traveled through Germany and France, enjoying the people and their wines; together, they have willingly met the challenges life has brought, including eight children (all but two in their twenties now) and wildly fluctuating crop sizes ("It's like going to Reno," he says).

The Blanchetts have twelve acres in grapes, eight in pears (they personally pick the Bartletts); they buy grapes from The Dalles and Bingen as

211

---

### ▓ HOOD RIVER VINEYARDS
4693 Westwood Drive
Hood River, OR 97031
386-3772

| | |
|---|---|
| Open to the public | 1-5 daily except Fri., May-Dec. |
| Tour groups | by appointment |
| Charge for tour groups | none |
| Picnic facilities at the winery | picnic tables under trees |
| Festivals/special events | Blossom Day, late April |
| Wines available (1984) | Riesling |
| | Gewurztraminer |
| | Pinot Noir |
| | Rose |
| | Blanchet Blanc |
| | Pear |
| | Raspberry |

---

well. "There's always something to do at the winery," Cliff says, without complaining. "But it usually isn't something that absolutely has to be done today."

A new tasting room will be built at the winery during 1984, which will make a visit to the Columbia Gorge all the more appealing. The winery holds an open house in late April to coincide with Hood River's Blossom Day, when visitors can follow a designated Blossom Route through the Hood River Valley's pear and apple orchards.

If you can't be in Hood River in spring, there's another chance for great natural beauty in August: a walk through the magnificent wildflower fields at Bird Meadows near Trout Lake. Dates change from year to year, depending on climate, so call the U.S. Forest Service at Trout Lake for more information. The fields are on land belonging to the Yakima Indian Nation, which collects a modest fee from visitors.

As for Hood River Vineyards, it has doubled its production in the past year, and has added a rose, a Blanc de Pinot Noir, and a blended white called Blanchet Blanc to its original line of wines. We also tasted tank samples of Sauvignon Blanc and two Rieslings (which Blanchett will probably blend). Nineteen eighty-three, he points out, was a vintage year, with especially well-balanced wines. And Rieslings figure heavily in his expansion plans.

**HOOD RIVER VINEYARDS**

| | |
|---|---|
| Owners | Cliff & Eileen Blanchette |
| Winemaker | Cliff Blanchette |
| Year bonded | 1981 |
| Year first planted | 1974 |
| Vineyard acreage | 12 |
| Principal varieties, acres | Pinot Noir, 4 |
| | Riesling, 2.5 |
| | Gewurztraminer, 2.5 |
| | Chardonnay, 2.5 |
| Year of first crush | 1981 |
| Production capacity | 8,000 gallons |
| Production in 1983 | 6,000 gallons |
| Expansion plans | 20 acres of vineyards |
| Awards, 1983 | |
| 1981 White Riesling: | Silver, Oregon State Fair |

As always, the varietal wines have a most appealing color, nose, and taste. We suspect, too, that many visitors will enjoy Hood River's prize-winning Pear and Raspberry wines. Especially the Raspberry!

# *Mont Elise Vineyards*

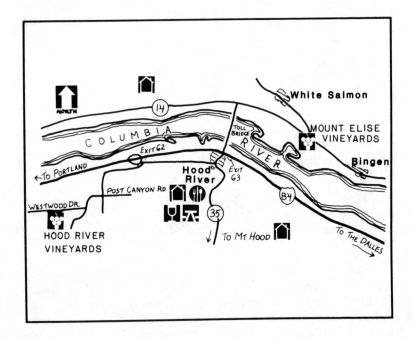

The Columbia Gorge is influenced by two distinct climates: the dry air that blows down the Gorge from the eastern Washington desert, and the moist, marine influence that comes upriver from the Pacific Ocean. The two climates converge between Hood River and The Dalles, creating a remarkable microclimate with as much as thirty inches of rain at the western end and only half as much on the eastern end.

On the Washington side is the town of Bingen, a friendly community settled by German immigrants and named for the German wine town of Bingen am Rhein. It's been done up in quaint mock-Bavarian facades, a device designed to attract tourists. (Some of the original German families aren't impressed.) The trip across the toll bridge from Hood River to Bingen is short but breathtaking. About halfway across, there's a stunning view downriver as the broad ribbon of water snakes through the canyon walls of the Columbia River Gorge. In a majestic setting like this, how can a winery be anything but superb?

---

**█ MONT ELISE VINEYARDS**
315 West Steuben
Box 28
Bingen, WA 98605
509/493-3001 or 493-1880

| | |
|---|---|
| Open to the public | 12-4:30 Thurs., Fri., Sat. and by appointment |
| Tour groups | by appointment |
| Charge for tour groups | $1 per person (groups over 15) |
| Festivals/special events | Mayfest, third Sat. in May; Huckleberry Fest, third Sat. in Aug.; Pre-Christmas sale, second Sun. in Dec. |
| Wines available (1984) | Pinot Noir |
| | Gewurztraminer |
| | Gamay |
| | Pinot Noir Blanc |
| | Chenin Blanc |
| | Riesling |

---

Chuck Henderson, a cherry grower and practical man, was more impressed by the unique climate than by the view in 1964, when he began planting some experimental vines on his 300-acre orchard overlooking the Gorge. Though the winters were cold and the ground often dry, his vines flourished. Henderson has practiced agronomy all his life; he is a man of the soil who takes pride in having spent a lifetime producing basic foods. Wine is almost an adventure for him, the icing on the cake.

The varieties Henderson planted on his steep hillside—Gewurztraminer and Pinot Noir—have been supplemented in recent years with Chardonnay, Riesling, and even some Cabernet Sauvignon. There's no need for irrigation, even during the long summers, when the ground is bone-dry; at root level, nine feet underground, the earth remains moist and free of frost.

Henderson does his own research into the geography and geology of the Northwest. "There's more to soil than 'the stuff that holds up the vine,'" he says. His splendid Gewurztraminers alone are testimony to his skill as a grape grower and winemaker. Coming up before long, from the existing vines, will be sparkling wines from the Chardonnay and the Pinot Noir.

**MONT ELISE VINEYARDS**

| | |
|---|---|
| Owners | Charles V. Henderson family |
| Winemaker | Charles V. Henderson |
| Year bonded | 1975 |
| Year first planted | 1972 |
| Vineyard acreage | 31 |
| Principal varieties, acres | Pinot Noir, 10 |
| | Gewurztraminer, 9 |
| | Gamay Beaujolais, 5 |
| | Chardonnay, 4 |
| | Riesling, 3 |
| Year of first crush | 1975 |
| Production capacity | 12,000 gallons |
| Production in 1983 | 8,000 gallons |
| Awards, 1983 | |
| 1982 Gewurztraminer: | Bronze, Tri-Cities |
| | Bronze, San Francisco |
| 1981 Chenin Blanc: | Bronze, Tacoma |

For a number of years, Mont Elise was known as Bingen Wine Cellars. The Hendersons had named their vineyard "Mont Elise" after their daughter Elise; now it's the winery's formal name, too. Their son Charles is getting a degree in enology at the University of California at Davis, and helps run the winery on his vacations.

The Mont Elise winery, with a squat, gabled tower, is housed in a former apple and pear warehouse decorated with southern German half-timbering. The woman who pours the wines in the tasting room is attired in a Bavarian dirndl. Why the showmanship? "I've learned that people won't pay beans for what they need, but will pay almost anything for what they want," Henderson says to explain the costume drama.

He need not worry. He is making a significant contribution to the Northwest's enology just by growing and producing wine where he is. It's the soil that counts, not the dirndl.

# *Mont Elise Vineyards*

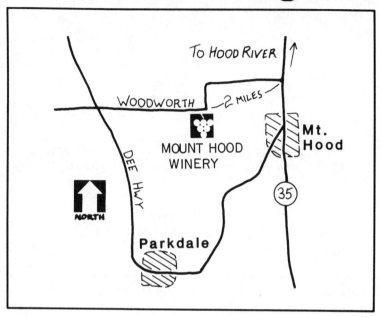

When Lester Martin retired fifteen years ago from a hectic career as a chemical engineer in Southern California, he wanted nothing more than a peaceful retirement along a fishing stream somewhere in the Northwest woods. So he bought himself an orchard overlooking the east fork of the Hood River. But instead of casting for trout he planted blackberries and raspberries; instead of a lazy retirement, he found a new occupation: making wine from the apple, pear, and berry crop.

Having studied winemaking from the standpoint of its engineering process, Martin concluded that the notion of making wine from grapes rather than other fruits is no more than a historical accident. In the cozy tasting room of his winery, overlooking the rushing river, Martin explained his thesis.

The nomadic tribes of pre-Biblical times needed a source of liquid to supplement fresh water or milk available from domestic animals, something they could pour into their goatskins and carry across the plains. Fruit juices wouldn't stay fresh, and even in a fermented state they deteriorated rapidly. All except the juice of one fruit: grapes.

217

---

**🍇 MOUNT HOOD WINERY**
4655 Woodworth Drive
Mount Hood, OR 97401
352-6465

| | |
|---|---|
| Open to the public | 1-5 Tues.-Sat., summer; other seasons by appointment |
| Tour groups | by appointment |
| Charge for tour groups | no charge |
| Picnic facilities at the winery | deck overlooking river; small barbecue |
| Wines available (1984) | Ganzapfel |
| | Buerre d'Anjou (Pear) |
| | Strawberry |
| | Blueberry |
| | Loganberry |
| | Raspberry |
| | Plum |
| | Cherry |

---

The reason, we now know, is that ripe grapes contain about 24 percent sugar, more than almost any other fruit. Fermentation—whether by wild yeasts or a winemaker's design—converts this sugar into (roughly) half alcohol and half carbon dioxide. Only if the alcohol level is high enough, 12 percent or so, will the resulting juice (which we now call wine) be "stable." If it's much less, the wine will deteriorate and spoil.

So it was to create a sound and stable beverage in the days before refrigeration or pasteurization that grapes were first fermented, Lester Martin says, that grapes, rather than apples, berries, or other plants, were cultivated to fill the goatskins and ceremonial gourds of the ancients.

But there is no need for grapes to remain the exclusive basis for wine today. Oregon is a huge fruit basket, and the Hood River Valley provides an abundant supply of luscious, ripe apples, pears, blueberries, blackberries, strawberries, and cherries. True, their sugar doesn't reach the requisite level at harvest, but there's plenty of refined sugar available these days to stir into the crushed fruit and "ameliorate" the juice. Modern filtration techniques make it relatively simple to remove impurities from the finished wine, to highlight the fruit flavors and eliminate the defects.

So now there's a winery in what was once Lester Martin's garage, with a spanking new, gleaming chrome centrifuge occupying a position of honor

**MOUNT HOOD WINERY**

| | |
|---|---|
| Owner & winemaker | Lester Martin |
| Year bonded | 1974 |
| Year of first crush | 1974 |
| Production capacity | 5,000 gallons |
| Production in 1983 | 4,500 gallons |

near the entrance. Across a breezeway in the tasting room, Martin's proclivity for items from the past shows up: a potbellied stove, a baking table with tin drawers, a phonograph that could have been the model for His Master's Voice. It's almost as if you'd stepped into somebody's grandmother's kitchen. Then you notice the stained glass panel in the window, studded with brilliantly colored blueberries, pears, and apples; it's the sort of panel we've seen in other wineries, except Lester Martin's doesn't include grapes.

What a lovely spot it is for a tasting of these "Mountain Grown" fruit wines. The sliding door at the back of the tasting room opens to a deck where the river's whispering waters can be heard through the pines. A backyard barbecue stands ready for visitors. How fortunate that Lester Martin decided there was more to retirement than fishing!

# St. Josef's Weinkeller

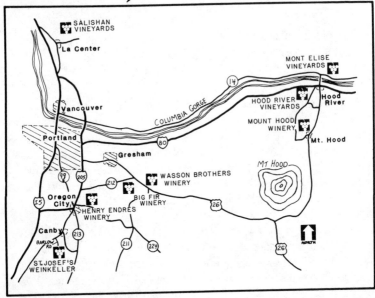

You can get to Canby, which calls itself "Oregon's Garden Spot," by following the river south from Oregon City, or by crossing the Willamette on the Canby Ferry from the west side of the river between Wilsonville and West Linn, or by coming up Highway 99 East from Woodburn, Hubbard, and Aurora. Just south of Canby is the old Barlow House, from which Barlow Road winds eastward through a landscape of plowed fields, paddocks, and gentle grassy slopes. Mount Hood looms over the fields, with Mount Adams perched on its shoulder. Cows and horses stand in front of rustic barns or beside still ponds; geese fly overhead. The picture-book scenery prepares you for the Old World experience awaiting visitors to St. Josef's Weinkeller, where Josef Fleischmann and his wife, Lilli, bonded their winery just in time for the 1983 crush.

The driveway, dividing vineyards of Chardonnay and Gewurztraminer, leads to a turn-of-the-century, carefully restored farmhouse with an Alsatian facade and a swimming pool out back. Also in back is the winery, where the name St. Josef's Weinkeller is stenciled in proud Gothic script on the side of an old cow barn. The Fleischmann family is growing ten acres of grapes on their sixty-five acre property, doing it not the way the book says, necessarily, not the Gospel According to Davis, but the way Joe

220

## ST. JOSEF'S WEINKELLER
28836 S. Barlow Road
Canby, OR 97013
651-3190

| | |
|---|---|
| Open to the public | 1-5 daily |
| Tour groups | yes, by appointment |
| Picnic facilities at the winery | 11 redwood tables, 2-acre lake, walkway to hillside vineyard |
| Festivals/special events | Grape Stomping Fest, Oct. |
| Wines available (1984) | French Colombard |
| | Zinfandel |
| | Late Harvest Zinfandel |
| | Chardonnay |
| | Cabernet Sauvignon |

Fleischmann thinks it should be done, his own way, with his own money, with his own name on the label.

Joe Fleischmann, aspiring winemaker, is a retired baker. Born in Hungary and raised in Germany, Fleischmann learned the baker's trade in the resorts around Lake Constance. In the mid-fifties, he and Lilli emigrated to Chicago, where he worked for Sara Lee before moving to Oregon in 1970 and buying his own bakery in Canby. Fleischmann was such a successful baker, with thirty-six varieties of bread, and doughnuts celebrated throughout the area, that he ended up owning a string of bakeries in Clackamas County. But he sold them all and switched to wine, a subject he had learned about at his grandfather's knee.

"Dough and wine are both live products," he told us. In the fermentation process, "a lot depends on time and temperature . . . and luck." Fleischmann will not use any chemicals in his winemaking. There will be no sulphur dioxide to control bacteria, no inoculation of his crushed grapes with any store-bought yeasts. Fermentation will take place spontaneously with wild yeasts. This means Fleischmann will have to be meticulous in filtering his wines to produce a commercially stable product; conditions in warehouses and retail stores vary greatly, and are hard on delicate wines. But the temptation to buy St. Josef wines will be great: "You'll never get a headache from one of my wines," Fleischmann promises.

The wines we tasted, barrel samples from his first commercial crush, were all dry, with the Chardonnay, Zinfandel, and Cabernet Sauvignon showing clean aromas with little wood character at that time. The Zinfandel

---

**ST. JOSEF'S WEINKELLER**

| | |
|---|---|
| Owners | Josef & Lilli Fleischmann |
| Winemaker | Josef Fleischmann |
| Year bonded | 1983 |
| Year first planted | 1980 |
| Vineyard acreage | 10 |
| Principal varieties, acres | Pinot Noir, 4 |
| | Gamay, 2 |
| | Gewurztraminer, 1.5 |
| | Chardonnay, 1 |
| | Cabernet Sauvignon, 1 |
| Year of first crush | 1983 |
| Production capacity | 5,000 gallons |
| Production in 1983 | 5,000 gallons |

---

contributes a great deal to Fleischmann's reputation. In August, 1984, he plans to release a late harvest Zin made with California grapes that was bottled with nearly 16 percent alcohol.

It won't be long now before the wines reach the public; the winery cellar is spanking clean, stuffed to its beamed ceiling with American oak brandy barrels. The tasting room, under construction upstairs when we visited, is an endeavor of the whole Fleishmann family, including grandparents on an extended visit from Germany. They have envisioned a setting like a German *Keller*: oiled oak floors, beamed ceilings, a long counter, a table for "regulars." The room and its adjacent deck overlook a spring-fed lake and the hillside beyond where more vines are growing; Fleischmann hopes visitors will stroll around the grounds after a picnic. It's hard to imagine a more enjoyable or welcoming site.

A final word about the winery's name. It honors St. Josef, patron saint of family providers. The Fleischmanns' parish priest was delighted by the idea.

# Salishan Vineyards

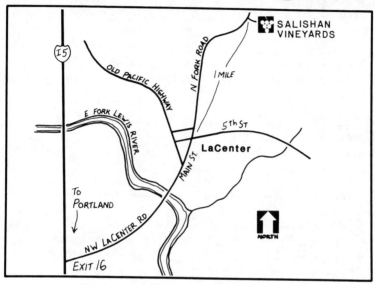

La Center is a bucolic place whose geography and climate are influenced by the nearby Columbia River and by Oregon's Willamette Valley, twenty miles to the south. The result is a reasonably long, cool (2,100 heat units) growing season, without as much rain as Bordeaux. The steelheading in nearby lakes and streams is sensational, and the freezer chest in the town grocery offers "Frozen Bait" next to the TV dinners.

In 1971, Joan and Lincoln Wolverton bought thirty acres of land overlooking the Lewis River near La Center, three hours from their home in Seattle, but only fifteen minutes from Vancouver, Washington, and began spending weekends planting a twelve-acre vineyard. They named their property Salishan after the Salish Indians who once roamed the Oregon coast.

Joan left her work at *The Seattle Times* in 1976, Lincoln found a position in Portland as director of technical projects for the Public Power Council. The Wolvertons moved into a tiny house on the property so that Joan, a tall, outgoing woman with boundless energy and a delightful sense of humor, could direct herself full-time to tending the vineyard and, after 1980, making the wine. Their comfortable modern home, which overlooks the vineyard and some of the state's loveliest countryside—the Portland skyline, Mount Hood, and Mount Jefferson—is a recent luxury.

---

**SALISHAN VINEYARDS**
North Fork Road
Route 2, Box 8
LaCenter, WA 98629
(206) 263-2713

| | |
|---|---|
| Open to the public | 1-5 weekends, May 1 to Dec. 30 |
| Tour groups | by appointment |
| Charge for tour groups | none |
| Festivals/special events | LaCenter Jamboree, late July |
| Wines available (1984) | 1980 Pinot Noir |
| | 1982 & 1983 Riesling |
| | 1982 Chardonnay |
| | 1982 White Table Wine |

---

Just *growing* grapes (Pinot Noir, Chardonnay, Riesling, Cabernet, Chenin Blanc) costs $1,100 an acre, Joan points out. And building a winery, as they've done now, is also very expensive. To raise the money for the venture, they've been selling their white grapes, mostly Chardonnay, to Amity Vineyard and others. Now that the Wolvertons have dealt with nuisances like deer, rabbits, robins, and volcanic dust, some of their neighbors are planning to put in vineyards themselves.

Early in 1981, the Wolvertons released the Salishan Vineyards 1978 Pinot Noir, made from their own grapes but produced and bottled by Dick Ponzi at the Ponzi Vineyard in Beaverton, Oregon. It won immediate attention and was acclaimed in the same breath as the best Pinots from The Eyrie Vineyard and Knudsen-Erath. The 1979 Pinot was even better—one of the best examples of a "Willamette Valley" style we've tasted, yet richer, earthier, fuller.

The 1979 Pinot recently won Best of Show honors at the Fort Lewis wine festival; the 1980 has already won Best of Show at the Tacoma wine festival. Both these wines were also made by Dick Ponzi; the 1980 was aged and bottled at Salishan, which opened its own winery in September of 1982.

The winery has a capacity of 10,000 gllalons, allowing the Wolvertons to use outside grapes, if they choose to. And they might: the 1983 harvest was "dismal," as Joan puts it, with thirteen inches of rainfall between late June and early July. The crop was decimated, down from thirty tons in 1982 to only seven tons in 1983. Still, quality was high, and the Wolvertons will

**SALISHAN VINEYARDS**

| | |
|---|---|
| Owners | Joan & Lincoln Wolverton |
| Winemaker | Joan Wolverton |
| Year bonded | 1982 |
| Year first planted | 1971 |
| Vineyard acreage | 12 |
| Principal varieties, acres | Pinot Noir, 5.5 |
| | Chardonnay, 2 |
| | Riesling, 2 |
| | Cabernet Sauvignon, 2 |
| Year of first crush | 1982 |
| Production capacity | 10,000 gallons |
| Production in 1983 | 2,000 gallons |
| Awards, 1983 | |
| 1979 Pinot Noir: | Gold & Best of Show, Tacoma |
| 1980 Pinot Noir: | Gold & Best of Show, Fort Lewis |
| | Silver, Tacoma |

"press" on. Especially since the last two festivals they entered honored their wines with Best of Show medals!

Salishan Vineyards will have a new tasting room in 1984, so visitors can taste the Wolvertons' wines and admire their view. They've been sharing their crop of grapes with others—birds, rabbits, and raindrops—for so long, it's nice they're finally getting the opportunity to share the fruits of their labors with the proper audience: appreciative wine drinkers.

# *Wasson Brothers Winery*

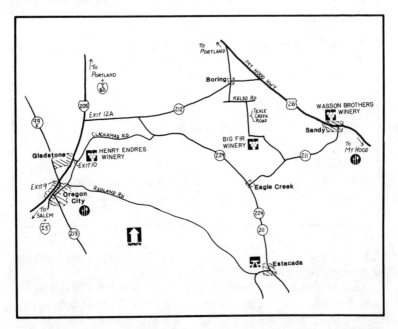

The Wasson brothers, Jim and John, have come to the winemaking business with the same spirit of cooperation that marked their earlier venture as Clackamas County farmers. And there's a remarkable coincidence: the Wassons, like Ted and Terry Casteel of Bethel Heights Vineyard, are identical twins.

It all began when their sister in Illinois got them interested in home winemaking. Turned out they were good at it; they won first prize at the Oregon State Fair in the amateur division. Encouraged by their success, they "turned pro." They began with a Rhubarb wine, which won a silver medal, then expanded their product line: more fruit wines in 1982, with a gold medal for the Apricot, then varietal wines in 1983. And the medals kept coming: gold for the Loganberry, gold for the Pinot Noir. The Pinot Noir was also named Best of Show in a consumer judging at nearby Clackamas Community College; it has a warm, berry-like aroma, and is nicely balanced.

**WASSON BROTHERS WINERY**
37675 Highway 26
Sandy, OR 97055
668-3124

| | |
|---|---|
| Open to the public | 9-5 daily |
| Tour groups | yes |
| Charge for tour groups | none |
| Wines available (1984) | Oregon White Riesling |
| | Northwest White Riesling |
| | Pinot Noir |
| | Red & White Table Wines |
| | Loganberry |
| | Blackberry |
| | Raspberry |
| | Rhubarb |
| | Bing Cherry |

The Wassons had planted a vineyard on their farm in 1978, on a rather cool and wet site, and, lo and behold, they got three tons of Pinot Noir and three and a half tons of Chardonnay to the acre with their second commercial crop in 1983. Jim Wasson reports that the harvest was bountiful, even with the wet summer, high winds, and attacks by voracious birds.

Jim, who used to be a plumber and now runs the winery, and John, a lock and dam operator for the Corps of Engineers at West Linn, originally found themselves stymied when they wanted to move to Sandy; there was a moratorium on new building permits. But they must have waged a successful campaign with the local citizenry, because even the Seventh Day Adventists endorsed their application for a liquor license. John figures that the people who live out this way grew up with fruit wines and like the idea of having their own winery around.

So there they are, the Wasson brothers, with a brand new winery and tasting room on the western outskirts of Sandy, next to Janz Berryland. It's a large building, with board-and-batten siding, a peaked roof, wide ramps and doorways to accommodate wheelchairs, and plenty of parking. By summer, a grape arbor will protect the picnic tables, and the Wassons will sell wine by the glass to be enjoyed with (or without) packed lunches.

Inside, the back wall of the tasting counter is already generously bedecked with ribbons and medals proclaiming the Wassons' success dur-

**WASSON BROTHERS WINERY**

| | |
|---|---|
| Owners | Jim Wasson, John Wasson |
| Winemaker | Jim Wasson |
| Consulting enologist | David Wirtz |
| Year bonded | 1982 |
| Year first planted | 1978 |
| Vineyard acreage | 7 |
| Principal varieties, acres | Gewurztraminer, 2.5 |
| | Early Muscat, 2.5 |
| | Chardonnay, 1 |
| | Pinot Noir, 1 |
| Year of first crush | 1982 |
| Production capacity | 9,000 gallons |
| Production in 1983 | 4,800 gallons |
| Expansion plans | picnic facilities, 1984 |
| Awards, 1983 | |
| 1982 Pinot Noir: | Gold, Clackamas County |
| White Riesling: | Silver, Clackamas County |
| Loganberry: | Gold, Oregon State Fair |
| | Gold, Oregon Wineries Showcase |
| Rhubarb: | Silver, Oregon State Fair |

ing their first two years of commercial winemaking. Be sure to try the superb, non-vintaged Pinot Noir, and the two delicious Rieslings. The Wassons will have many more medals before long.

# *Lodging*

## *Welches*

### *Rippling River Resort*
68010 E. Fairway
622-3101 (from Portland, 224-7158; toll free, 800-547-8054)

A long, long time ago, it seems, this was a simple golf course. Then the Bowmans added a few cabins, then another nine holes of golf, until now it's a full-fledged resort with what they call "townhouse elegance." Nostalgia aside, it's very handsome, with an airy lodge in bleached woods and earth-tone furnishings, and rates that seem quite reasonable, especially for winter ski packages.

The dining room turns out interesting fare. For those who expect to have only eggs and bacon or French toast at breakfast, there's a Sunday brunch which willingly complies. But for the more adventurous, brunch also offers smoked salmon, oysters on the half shell, herring in sour cream, poached salmon, blini, and a groaning board of desserts, including a tempting tray of cream puffs oozing custard.

## *Government Camp*

### *Timberline Lodge*
Six miles north of Highway 26
272-3311 or (toll free) 800-547-1406

A National Historic Monument, built by the W.P.A. during the 1930s, this imposing structure belongs so completely to the mountain that it could have been carved from the rock itself. Inside, the preoccupation with detail—beams, window frames, mantels, walls, stairways, fireplaces, floors—puts one in mind of the total art form of the medieval cathedral. Everywhere you look is the work of a fine craftsman, sculptor, painter. You can sit for an hour (in the Ram's Head bar in the balcony, for instance) and relish their work, or stroll on the wide-planked oak floors, caressing the figures of Oregon wildlife revealed in the carved newel posts.

The lodge's traditional St. Bernards will welcome you, but the park wardens may turn your car away: there's a limit of 800 parking places, so come early if the weather's glorious.

## *Hood River*

### *Columbia Gorge Hotel*
4000 Westcliff Drive
386-5566

This imposing hotel was built by Portland lumber baron Simon Benson in 1921 to provide a destination at the end of the newly completed Columbia River Scenic Highway. In 1982 it was acquired by the company that runs Snoqualmie Falls Lodge outside of Seattle; they spruced up the rooms and grounds and began improving the kitchen, importing the trademarked Snoqualmie Falls World Famous Farm Breakfast.

The public spaces in the hotel are grand, with windows that look across (but not down) the Gorge. Rooms are expensive; the refurbishing begun a year ago is almost complete. The hotel's Cadillac limousine seems to be permanently parked across the entrance portico, which makes disembarking in winter rather inconvenient, but doormen will be available in summer to carry your bags.

### *Hood River Inn*
Interstate 84 at exit 64
386-2200

A lovely location with very comfortable rooms made immensely appealing by their setting right on the river. A drink at sunset on your waterfront patio could be one of life's peak experiences.

### *Vagabond Motel*
4070 Westcliff Drive
386-2992

A family-run motel where nine of the seventeen units have a view of the river. Prices are low, and the family is proud of the service they give their guests.

## *White Salmon, Washington*

### *Inn of the White Salmon*
172 W. Jewett
509/493-2335

Bill Hopper, an airline pilot, and his wife, Loretta, stayed in this building some ten years ago when it was the Hoodview Hotel (you can see the Mount Hood from the second-floor rooms); they bought the place in 1976. Since then, they've restored it to cozy Victorian opulence, with twenty-five rooms decorated with antiques and furnished with personal touches like perfume, shaving mugs, and bathrobes.

The Inn arranges rafting, fishing, and wilderness backpacking trips for its guests. The float trips on the White Salmon River pass through some of the loveliest scenery imaginable.

## Bingen, Washinton

### The Grand Old House
1860 Highway 14
509/493-2838

A gracious, twin-towered old dame of the Victorian era, she is celebrating her 124th birthday with a fresh coat of paint and a new role as a bed & breakfast establishment. Owners Gregory and Cyndy de Bruler have organized six rooms, two in the towers, and three baths, at prices ranging from $30 to $50 per couple, including a hearty breakfast.

The de Brulers plan to open a moderately priced restaurant in the house by summer, 1984, with the menu changing nightly from French to Chinese to Middle Eastern to seafood.

## Carson, Washington

### Carson Hot Springs Resort
One mile north of Highway 14 at Wind River Junction
509/427-8292

This is neither a European spa nor a typical American resort. Good grief, where's the TV? What you get, for less than $15, is a very plain room in the "hotel" or, for $20, a simple housekeeping cabin. Hiking trails along the nearby Wind River take you downstream to the Columbia or upstream into the wilderness.

For $4 you can take a bath in the hot mineral springs (separate facilities for men and women) with attendants to bring you a drink of mineral water, wrap you up, or dry your back.

# *Restaurants*

## *Aurora*

### Chez Moustache
224 Highway 99 East
678-1866

Gene and Barbara Kretz manage this roadside cottage with genuine old world charm and value. The charm is in the posters of France and Switzerland, the small rooms and verandas filled with oil-cloth covered tables, the involvement of the family. The value is in the food, prepared by Gene and served by Barbara, at astonishingly low prices considering the high quality of the ingredients.

## *Oregon City*

### Merulli's
76 Oregon City Shopping Center
657-3037

Neither the shopping-mall setting nor the interior decor prepare you for the care that Roger and Bonnie Merulli pour so profusely into the selection of ingredients and the preparation of each menu item. The pana fino (cracker bread) is baked in their pizza oven at 500 degrees for thirty seconds on each side, then rushed to the table; it gets crunchier as it cools. Into Merulli's tomato sauce go plum tomatoes custom-packaged in San Jose, with olive oil, carrots, onions, and parsley, all slow-cooked for two days to emerge with a lovely fresh and intense flavor.

## *Sandy*

### Forest Inn at Aldercreek
54737 Highway 26
668-6079, or 622-3426 from Portland

Richard Estes came here after training with the Western Hotels chain. His restaurant is comfortable, his food is beyond reproach, his wine list enviable. The cuisine is in the mold of the London Grill at its 1960s best: seafood, steaks, veal Cordon Bleu, filet mignon Oscar. The restaurant again won the Travel-Holiday Magazine Fine Dining Award last year, one of only six in Oregon to achieve that honor, confirming its long-standing popularity with fans who regularly drive from Portland or Lake Oswego for dinner here.

## Zig Zag

### Barlow Trail Inn
Highway 26
622-3877

A log cabin beside the highway surrounded by cars, campers, and pickups, this establishment has earned its popularity. A stone fireplace welcomes visitors inside, a barbecue deck provides lots of summer seating outside.

## Mount Hood

### Elkhorn Inn
4780 Highway 35
354-1294

You could whip right past this little roadside restaurant on the Mount Hood loop and never be aware of the welcome and value inside. Being hungry would make your mistake greater, for Texan Ken Hawkins and his Australian wife, Lucia, prepare slow-roasted prime barbecue ribs in original Texas sauce, as well as prime rib, pizza, and a full menu of American standards at rock-bottom prices. Portions are large, too.

## Hood River

### Stonehedge Inn at Wildwood Acres
3405 Cascade Drive
386-3940

A cozy turn-of-the-century home in the trees above Hood River, where dinner can be very gracious. One of the rooms is a porch overlooking a pretty garden; another is the comfortable library bar. The wine list, which includes local wines, is reasonably priced, the service attentive, and the food (despite a change in chefs) well prepared and attractively presented.

## The Old Rockford Store
1476 Markham Road
386-3844

An inviting interior, with easy chairs and a sofa on an old Oriental rug in the entry hall, and a fine counter with an espresso machine. Owner Charlie Capovilla and chef Patrick Edwards have been here since the summer of 1983, serving an all-Italian menu of calzone, fettuccine, ravioli, and pizza dinners.

## Charburger
4100 Westcliff Drive
386-3101

Old West decor, but with a sense of humor: there's a life-size carving of a pioneer couple on the bench outside, and an Indian couple inside. The atmosphere is cozy and warm. The menu runs to country-style breakfasts, burgers, steaks.

# BZ Corner, Washington

## The Logs
Highway 141
509/493-1402

You head out of White Salmon for Trout Lake and the lava caves, leaving behind the beautiful Gorge with vistas of the shining, slithering river bordered by layers of gray hills. Snow-covered Mount Adams is straight ahead, along with some unusual roadside signs: "Taxidermy Done Here" and "We Buy Porcupines."

The Logs, which could be a cabin in the Black Forest, opened in 1932 and has remained virtually unchanged since, except that the willow tree planted at the front door has grown as big as the place itself. True, the video game inside is new, but the sign over the cash register still advises patrons to keep their knives and handguns outside. This is a hangout for hunters, loggers, farmers, schoolteachers, travelers of all sorts; the regulars have their Polaroid pictures tucked under the glass-topped bar.

What keeps everyone coming back is the chicken: deep-fried under pressure, like Colonel Sanders makes, only lots better. Six hundred orders a week, served with jo-jos (deep-fried potato slices), toast, and coleslaw.

## Vancouver, Washington

### Hidden House
100 W. 13th Street
206/696-2847
 Dining rooms are on two floors of this old brick house, widely considered Vancouver's best. Fresh soups, crepes, and lighter fare at lunch; excellent seafood at dinner. In summer, you can eat outside on the porch, too. The wine list is well thought out.

### Who-Song & Larry's Cantina
111 Columbia Way
206/695-1198
 If you're making the entire Mount Hood Loop, returning to Portland along the Gorge Highway, you just might be ready for this zany place, a stone's throw east of the Interstate bridge. The waiters have been known to dance on the tables, ride a unicycle, and serenade the guests. The food is good, and the menu goes on for pages. Older children will like this place, and the view of the river is very pleasant. It's open Sundays, and has a cocktail license, so this may even be the place to forget your commitment to wine and have a Margarita or two.

# Wine Shops and Delicatessens

## Sandy

### Janz Berryland
37601 Highway 26
668-7414
 A large roadside operation with the Wasson Brothers Winery in the parking lot next door. A good place to buy produce, especially apples and such, as well as wines. Good Northwest selection.

## Hood River

### The Fruit Tree
Hood River Village Exit 64 from Interstate 84
387-4122

Until recently an outlet for the Diamond Fruit Company, this spacious store has been leased by Chuck and Jackie Betts, who will add several lines of resort-type gifts and sportswear. Local produce and wines will continue to be featured.

### The Coffee Spot
12 Oak Street
386-1772

No wine here (because of a prohibitionist covenant on the property), but there's plenty to make up for it at this popular new spot in downtown Hood River: a dozen interesting sandwiches to choose from, a pleasant place to sit, fine espresso, and home-baked goodies. If you're planning a picnic there are meats, cheeses, salads, croissants, and bagels to take along.

## Vancouver, Washington

### Keil's
two locations:
303 N.E. 78th Street (Hazel Dell)
Fourth Plain Boulevard at Andresen Road

These supermarkets have excellent delicatessen sections and the most extensive selection of wines in Clark County. Yes, Virginia, there is a Hazel Deli.

# Picnic Spots

## Oregon City

### Clackamette Park
Here's a lovely spot at the confluence of the Clackamas and Willamette Rivers, with plenty of picnic tables and running room for kids.

## Milo McIver State Park

Highway 211, 5 miles west of Estacada

You can get here with just a short detour out of Sandy, or directly from Oregon City. It's one of the region's most popular parks, with camping facilities, boating on the Clackamas River, viewpoints, horseback riding, and picnic facilities.

# Highway 26

## Timberline Lodge

The massive stone and timber lodge is now reserved for overnight guests, but there's a new day lodge across the parking lot for skiers and transient travelers. Bring your own picnic fixings and buy bowl of hot soup here, then enjoy the unmatched view of the Cascades from the grassy (or snow-covered) slope outside the lodge.

# Hood River

## Panorama Point

The thing to do is to take the entire scenic loop, a one-hour drive. From Hood River, Highway 35 winds through pear and apple orchards to Panorama Point itself, which offers a view of the entire valley.

# Columbia Gorge

Beacon Rock is the most impressive of the sights on the Washington side of the Gorge, accessible via Highway 14 out of Bingen. There's a trail that winds to the top of the monolith, and a few picnic sites.

On the Oregon side, where you have a choice of the speedy, river-level Interstate 84 freeway or a winding scenic route through the cliffs, the best picnic sites are the parks at Eagle Creek, Benson State Park, and Rooster Rock. They all have waterside views of the Gorge. Multnomah Falls is well worth seeing; it's the closest thing to Niagara on the West Coast. Latourelle Park, on the Scenic Highway, has picnic tables with a view, and trails to its own falls.

# Eastern Oregon

We are just beginning to learn that the climate and geography of the Pacific Northwest includes tens of thousands of acres that might be suitable for viticulture. There's Oregon's Willamette Valley and the rest of the relatively cool microclimates west of the Cascades; those western regions will undoubtedly continue to produce wines of the highest quality. But the region that offers even more potential for viticulture, some say, is the Columbia Basin.

The broadest definition of the Columbia Basin encompasses literally millions of square miles, from Hood River to Lewiston, from the Wallowa Mountains to Wenatchee. The basin takes in Washington's fertile Yakima Valley, the burgeoning vineyards of the Wahluke Slope, the temperate regions around Walla Walla, the banks of the Columbia east of the Gorge. Most of the land lies in Washington State, but the southern strips are firmly in Oregon.

Within this great basin there are, no doubt, variations of climate, of soil. But there are common characteristics, too: no native trees, little rainfall, no cloud cover during the growing season. From a satellite, this area looks like North America's bald spot. It is a desert, with less natural rainfall than the Sahara. Fortunately, the waters of the Columbia and its tributaries have made agriculture possible here, turning the sagebrush into garden spots of apple orchards and circle farms of alfalfa, corn, and potatoes.

And now, grapes. Eastern Washington is crawling with consultants analyzing the soil to determine which patches of ground will make the best potential vineyards. The interest has spread to the Oregon side of the Columbia, where irrigation, from wells dug on the banks of the Columbia, is already in place for 200,000 acres of farmland suitable for grape growing.

All that's needed is an economic reason for farmers to convert their acreage, and the poor market for cash crops is making farmers look at their options. It takes between five and seven years for a piece of land to be converted from a farm crop like alfalfa or potatoes to a commercially producing vineyard; not many farmers can wait that long. But the impetus exists in the form of tax shelters for wealthy investors.

Potato farmers are the likeliest prospects. As a crop, potatoes bring $1,500 to $2,000 per acre in a good year, but an acre of land can produce potatoes only once every five years. Grasses and alfalfa rotate on the "potato" acres for much less money, but with the same expensive irrigation equipment: those enormous "circular" sprinkler systems, pivoting over 125 acres of fields like mechanical spiders. Now, when those pivots wear out, a farmer has to determine whether to replace the system or replace the crop. Wine grapes entail a higher labor cost, but the potential return is greater: $2,000 and more per acre per year. And grapes, with drip irrigation from the existing water supply, can be planted over the entire 160-acre quarter-section, not just the 125-acre circle covered by the sprinkler system.

Corporate farmers and packagers of tax shelter investments are leading the way. Companies like Boardman Farms and Western Empire have planted 750 acres of wine grapes in Oregon's Morrow County in the past two years alone. Half a dozen individual growers are also getting involved. One tiny winery is already established in Boardman, and other investors are watching closely to see if it's a fluke or a trend.

The big question is not so much the productivity of the land but the quality of the wine. That will take time, and several issues need to be settled first. Among them is the demand for grapes; it makes little sense for growers to plant vineyards today hoping for $500 a ton five years from now if there are no wineries buying grapes at that price.

Then there's the rather esoteric question of the soil's pH level (a chemical measurement of free hydrogen ions, or degree of acidity) after the potato fields have been fertilized over a period of time with potassium. Some winegrowers in the eastern United States have reported pH problems with grapes grown on the site of old potato farms.

Finally, there's not much out here in the way of tourist facilities; you have to be pretty enthusiastic about vineyards and winemaking (or rodeos, maybe) to pay a visit.

Still, there's a good possibility that eastern Oregon could, within a decade or so, produce decent wines in large quantities: perhaps the elusive "Northwest Jug Wine" so many people seem to want. And tourist amenities, we know, follow tourist attractions. In that case, this chapter is just the beginning.

# La Casa de Vin

This winery represents Oregon's first outpost in the eastern part of the state. And the wines being produced here, especially the Riesling and Cabernet Sauvignon, show the best promise of developing into that elusive creature, a premium Oregon wine at a jug wine price.

Ed Glenn, an attorney in Boardman, has been making wine since 1971, starting with dandelions and rosehips until he got his hands on grapes in 1975. In 1980, he began planting his own vineyard. Last season he made the first commercial White Riesling ever produced in eastern Oregon from local Morrow County grapes, and he's looking forward to producing a good deal more. He's planted grapes in Umatilla County, too, near Milton-Free-water; that's part of the new bi-state Walla Walla winegrowing region, and Glenn's Cabernet Sauvignon vines yielded fruit at the astonishing rate of nine tons to the acre.

Glenn is proudest of his Morrow County Riesling. The wine finished fermenting with 5-percent residual sugar and nine degrees of alcohol, a lovely dessert wine which he bottled in half-size tenths. Until now, there's been little interest in using the irrigated acreage of eastern Oregon to produce wine grapes, but that's changing. La Casa de Vin's own acreage gets its water from a pipeline that crosses the property carrying Columbia River water; solid set sprinklers irrigate the grapes.

As important as the water is the warmth. Ed Glenn feels that the climate where he's located is almost identical to the south slope of Chateau Ste. Michelle's River Ridge, just seven miles away as the crow flies (the road takes four times that long). His vineyard gets 2,800 heat units, a measure of overall warmth during the growing season, compared with about 2,300 in the Willamette Valley and 2,600 in the warmest parts of the Yakima Valley.

Glenn admits he's still learning. Microbiological stability, a problem for any winemaker, is the hardest part of the job for him. On the other hand, he really enjoys tasting the wines and sharing them with his visitors. Not that he's got all that much wine to sell, mind you; 720 gallons isn't going to flood the market. But it's a start. Half of La Casa de Vin's production is sold at the winery, the balance directly to restaurants and retailers in Boardman, Hermiston, and Pendleton.

A tasting room is planned in time for fall of 1984, with a picnic area nearby. The tasting room will sell a lunch basket with wine, a nice touch. The winery is just south of Exit 165 from the Interstate 84 freeway, but the interchange was still under construction at press time. Coming from

---

### ▓ LA CASA DE VIN
East Wilson Road
P.O. Box 428
Boardman, OR 97818
481-3151

| | |
|---|---|
| Open to the public | by appointment |
| Tour groups | yes, by appointment |
| Charge for tour groups | none |
| Wines available (1984) | 1982 & 1983 White Riesling |
| | 1982 Morrow County White |
| | Riesling |
| | 1982 Chenin Blanc |
| | 1982 Oregon Cabernet Sauvignon |
| | Rose |
| Winemaker | Ed Glenn |
| Year bonded | 1982 |
| Year first planted | 1980 |
| Vineyard acreage | 9 producing |
| Principal varieties | Cabernet Sauvignon, 1.5 |
| | Sauvignon Blanc, 1.5 |
| | White Riesling, 1.5 |
| Year of first crush | 1982 |
| Production capacity | 1,000 gallons |
| Production in 1983 | 720 gallons |
| Expansion plans | additional 4,000 gallons of |
| | production capacity; 7,800 gallons |
| | of storage; tasting room by fall, |
| | 1984 |

Boardman, go south on Main Street and east on Wilson Road. The winery sign is at Laurel Lane.

"The real trend in the Pacific Northwest," Ed Glenn believes, "is going to be toward a very good wine, perhaps a nearly pure White Riesling, at an ordinary price." And how can an Oregon winery make a wine that's as good as California jug wine at a lower cost than currently possible?

"Look for some really big—big by Oregon standards—wineries over here in the next few years," Glenn predicts. "These wineries will supply the need for a premium wine . . . at a jug-wine price."

# *River Ridge*

## *(Chateau Ste. Michelle)*

Why is River Ridge, the largest winery in Washington, profiled in a book about the Oregon wine country?

Well, it's only a couple miles as the crow flies from Ed Glenn's La Casa de Vin, so if you're visiting Oregon's smallest winery in Boardman, you might want to check out River Ridge as well. This $26-million facility is now Chateau Ste. Michelle's primary processing plant; some of the wines are finished here, some are trucked to the Seattle suburb of Woodinville. It's also the site of the largest vineyard in the Northwest: 3180 acres of grapes on one farm, more than all Oregon's vineyards combined!

River Ridge produced 1.6-million gallons of wine for Chateau Ste. Michelle in 1983, an amount that's staggering by Northwest standards, yet average for premium domestic wineries. The winery has the scale of a farmhouse estate in the French wine country, with solid stone walls, enormous wooden gates, and a large inner courtyard. Vines are planted right up to the doors of the redwood-paneled tasting room, and the patio, overlooking the river, is set up for picnics. All in all, this is a first class tourist attraction as well as a working winery.

Kay Simon, a graduate of the University of California at Davis, is the winemaker in charge. A very capable staff runs the tasting room and tour program, and River Ridge is delighted to welcome tour groups. From the outside, visitors get little idea of the size of the place; most of it, a virtual forest of stainless steel fermenting tanks, is underground.

Chateau Ste. Michelle wines are more widely distributed than any other Northwest label, and they are consistently ranked with the nation's best. The company recognizes the role its wines play as ambassadors from the Northwest, and that its facilities play as tourist attractions; the region's winemakers and tourists all benefit from the quality of that vision.

**RIVER RIDGE**
(Chateau Ste. Michelle)
Highway 221
P.O. Box 231
Paterson, WA 99345
(509) 875-2061

| | |
|---|---|
| Open to the public | 10-4:30 daily (call for winter hours, Dec.-March) |
| Tour groups | yes (large groups are asked to call ahead) |
| Charge for tour groups | none (except for special arrangements) |
| Picnic facilities at the winery | tables on the terrace outside the winery and in the courtyard; retail shop for picnic supplies at the tasting room |
| Wines available (1984) | 1983 Johannisberg Riesling |
| | 1983 Chenin Blanc |
| | 1983 Semillon Blanc |
| | 1983 Grenache |
| | 1983 Rose of Cabernet |
| | 1982 Chardonnay |
| | 1982 Fume Blanc |
| | 1982 Gewurztraminer |
| | 1978 Cabernet Sauvignon |
| | 1978 Merlot |

Awards, 1983

| | |
|---|---|
| 1978 Cabernet Sauvignon, Chateau Reserve: | Gold, Reno |
| | Silver, Seattle |
| 1978 Cabernet Sauvignon: | Silver, London |
| | Silver, Tacoma |
| 1982 Rose of Cabernet: | Gold, Atlanta |
| 1981 Chardonnay: | Silver, Atlanta |
| 1982 Johannisberg Riesling: | Silver, New York |
| 1982 Chenin Blanc: | Silver, Seattle |
| | Gold, Central Wash. State Fair |
| 1982 Muscat Canelli: | Gold, Central Wash. State Fair |

# *Lodging*

## *Boardman*

### *Dodge City Inn*
100 First Street
481-2441
    This is the best spot in town, with forty units and a pool, a nice restaurant (the Nomad) overlooking the rodeo arena, and some of the best prime rib in the Northwest. La Casa de Vin's wines are available here, too.

## *McNary*

### *Desert River Inn*
705 Willamette
922-4871
    A large, very comfortable motel on the Columbia from the Oregon side of the McNary Dam, with a good restaurant and a golf course.

# *Picnic Spots*

## *Boardman*

### *Boardman Marina Park*
Marina Drive
    Plenty of room here to launch your boat (you brought one along, didn't you?) or park your camper. Picnic facilities, too, right on the Columbia River.

### *Crow Butte State Park*
Highway 14, ten miles west of Paterson, Washington
    Everything you need for a refreshing stop: picnic grounds, a roped-off area for swimming in the Columbia, and waterskiing.

# Bed & Breakfast Registries

Many bed-and-breakfast establishments are listed with central registries and don't show up on the listings of lodgings in the individual touring areas. Travelers who have a pretty good idea what their itinerary will be might consider contacting the registries to find out if they have any homes in the vicinity.

Generally, people who list their homes with a registry don't hang a shingle on the porch announcing that they take in overnight guests. Only in Ashland is there an abundance of bed and breakfast lodgings; elsewhere, it's not like Europe, where guest rooms are inexpensive and plentiful. B & Bs tend to be more elegant, and more expensive, in the United States. And don't let the talk of "shared bathrooms" discourage you. It's rare indeed that you'll have to share the shower. What you *won't* get is the Holiday Inn.

Listings are in alphabetical order.

## Bed & Breakfast Oregon
5733 S.W. Dickinson Street
Portland, OR 97219
245-0642

Homes are located in Portland, Mount Hood, Eugene, and on the coast. Rates, including breakfast, run from $16 to $35.

## Gallucci Hosts Hostels
P.O.Box 1303
Lake Oswego, OR 97034

Most of Betty Gallucci's homes are in the Portland area, but she has a couple in the Columbia Gorge and the Willamette Valley. Prices range from $12 to $50 a night. For a brochure, send $1 and a stamped, self-addressed return envelope.

## Northwest Bed & Breakfast
7077 S.W. Locust Street
Portland, OR 97223
246-8366

This service, run by Laine Friedman and Gloria Shaich, has more than 250 homes up and down the West Coast. They can arrange for accommodations in specific locations, or set up entire two-week tours: a loop from Seattle to Ashland along the coast, or up the Columbia Gorge, or down to San Francisco. To receive a coded roster of homes, families pay a $20 membership fee. Sample wine country listing (in Sheridan, near McMinnville): working farm, two-story, turn of the century farmhouse, four bedrooms, private baths, children welcome, $28 a night. The registry then collects a deposit and makes the reservation for you.

### Pacific Bed & Breakfast
701 N.W. 60th Street
Seattle, WA 98107
(206) 784-7920 or 784-0539
Irmgard Casteleberry will send you a free guide listing sample homes. Most of them are in Washington, however.

### PT International Bed & Breakfast
1318 S.W. Troy Street
Portland, OR 97219
In Oregon: 245-0440; toll-free (800) 547-1463
This company acts as an agent for individuals around the world. You can book a room in France, New Zealand, or the Lesser Antilles, stay on a farm in Australia or a homestead near London. Rates for B & B accommodations in Oregon range from $28 to $33.

### Travelers Bed & Breakfast
P.O. Box 492
Mercer Island, WA 98040
(206) 232-2345
Jean Knight publishes a directory of subscribers to her Bed & Breakfast service for $3. Most of the listings are in the Puget Sound area of Washington.

### West Coast Bed & Breakfast
11304 20th Place S.W.
Seattle, WA 98146
(206) 246-2650
Jean Hartzell's registry is dominated by Seattle-area homes, but she will make reservations for other cities.

# Index

247